# 101 Fabulous Small Quilts

# 101 Fabulous Small Quilts

Martingale®
Create with Confidence

101 Fabulous Small Quilts

© 2013 by Martingale & Company®

Martingale
19021 120th Ave. NE, Ste. 102
Bothell, WA 98011-9511 USA
ShopMartingale.com

Printed in China

18 17 16 15 14 13     8 7 6 5 4 3 2 1

**Library of Congress Cataloging-in-Publication Data is available upon request.**

ISBN: 978-1-60468-268-7

**MISSION STATEMENT**
Dedicated to providing quality products and service to inspire creativity.

**CREDITS**

PRESIDENT & CEO: Tom Wierzbicki

EDITOR IN CHIEF: Mary V. Green

DESIGN DIRECTOR: Paula Schlosser

MANAGING EDITOR: Karen Costello Soltys

COPY EDITOR: Sheila Chapman Ryan

PRODUCTION MANAGER: Regina Girard

COVER AND TEXT DESIGNER: Paula Schlosser

TEXT LAYOUT: Dianna Logan / DBS

PHOTOGRAPHER: Brent Kane

# Contents

# Introduction

Nothing warms a home like quilts. They suggest comfort, coziness, and caring. And while there's nothing quite like wrapping up in a well-loved quilt to keep the world at bay, small quilts play an equally important role. They add personality and friendliness to a room. They soften hard edges and bring a bit of sweetness and whimsy to any decor. And for the quiltmaker, they provide wonderful opportunities to play with ideas, experiment with new palettes and styles, and learn new techniques.

Whether you're a fan of piecing, appliqué, or a combination of the two, there are quilts in this collection that will have you itching to stitch. We combed through our archives to bring you the widest variety of styles and techniques we could find. It's like a quilt show between the covers of a book. You'll find quilts for walls, tables, and doll cribs, from a generous 48" square to a petite 14" x 17". Some are quick and easy, while others may challenge your skills. Looking for a perfect fat-quarter quilt? It's in here. Do you love charm squares? We've got you covered. Searching for that perfect little project to use up some scraps from your stash? You'll find that here too. And once you stitch up one or two of these little beauties, you may find yourself unable to resist making more.

Small quilts can be used in so many ways. They're the perfect way to decorate for a special occasion, celebrate a season, or brighten a dark corner. And they make lovely and welcome gifts, especially for your quilting friends.

If you share our passion for quilts, you'll love this collection. Brimming with ideas, inspiration, and wonderful designs, it will bring you many happy hours of stitching pleasure.

# Oso

*Carrie's mom said these blocks looked like Bear's Paw blocks. So this quilt needed a bear-related name. Oso is Spanish for "bear."*

By Carrie Nelson; machine quilted by Sharon Brooks

FINISHED QUILT SIZE: 33¾" x 40"     FINISHED BLOCK SIZE: 4½" x 4½"

## Materials

*Yardage is based on 42"-wide fabric unless otherwise noted.*

⅝ yard of cream print for block backgrounds

⅔ yard of tan print for block backgrounds and setting triangles

32 assorted 5" squares for blocks

31 assorted 5" squares for borders

⅜ yard of fabric for binding

1⅜ yards of fabric for backing

39" x 45" piece of batting

## Cutting

*All measurements include ¼"-wide seam allowances.*

**From the cream print, cut:**

3 strips, 5" x 42"; crosscut into 20 squares, 5" x 5"

1 strip, 2" x 42"; crosscut into 20 squares, 2" x 2"

**From the tan print, cut:**

2 strips, 5" x 42"; crosscut into 14 squares, 5" x 5". Cut *2 of the squares* in half diagonally to make 4 corner triangles.

1 strip, 7¾" x 42"; crosscut into 4 squares, 7¾" x 7¾". Cut the squares into quarters diagonally to make 16 side triangles (2 will be extra).

1 strip, 2" x 42"; crosscut into 12 squares, 2" x 2"

**From *each of 30* assorted squares for borders, cut:**

1 strip, 2¼" x 5" (30 total)

1 strip, 2½" x 5" (30 total)

**From the 1 remaining assorted square for borders, cut:**

2 strips, 2½" x 5"

**From the binding fabric, cut:**

160" of 2"-wide bias binding

## Making the Blocks

Use a scant ¼"-wide seam allowance throughout. After sewing each seam, press the seam allowances in the direction indicated by the arrows.

1 Referring to "Making Half-Square-Triangle Units" on page 10 as needed, pair an assorted square with a cream or tan 5" background square and make one large half-square-triangle unit and four small half-square-triangle units. Trim the large half-square-triangle unit to measure 3½" square.

Trim the small half-square-triangle units to measure 2" square.

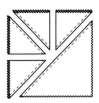  

2 Lay out the units from step 1 and a 2" cream or tan background square as shown. Join the pieces into rows, and then sew the rows together to complete the block. The block should measure 5" square. Repeat to make a total of 20 cream blocks and 12 tan blocks.

Make 20.     Make 12.

## Assembling and Finishing the Quilt

1 Lay out the cream blocks, tan blocks, side triangles, and corner triangles in diagonal rows as shown. Sew the pieces together into rows. Press the seam allowances as indicated by the arrows.

2 Sew the rows together and press the seam allowances in one direction. The setting triangles have purposely been cut a bit oversized.

3 Before attaching the border, trim and straighten the quilt top. Align the ¼" line on your long ruler with the outermost points of the blocks. Use a rotary cutter to trim any excess fabric, leaving a ¼"-wide seam allowance and making sure the corners are square.

4 For the inner border, sort the 2¼" x 5" strips into the following groups:

- Side borders: two groups of eight strips each
- Top and bottom borders: two groups of seven strips each

Join each group of strips end to end to make four long strips. Press the seam allowances in one direction. For the side borders, trim the longer strips to measure 2¼" x 32½". For the top and bottom borders, trim the shorter strips to measure 2¼" x 29¾".

5 Sew the pieced inner-border strips to the sides, and then the top and bottom of the quilt top. Press the seam allowances toward the inner border.

6 For the outer border, sort the 2½" x 5" strips into four groups: two groups of eight strips and two groups of seven strips. Join each group of strips end to end to make four long strips. Press the seam allowances in one direction. For the side borders, trim the two longest strips to measure 2½" x 36". For the top and bottom borders, trim the two remaining strips to measure 2½" x 33¾".

7 Sew the pieced outer-border strips to the sides, and then the top and bottom of the quilt top. Press the seam allowances toward the outer border.

8 Layer, baste, and quilt as desired. Using the 2"-wide binding strips, make and attach binding.

## Making Half-Square-Triangle Units

1 Select one light square and one dark square; both will be 5" squares. Draw a diagonal line from corner to corner on the wrong side of the light square using a permanent pen, pencil, or chalk marker.

2 Draw a second diagonal line from one corner to the center of the square, stopping at the first line as shown.

3 Draw a horizontal line and a vertical line from the center of the square to the outer edge as shown. These lines will fall along the midpoint of the square, 2½" from the outer edges. All of the drawn lines *are cutting lines,* not stitching lines.

4 Layer the marked square with the dark square, right sides together and raw edges aligned. Stitch a scant ¼" seam allowance on both sides of the diagonal lines exactly as shown. Only stitch along diagonal lines.

5 Cut the squares apart on the long diagonal line. Set aside the large triangle to avoid any accidents.

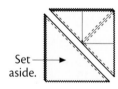

Set aside.

6 Cut the remaining triangle apart on the drawn lines, cutting on the diagonal, horizontal, and vertical lines. You'll have four small triangles.

7 Press the seam allowances on the half-square-triangle units toward the dark triangle.

# Diamond Maze

*The triangles in these blocks are great for showing off your favorite fabrics. Use small-scale prints or solids in the smaller, dark triangle portions of the blocks. When the blocks are sewn together, this setting gives the illusion of a maze.*

By Ellen Pahl

FINISHED QUILT SIZE: 42" x 42"    FINISHED BLOCK SIZE: 5" x 5"

## Materials

*Yardage is based on 42"-wide fabric unless otherwise noted.*

1½ yards *total* of 12 to 16 medium to dark large-scale prints for large triangles

½ yard *total* of 9 medium to dark solids for narrow accent border

¼ yard OR fat quarter *each* of 8 light prints for background

Scraps OR ½ yard *total* of 12 to 16 medium to dark small-scale prints for small triangles

½ yard of fabric for binding

2 yards of fabric for backing

46" x 46" piece of batting

5½" x 5½" square of template plastic

## Cutting

*All measurements include ¼"-wide seam allowances.*

**From *each* of the 8 light prints, cut:**

4 squares, 3⅜" x 3⅜"

8 rectangles, 3" x 4"

**From the medium to dark small-scale prints, cut:**

32 squares, 3⅜" x 3⅜"

**From the medium to dark large-scale prints, cut:**

32 rectangles, 5½" x 6½"

**From the medium to dark solids, cut:**
3 strips, 1¼" x 21¼"
1 strip, 1¼" x 20½"
1 strip, 1¼" x 16¼"
2 strips, 1¼" x 15½"
1 strip, 1¼" x 10½"
5 strips, 1¼" x 5½"
**From the binding fabric, cut:**
5 strips, 2½" x 42"

## Making the Blocks

Work with one background fabric at a time to make the eight blocks for each row.

1 Layer a light 3⅜" square with a medium 3⅜" square, right sides together. Draw a line diagonally from corner to corner on the wrong side of square.

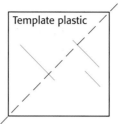

2 Stitch ¼" from the drawn line on both sides. Cut apart on the drawn line to create two triangle squares. Press the seam allowances toward the darker fabric.

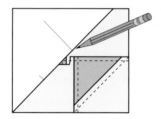

3 Sew a triangle square to each corresponding light 3" x 4" rectangle as shown. Press.

4 Sew pairs of these units together as shown. The triangles in this quilt were mixed and matched so that the two resulting blocks did not have the same fabric used for the small triangles. The dark triangles should be on the outer corners of the unit. Clip the seam allowance to the seam line in the center so that you can press the seam allowances away from the triangle-square units.

5 Cut the 5½" square template in half diagonally.

6 To mark the sewing line, place the template on the wrong side of your pieced rectangle, with the corner of the template on the triangle square. Draw the diagonal line as shown below. Place the template on the opposite corner, again with the corner of the template on the triangle square. Mark a second sewing line.

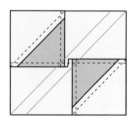

Mark stitching lines.

7 Pair the units from step 6 with the medium and dark 5½" x 6½" rectangles. Sew on each of the lines you drew, and then cut between them. Press the seam allowances toward the large triangles.

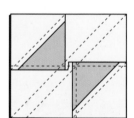

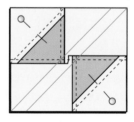 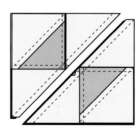

Makes 2.

8 You will make 8 blocks from each background fabric for a total of 64 blocks. You may want to wait until after you arrange your blocks before pressing the diagonal seam so that you can press the seam allowances in adjoining blocks in opposite directions for easier assembly.

Make 8 of each background
(64 total).

## Assembling the Quilt

1 Arrange the blocks and accent border as shown in the assembly diagram. Eight blocks with matching background fabric should create one vertical row. Rearrange your blocks until you're pleased with the overall look of your quilt. Press the diagonal seam allowances of the blocks in opposite directions from block to block.

2 Piece the accent border strips as shown in the assembly diagram below. Border seam allowances should be pressed in the opposite direction from the neighboring blocks.

3 Sew the six rows of six blocks together for the quilt center. Press the seam allowances in opposite directions from row to row. Sew the border blocks together into two horizontal and two vertical rows.

4 Join the border blocks with the accent border strips as shown in the assembly diagram to create four border units.

5 Add the border units one at a time, using a partial-seam technique for the first border. Refer to the assembly diagram for guidance. Start at one corner and pin the border unit to the quilt center. Sew the seam until you reach the last block. Stop stitching and remove the quilt from the sewing machine.

6 Attach the next border unit, again referring to the assembly diagram for the sewing order. You'll be able to sew the complete border seam if you rotate your quilt in a clockwise manner and attach the border units in that sequence.

7 After adding the last border unit, you can go back to the first border unit and complete the seam.

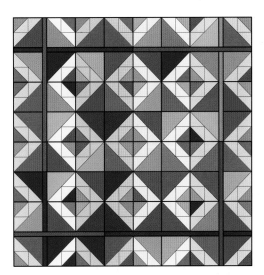

## Finishing the Quilt

1 Layer the quilt top with batting and backing; baste the layers together.

2 Hand or machine quilt as desired. The quilt shown was machine quilted with meandering in the light fabrics. Straight parallel lines were quilted in the large and small squares formed where the dark triangles meet.

3 Trim the batting and backing even with the edges of the quilt top. Sew the binding to the quilt.

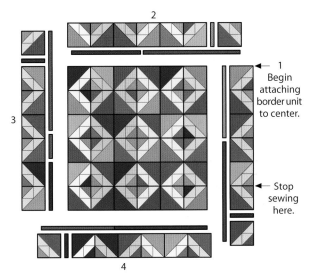

2

1
Begin attaching border unit to center.

3

Stop sewing here.

4

Quilt assembly

# Japanese Circles

*Inspired by a photo of an appliquéd purse in a Japanese quilting magazine, this little quilt features assorted print circles appliquéd onto a checkerboard background of alternating dark- and medium-brown squares.*

Pieced and quilted by Karen Costello Soltys; hand appliquéd by Karen Clifton
FINISHED QUILT SIZE: 17½" x 20½"    FINISHED BLOCK SIZE: 3" x 3"

## Materials

*Yardage is based on 42"-wide fabric unless otherwise noted.*

½ yard of subtle brown print for blocks and borders

1 fat quarter of brown striped fabric for blocks

Scraps of 20 colored fabrics, about 6" x 6" each, for appliqués and pieced border

⅝ yard of fabric for backing

20" x 23" piece of batting

3" x 3" square of template plastic

Freezer paper

Fine-point permanent marker

White embroidery thread (optional)

## Cutting

*All measurements include ¼"-wide seam allowances.*

**From the brown print, cut:**

10 squares, 3½" x 3½"

2 border strips, 1" x 42"

2 border strips, 1½" x 42"

31 squares, 1½" x 1½"

**From the brown striped fabric, cut:**

10 squares, 3½" x 3½"

**From the colored scraps, cut:**

31 squares, 1½" x 1½"

## Appliquéing the Blocks

1 Make a plastic template using the circle pattern on page 16. Trace the pattern onto the dull side of freezer paper 20 times using the fine-point marker. Cut out the freezer-paper templates exactly on the drawn line.

2 Press the freezer-paper circles onto the wrong side of the colored fabric scraps. Cut out each circle, leaving a scant ¼" (or less) seam allowance. Hand baste a ring of gathering stitches around the paper, sewing in the seam-allowance area. Pull the thread to gather the seam allowance over the edge of the paper. Hand baste the seam allowance in place, stitching through both paper and fabric. Ease in the excess fabric as you go. The narrower the

seam allowance, the easier it will be to ease in the fabric. Press.

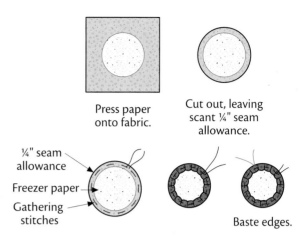

Press paper onto fabric.

Cut out, leaving scant ¼" seam allowance.

¼" seam allowance

Freezer paper

Gathering stitches

Baste edges.

3 Fold a brown fabric square in half vertically and horizontally and finger-press to mark the center. Fold a circle in half in the same manner and crease. Matching the vertical and horizontal creases, center the circle on the brown square and pin in place.

Match centers and pin in place.

4 Appliqué the circle in place using a small invisible stitch and thread to match the appliqué fabric. When you have about 1" to go, remove the basting stitches, pull out the freezer paper with tweezers (or fingers), fold the seam allowance back under the appliqué, and finish stitching in place.

5 Repeat steps 3–4 to make 20 blocks, 10 using the brown-print background squares and 10 using the brown-striped squares.

## Assembling the Quilt

1 Lay out the appliquéd squares in five rows of four blocks each, alternating the background fabrics. When you're satisfied with the color arrangement, sew the blocks together into rows. Press the seam allowances in opposite directions from one row to the next. Then sew the rows together and press the seam allowances in one direction.

2 Measure the length of the quilt top through the middle. Cut a brown-print 1" strip into two strips of this length. Sew the strips to the sides of the quilt top and press the seam allowances toward the brown borders. Measure the width of the quilt and cut the remaining brown-print 1" strip into two strips of that length. Sew to the top and bottom of the quilt and press.

3 To make the top and bottom pieced borders, lay out the brown and colored 1½" squares, alternating them. The top border starts and ends with brown squares. The bottom border starts and ends with colored squares. Each border has a total of 13 squares. Sew the squares together; press the seam allowances in one direction. Sew these borders to the quilt and press the seam allowances toward the brown inner border.

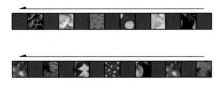

Make 1 of each.

4 Make two side borders with 18 squares each, alternating brown and colored 1½" squares. Press the seam allowances in one direction. Add these borders to the sides of the quilt, positioning them so that the brown squares are next to a colored square in the top and bottom borders. Press the seam allowances toward the brown inner border.

Make 2.

5 Measure the length of the quilt top. Cut a brown-print 1½" border strip into two strips of this length. Join them to the sides of the quilt and press the seam allowances toward the brown border. Measure the width of the quilt in the same manner. Cut two strips to fit from the remaining brown-print strip. Sew them to the top and bottom of the quilt, and press.

## Finishing the Quilt

1 Mark any quilting designs on the quilt top.

2 Trim the backing fabric to the same size as the quilt top. Place the batting on the table or floor, smoothing out any wrinkles. Layer the pressed quilt top on the batting, right side up. Finally, add the quilt backing, right side down, on top. Smooth and pin the layers together around the perimeter.

3 Using a walking foot on your machine, stitch around the perimeter of the quilt with a ¼" seam allowance. Leave an opening on one side for turning. Trim the excess batting from the corners and turn the quilt right side out. Smooth out any wrinkles, press the edges flat, and hand stitch the opening closed.

4 Baste the layers and quilt by hand or machine. The quilt shown was machine quilted in the ditch between the blocks and along the border seam lines to hold everything in place. Then, using one strand of white embroidery floss, stitching was added around the appliquéd circles using a longer-than-normal quilting stitch to simulate the look of Sashiko (traditional Japanese quilting).

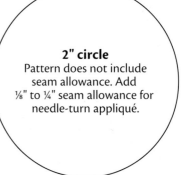

**2" circle**
Pattern does not include seam allowance. Add ⅛" to ¼" seam allowance for needle-turn appliqué.

# Never Wear Gloves at the Table

*Gloves seem too formal to wear while seated at a table covered with this little quilt. It's a casual, scrappy quilt that would make anyone feel at ease.*

By Mary Etherington and Connie Tesene of Country Threads

FINISHED QUILT SIZE: 24" x 31"     FINISHED BLOCK SIZE: 4" x 4"

## Materials

*Yardage is based on 42"-wide fabric unless otherwise noted. Charm squares are 5" x 5".*

42 assorted charm squares in cream, tan, pink, brown, and red for blocks and border

½ yard of dark print for block squares and binding

1 yard of fabric for backing

30" x 37" piece of batting

## Cutting

*All measurements include ¼"-wide seam allowances.*

**From each charm square, cut:***

1 rectangle, 3" x 4½"

1 rectangle, 2" x 3"

1 square, 2" x 2" (You only need 32.)

**From the dark print, cut:**

2 strips, 2" x 42"; crosscut into 42 squares, 2" x 2"**

3 strips, 2¼" x 42"

*Keep pieces of the same fabric together.*

**If you have less than 42" of usable fabric you'll need to cut 3 strips.*

## Making the Blocks

Each block uses a dark-print 2" square plus a 3" x 4½" rectangle and a 2" x 3" rectangle of the same fabric.

1 Sew a dark-print 2" square to a charm 2" x 3" rectangle. Press the seam allowances toward the dark print.

2 Sew a matching charm 3" x 4½" rectangle to this unit to make a block. Press toward the larger rectangle. Make 42 blocks.

Make 42.

## Assembling the Quilt

1 Sew the blocks together into seven rows of six blocks each, orienting the blocks as shown. Press the seam allowances in opposite directions from row to row. Sew the rows together and press.

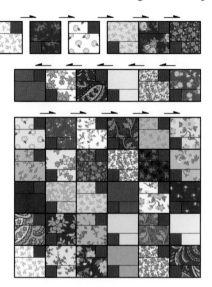

2 Sew 16 charm 2" squares together to make a border for the top of the quilt. Repeat for the bottom border, adjusting seams as necessary to fit the quilt. Sew the border strips to the top and bottom of the quilt and press the seam allowances away from the borders.

## Finishing the Quilt

1 Make a quilt back approximately 30" x 37". Layer the quilt top with batting and backing. Baste, and then quilt as desired.

2 Trim the excess batting and backing and bind the quilt with the dark-print 2¼"-wide strips.

# Blueberry Buckle

*This cheerful little quilt is made in a traditional blue-and-white color scheme.*
*Two variations of the same block are made by reversing the color positions.*

By Cathy Wierzbicki

FINISHED QUILT SIZE: 48½" x 48½"    FINISHED BLOCK SIZE: 6" x 6"

## Materials

*Yardage is based on 42"-wide fabric unless otherwise noted.*

2⅛ yards *total* of assorted dark-blue fabrics for blocks

2⅛ yards *total* of assorted light fabrics for blocks

½ yard of fabric for binding

3 yards of fabric for backing

54" x 54" piece of batting

## Cutting

*All measurements include ¼"-wide seam allowances.*

**From the assorted dark-blue fabrics, cut:**

12 squares, 5¼" x 5¼"; cut into quarters diagonally to yield 56 triangles (B)

18 squares, 4⅞" x 4⅞"; cut in half diagonally to yield 36 triangles (E)

28 squares, 4½" x 4½" (A)

36 squares, 2⅞" x 2⅞"; cut in half diagonally to yield 72 triangles (D)

108 squares, 2½" x 2½", in matching sets of 3 (C)

**From the assorted light fabrics, cut:**

18 squares, 5¼" x 5¼"; cut into quarters diagonally to yield 72 triangles (B)

14 squares, 4⅞" x 4⅞"; cut in half diagonally to yield 28 triangles (E)

36 squares, 4½" x 4½" (A)

28 squares, 2⅞" x 2⅞"; cut in half diagonally to yield 56 triangles (D)

84 squares, 2½" x 2½", in matching sets of 3 (C)

**From the binding fabric, cut:**

6 strips, 2½" x 42"

## Making the Blocks

You'll make a total of 64 blocks for this quilt in two variations. Each block is made from two fabrics: one light and one dark blue. For 36 blocks, the T motif is light and the background is dark blue (block 1). For 28 blocks, the T motif is dark blue and the background is light (block 2).

## Block 1

1 With right sides together, align matching dark C squares on opposite corners of one light A square as shown. Sew, trim, and press. Repeat to sew a matching C square to one remaining corner.

2 Sew a matching dark D half-square triangle to a matching light B quarter-square triangle as shown; press. Make one of each.

Make 1 of each.

3 Sew the units from step 2 to the unit from step 1 as shown; press. Sew one matching E half-square triangle to the unit to complete the block; press.

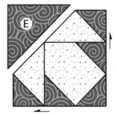

Block 1

4 Repeat steps 1–3 to make a total of 36 of block 1.

## Block 2

Reversing the dark-blue and light pieces, repeat "Block 1," steps 1–3, to make 28 of block 2.

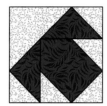

Block 2

# Assembling the Quilt

1 Arrange and sew four of block 1 together, rotating the blocks as shown; press. Make nine.

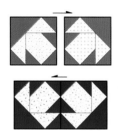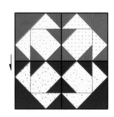

Make 9.

2 Arrange the units from step 1 into three horizontal rows of three units each as shown in the assembly diagram. Sew the units together into rows; press. Sew the rows together; press.

3 For the side borders, arrange and sew six of block 2, rotating the blocks as shown; press. Make two. For the top and bottom borders, arrange and sew eight of block 2, rotating the blocks as shown; press. Make two.

Make 2.

Make 2.

4 Sew the borders to the quilt top.

Assembly diagram

# Finishing the Quilt

1 Layer the backing, batting, and quilt top; baste.

2 Hand or machine quilt as desired.

3 Use the 2½"-wide strips to bind the quilt edges.

# Harvest Star

*With fall colors and autumn-themed prints, this star quilt*
*makes a fitting table topper or wall hanging for the fall season.*

By Sara Diepersloot; quilted by Deborah Rasmussen
FINISHED QUILT SIZE: 47" x 47"

## Materials

*Yardage is based on 42"-wide fabric. Fat eighths are 9" x 21".*

⅞ yard of gold leaf print for blocks

¾ yard of tan leaf print for border 4

⅝ yard of large-scale pumpkin print for blocks

⅝ yard of brown plaid for border 2 and binding

⅓ yard of rust print #1 for blocks

⅓ yard of rust print #2 for border 1

¼ yard of tiny-pumpkin print for blocks

¼ yard of gold star print for border 3

⅛ yard of brown pumpkin print for blocks

⅛ yard of gold-dot print for blocks

1 fat eighth *OR* 5" x 5" piece of pumpkin plaid for center square

3⅛ yards of fabric for backing

55" x 55" piece of batting

## Cutting

*All measurements include ¼"-wide seam allowances.*

**From the gold-dot print, cut:**

1 strip, 2½" x 42"; crosscut into 8 squares, 2½" x 2½"

**From the brown pumpkin print, cut:**

1 strip, 2½" x 42"; crosscut into 4 rectangles, 2½" x 4½", and 4 squares, 2½" x 2½"

**From the pumpkin plaid, cut:**

1 square, 4½" x 4½"

**From the tiny-pumpkin print, cut:**

1 strip, 4½" x 42"; crosscut into 8 squares, 4½" x 4½"

**From rust print #1, cut:**

2 strips, 4½" x 42"; crosscut into 4 rectangles, 4½" x 8½", and 4 squares, 4½" x 4½"

**From the large-scale pumpkin print, cut:**

2 strips, 8½" x 42"; crosscut into 8 squares, 8½" x 8½"

**From the gold leaf print, cut:**

3 strips, 8½" x 42"; crosscut into 4 rectangles, 8½" x 16½", and 4 squares, 8½" x 8½"

**From rust print #2, cut:**

4 strips, 2" x 42"

**From the brown plaid, cut:**

4 strips, 1½" x 42"

5 strips, 2¼" x 42"

**From the gold star print, cut:**

4 strips, 1¼" x 42"

**From the tan leaf print, cut:**

5 strips, 4½" x 42"

## Making the Blocks

1 Draw a diagonal line from corner to corner on the wrong side of the gold-dot 2½" squares.

2 Lay a marked square on one end of a brown pumpkin 2½" x 4½" rectangle, right sides together. Sew on the drawn line. Trim off the excess ¼" from the stitching line. Press the seam allowances toward the triangle. Repeat on the other end of the rectangle, orienting the diagonal line in the opposite direction. Make four of these star-point units.

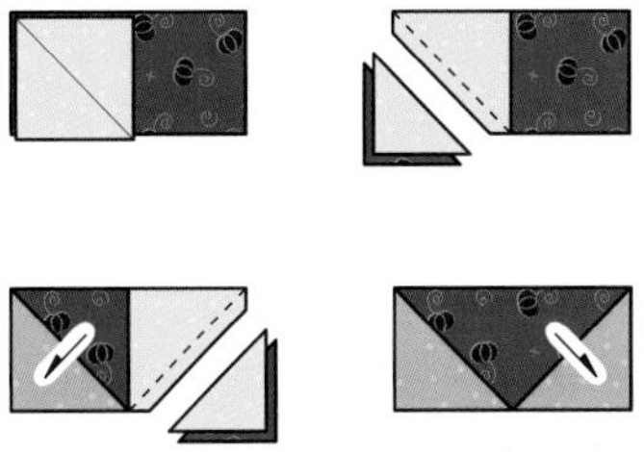

Make 4.

3 Arrange the brown pumpkin 2½" squares, the star-point units, and the pumpkin plaid 4½" square as shown. Join the units into rows, and then sew the rows together. Press, following the arrows in the diagram.

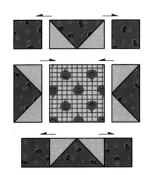 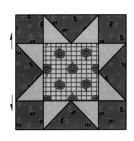

4 Draw a diagonal line from corner to corner on the wrong side of the tiny-pumpkin 4½" squares. Repeat step 2, placing the squares on a 4½" x 8½" rust print #1 rectangle. Make four of these star-point units.

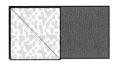 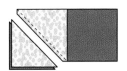
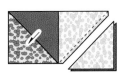 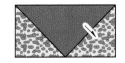

Make 4.

5 Arrange the 4½" rust #1 squares, the star-point units, and the unit made in step 3 as shown. Join the units into rows; sew the rows together. Press.

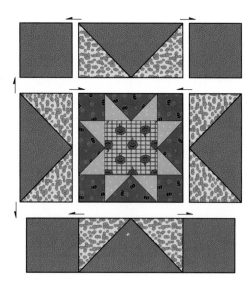

6 Draw a diagonal line from corner to corner on the wrong side of the large-scale pumpkin 8½" squares. Repeat step 2, placing the squares on a gold leaf 8½" x 16½" rectangle. Make four of these star-point units.

7 Arrange the gold leaf 8½" squares, the star-point units, and the step 5 unit as shown. Join the units into rows and sew the rows together. Press.

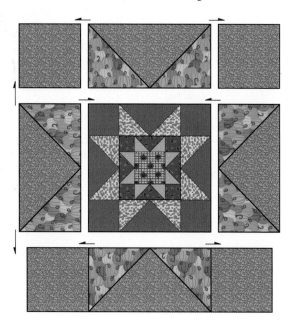

## Assembling the Quilt

Add the four borders in this order: rust print #2, brown plaid, gold star print, and tan leaf print.

## Finishing the Quilt

1 Layer the quilt top with batting and backing and quilt as desired. The quilt shown uses an overall pattern of vines and leaves in keeping with the harvest theme.

2 Bind the edges of the quilt using the 2¼"-wide brown-plaid strips.

# Don't Break Bread into Your Soup

*All your guests will use their best table manners in a dining room graced with this elegant quilt.*

By Mary Etherington and Connie Tesene of Country Threads

**FINISHED QUILT SIZE: 27" x 27"    FINISHED BLOCK SIZE: 4½" x 4½"**

## Materials

*Yardage is based on 42"-wide fabric unless otherwise noted. Charm squares are 5" x 5".*

18 charm squares in dark values
18 charm squares in medium values

⅞ yard of aged muslin for background*
¼ yard of dark-blue fabric for binding
1 yard of fabric for backing
31" x 31" piece of batting
*If aged muslin is not available, you can substitute regular muslin or an off-white tone-on-tone print.*

## Cutting

*All measurements include ¼"-wide seam allowances.*

Sort the charm squares into pairs of a medium- and a dark-value fabric (two contrasting fabrics).

**From *each* charm square, cut:**

4 squares, 2⅜" x 2⅜"; crosscut in half diagonally to make 2 triangles (8 per fabric; 288 total). Keep medium- and dark-value pairs of fabrics together.

**From the muslin, cut:**

7 strips, 2⅜" x 42"; crosscut into 108 squares, 2⅜" x 2⅜". Cut each square in half diagonally to make 2 triangles (216 total).

4 strips, 2" x 42"; crosscut into 72 squares, 2" x 2"

**From the dark-blue fabric, cut:**

3 strips, 1½" x 42"

## Making the Blocks

Work with one medium/dark fabric pair at a time. Each pair will make two identical blocks.

1 Sew a dark fabric triangle and a muslin triangle together as shown. Make three. Repeat with medium fabric triangles and muslin triangles to make three more triangle squares. Make one triangle square with a dark and a medium triangle. Press the seam allowances toward the darker fabrics.

Make 3.    Make 3.    Make 1.

2 Arrange the triangle squares from step 1 with two muslin squares, being careful to position the dark and medium triangles accurately. Sew the units into rows; then sew the rows together. Press. Pressing the seam allowances open makes it easier to match the points. Repeat to make 36 blocks (18 sets of two identical blocks).

Make 2 identical blocks.

## Assembling the Quilt

1 Choose two sets of two identical blocks for each four-block unit. Position the blocks to form a "circle" and sew together. Press. Make nine four-block units.

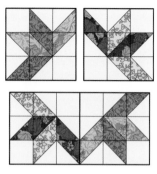

4-block unit.
Make 9.

2 Sew the four-block units together into three rows of three units each. Press in opposite directions from row to row. Sew the rows together and press.

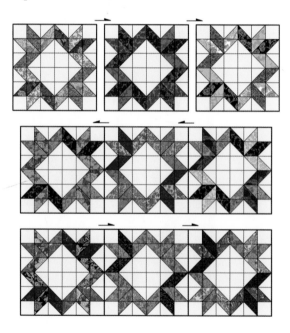

## Finishing the Quilt

1 Layer the quilt top with batting and backing; baste the layers together.

2 Quilt as desired. Sew the dark-blue 1½"-wide strips together end to end to make one long strip. Use this strip to bind your quilt.

# Vines and Flowers

*Select pale, muted tones for the Double X blocks to create
an unexpected background for the appliqué.*

By Lori Smith of From My Heart to Your Hands

FINISHED QUILT SIZE: 16" x 20"    FINISHED BLOCK SIZE: 4½" x 4½"

## Materials

*Fat quarters measure approximately 18" x 21"; fat eighths measure 9" x 21".*

1 fat quarter *OR* scraps of off-white prints for blocks

1 fat quarter of dark-green print for bias vine and leaves

1 fat quarter of rose floral for border

1 fat quarter *total* of assorted scraps of 12 light- to medium-green prints for blocks and leaves

1 fat eighth *total* of assorted scraps of medium- to dark-red prints for flowers

1 fat quarter of fabric for binding

1 fat quarter of fabric for backing

18" x 22" piece of batting

## Cutting

*All measurements include ¼"-wide seam allowances.*

**From the off-white prints, cut a total of:**

36 squares, 2⅜" x 2⅜"; cut in half diagonally to make 72 triangles

24 squares, 2" x 2"

**From *each* of the 12 light- to medium-green prints, cut:**

3 squares, 2⅜" x 2⅜"; cut in half diagonally to make 6 triangles (72 total)

1 square, 2" x 2" (12 total)

**From the dark-green print, cut:**

1¼"-wide bias strips to total 66"

**From the rose floral, cut:**

1 strip, 2½" x 14"

2 strips, 1¾" x 20½"

**From the binding fabric, cut:**

4 strips, 1¾" x 20"

## Making the Blocks

1 Sew an off-white 2⅜" triangle and a green 2⅜" triangle together to make a half-square-triangle unit. Make six for one block.

Make 6.

2 Arrange the units from step 1, two off-white 2" squares, and one matching green 2" square in rows as shown. Sew the units into rows; sew the rows together to make a block. Repeat to make a total of 12 blocks.

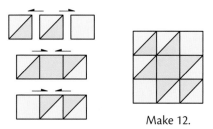

Make 12.

3 Arrange the blocks into four rows of three blocks each. Sew the blocks into rows and sew the rows together. Press.

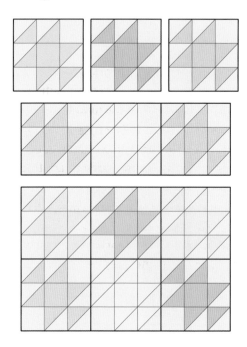

## Appliquéing the Flowers and Vines

1 Draw lines freehand on your quilt top as shown for the placement of the bias vines. Skip alternating diagonal rows, allowing each one to be

different. This will give a casual and natural appearance to your vines.

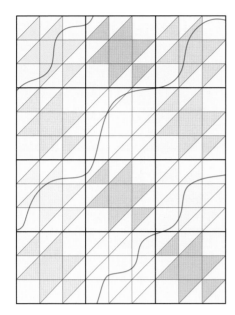

2 Prepare the vines using the dark-green bias strips. Pin or baste the vines in position and appliqué them in place on the quilt top.

3 Prepare the flower and leaf pieces using your favorite appliqué technique. Cut some of the leaves different shapes and sizes for variety and a natural look.

4 Arrange the leaves along the vines, adding or subtracting flowers and leaves as desired. When you're pleased with the arrangement, appliqué the pieces in place. Press the quilt top after the appliqué is complete.

## Finishing the Quilt

1 Sew the rose-floral 2½" x 14" strip to the bottom of the quilt; press. Sew a rose-floral 1¾" x 20½" strip to each side; press.

2 Layer the quilt top, batting, and backing. Baste the layers together and quilt as desired.

3 Add the binding and enjoy.

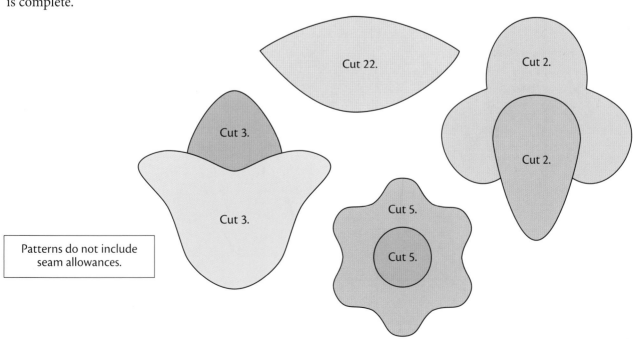

Cut 22.

Cut 2.

Cut 3.

Cut 2.

Cut 5.

Cut 3.

Cut 5.

Patterns do not include seam allowances.

# Asian Influences

*Terry loves to collect Asian-themed fabric, especially in shades of red, black, and white. These fabrics worked perfectly in this Japanese-type banner.*

By Terry Martin

FINISHED QUILT SIZE: 25½" x 47¾"    FINISHED BLOCK SIZES: 4½" x 4½" and 9" x 9"

## Materials

*Yardage is based on 42"-wide fabric.*

⅝ yard of large-scale floral for blocks and border

⅝ yard of black print for blocks, borders, and
   binding

⅝ yard of white print for blocks and background

¼ yard of red crane print for blocks

¼ yard of red character print for blocks

1½ yards of fabric for backing

30" x 52" piece of batting

2 squares of template plastic: 5" and 9½"

## Cutting

*All measurements include ¼"-wide seam allowances.*

**From the large-scale floral, cut:**

3 rectangles, 9½" x 10½"

1 strip, 6" x 25½"

**From the black print, cut:**

14 squares, 2¾" x 2¾"

1 strip, 1½" x 25½"

1 strip, 3" x 25½"

4 strips, 2½" x 42"

**From the white print, cut:**

6 rectangles, 5" x 6"

14 rectangles, 2¾" x 3¾"

2 squares, 7¼" x 7¼"; cut in half diagonally to make
   4 corner triangles

3 squares, 7¾" x 7¾"; cut into quarters diagonally to
   make 12 side triangles

**From the red crane print, cut:**

6 squares, 5" x 5"

**From the red character print, cut:**

7 rectangles, 5" x 6"

## Making the Blocks

1 For the 9" blocks, sew a crane-print 5" square to
   one end of each 5" x 6" rectangle.

2 Sew the pieced strips into pairs as shown. Make
   three paired rectangles.

 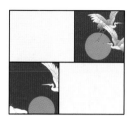

Make 3.

3 Clip the seam allowances to the seam line
   between the crane-print squares. Press the seam
allowances away from the squares, changing the
direction of the seam at the center cut.

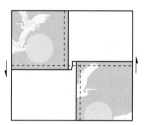

4 Cut the 9½" square of template plastic in half
   diagonally.

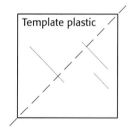 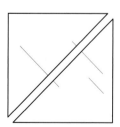

Template plastic

5 To mark the sewing line, place the template on the wrong side of your pieced rectangle, with the corner of the template on the square. Draw a diagonal line as shown below. Place the template on the opposite corner, again with the corner of the template on the square. Mark a second sewing line.

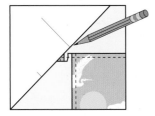 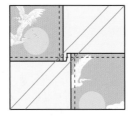

Mark stitching lines.

6 Pair the units from step 5 with the floral 9½" x 10½" rectangles, right sides together. Sew on each of the lines you drew, and then cut between them. Press the seam allowances toward the floral triangles. Make six blocks.

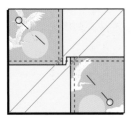 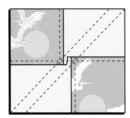

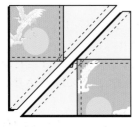 

Makes 2.

9" block.
Make 6.

7 Repeat steps 2–6 to make 4½" blocks using the black 2¾" squares, the white 2¾" x 3¾" rectangles, and the character-print 5" x 6" rectangles. Make 14 blocks.

4½" Block
Make 14.

## Assembling the Quilt

1 Sew white side triangles to the red sides of six of the 4½" blocks.

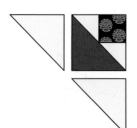 

Make 6.

2 Sew the remaining 4½" blocks together in sets of four to create two large blocks, as shown.

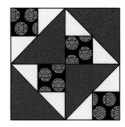

Make 2.

3 Lay out the blocks and corner triangles and sew them into rows as shown.

Quilt assembly

4 Sew the rows together. Sew the four white corner triangles to the corners of the quilt top.

5 Join the black 1½" x 25½" strip and the floral 6" x 25½" strip along their long edges. Sew the strip unit to the bottom of the quilt top, with the black strip next to the quilt top. Press the seam allowances toward the floral strip.

6 Join the black 3" x 25½" strip to the top of the quilt to complete the quilt top. Press the seam allowances toward the border.

# Finishing the Quilt

1 Layer the quilt top with batting and backing; baste the layers together.

2 Hand or machine quilt as desired. The quilt shown was machine quilted using an outline stitch in the small white triangles and around motifs in the floral print. A crane motif was quilted in the corner triangles.

3 Trim the batting and backing even with the edges of the quilt top. Sew the binding to the quilt.

# Bento Box

*Beautiful Japanese prints are the focus of this quilt, with the dark-blue indigos in sharp contrast to the brightly colored floral prints.*

By Judy Turner

**FINISHED QUILT SIZE: 30" x 36"     FINISHED BLOCK SIZE: 6" x 6"**

## Materials

*Yardage is based on 42"-wide fabric.*

1 yard *total* of assorted Japanese indigo prints for blocks

½ yard *total* of assorted brightly colored Japanese floral prints for blocks

⅜ yard of indigo print for binding

1¼ yards of fabric for backing

34" x 40" piece of batting

## Cutting

*All measurements include ¼"-wide seam allowances.*

**From the assorted Japanese indigo prints, cut a total of:**

180 rectangles, 2" x 3½"

**From the assorted brightly colored Japanese floral prints, cut a total of:**

60 rectangles, 2" x 3½"

**From the indigo print for binding, cut:**

4 strips, 2½" x 42"

## Making the Blocks

You'll need a total of 30 pieced blocks for this quilt. Avoid duplicating prints within the blocks.

1  Arrange six indigo-print and two floral-print rectangles. Choose florals with colors and patterns that will blend subtly in the center of each block.

2  Sew the rectangles together as shown; press. Make 30 blocks.

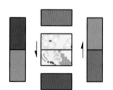

Make 30.

## Assembling the Quilt

1  Arrange the blocks in six horizontal rows of five blocks each.

2  Sew the blocks together into rows. Press the seam allowances in opposite directions from row to row.

3  Pin and sew the rows together; press.

Assembly diagram

## Finishing the Quilt

1  Center and layer the quilt top and batting over the backing; baste.

2  Quilt as desired.

3  Use the 2½"-wide binding strips to make the binding. Sew the binding to the quilt.

# Eat Slowly, It Took a Long Time to Prepare

*It may take a little longer to prepare than dinner, but this elegant little quilt is worth every minute!*

By Mary Etherington and Connie Tesene of Country Threads

FINISHED QUILT SIZE: 21" diameter

# Materials

*Yardage is based on 42"-wide fabric unless otherwise noted. Charm squares are 5" x 5".*

36 charm squares OR 18 assorted prints, 5" x 9"

⅛ yard of light-brown print for binding

¾ yard of fabric for backing

22" x 25" piece of batting

Template plastic OR half-hexagon acrylic template (available from your local quilt shop or Country Threads: www.CountryThreads.com)

# Cutting

*All measurements include ¼"-wide seam allowances.*

**From each charm square, cut:**

2 half-hexagons (72 total) using the pattern on page 38 and template plastic. You can stack up to 6 charm squares and cut all 6 at once.

**From the light-brown print, cut:**

2 strips, 1½" x 42"

# Making the Quilt

This project requires planning, and it's best to lay out all the pieces on your table or work wall before you start sewing. If you look at the photo on page 36 or the diagram above right, you'll notice three pieces are sewn together with a Y-seam to make an equilateral triangle. The matching half-hexagon is used in the equilateral triangle in the adjacent triangle or row. In addition, in every second triangle, the half-hexagons are arranged in a reversed (mirror) image of the preceding triangle. Each row consists of equilateral triangles sewn together with straight seams before the rows are sewn together—but all must match up correctly. (This is not a simple Nine Patch quilt!)

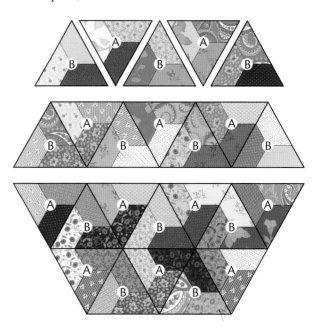

1 You may find it easiest to sew one triangle and put it back in place before sewing the next one. Flip one half-hexagon onto another, right sides together, and sew the first seam, stopping ¼" from the inner point. Finger-press the pieces open.

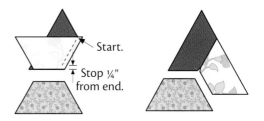

2 Add the third half-hexagon and sew the second seam the same way, stopping ¼" from the center.

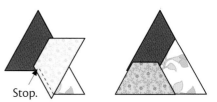

3 Sew the first and third half-hexagons together on the adjoining edge, stopping ¼" from the center. Press seam allowances open. You now have one equilateral triangle.

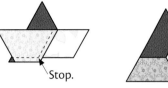

Triangle A.
Equilateral.

4 The triangles adjacent to the first one are a reversed image. Sew in the same manner as triangle A, stitching each seam and stopping ¼" from the center. Continue sewing three half-hexagons into equilateral triangles, being careful to sew the matching fabrics in the correct positions.

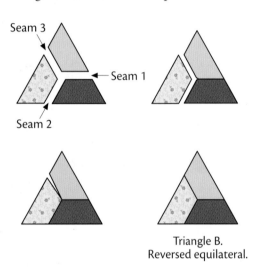

Triangle B.
Reversed equilateral.

5 Make 12 equilateral triangles and 12 reversed equilateral triangles (24 total).

6 Sew the triangles into rows; then sew the rows together and press.

## Finishing the Quilt

1 Layer the quilt top with batting and backing; baste. Quilt as desired.

2 Sew the light-brown 1½"-wide strips together end to end to make one long strip. Use this strip to bind your quilt, pivoting at each corner and then continuing on.

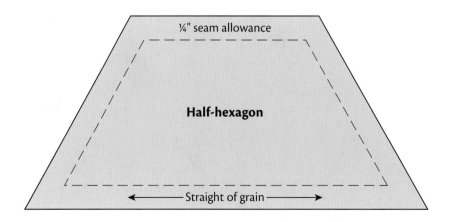

¼" seam allowance

**Half-hexagon**

Straight of grain

# Delectable Mountains

*Enjoy a sense of the beauty of nature while climbing the*
*"mountains" of this traditionally inspired quilt.*

By Lori Smith of From My Heart to Your Hands

FINISHED QUILT SIZE: 16" x 20"

## Materials

*Fat quarters measure approximately 18" x 21".*

1 fat quarter of light-green floral
1 fat quarter of dark-green print
1 fat quarter of violet print
1 fat quarter of off-white print
1 fat quarter of fabric for backing
18" x 22" piece of batting

## Cutting

*All measurements include ¼"-wide seam allowances. As you cut, keep all of the triangles separate and label them according to the size of the original square so that you can easily tell them apart after cutting.*

**From the light-green floral, cut:**

1 square, 2½" x 2½"
4 squares, 4⅞" x 4⅞"; cut in half diagonally to make 8 triangles
1 square, 5¼" x 5¼"; cut into quarters diagonally to make 4 triangles

**From the dark-green print, cut:**

4 squares, 1⅞" x 1⅞"; cut in half diagonally to make 8 triangles
13 squares, 3¼" x 3¼"; cut into quarters diagonally to make 52 triangles
8 squares, 2⅞" x 2⅞"; cut in half diagonally to make 16 triangles

**From the violet print, cut:**

3 squares, 5¼" x 5¼"; cut into quarters diagonally to make 12 triangles
8 squares, 1⅞" x 1⅞"; cut in half diagonally to make 16 triangles
4 strips, 1¾" x 20"

**From the off-white print, cut:**

13 squares, 3¼" x 3¼"; cut into quarters diagonally to make 52 triangles
4 squares, 1½" x 1½"
4 squares, 2⅞" x 2⅞"; cut in half diagonally to make 8 triangles
20 squares, 1⅞" x 1⅞"; cut in half diagonally to make 40 triangles

## Assembling the Quilt

1 Sew two dark-green 1⅞" triangles to an off-white 3¼" triangle as shown to make a star-point unit; press. Make four star-point units.

Make 4.

2 Arrange the off-white 1½" squares, the star-point units, and the light-green 2½" square as shown. Sew the units into rows; press. Sew the rows together to make the Sawtooth Star block; press.

3 Sew a large violet triangle to each side of the Sawtooth Star block; press.

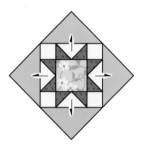

4 Sew dark-green 3¼" triangles, off-white 3¼" triangles, and off-white 2⅞" triangles together in rows as shown. Make two of each row.

Make 2.

Make 2.

5 Sew the shorter rows from step 4 to opposite sides of the unit from step 3; press. Sew the longer rows from step 4 to the remaining sides; press.

6 Sew a large violet triangle to each short side of the light-green 4⅞" triangle; press. Make four units.

Make 4.

7 Sew dark-green 3¼" triangles, off-white 3¼" triangles, and off-white 2⅞" triangles together in rows as shown. Make four of each.

Make 4 of each.

8 Sew one of each short row from step 7 to opposite sides of the units from step 6; press. Add a long row from step 7 to one remaining side as shown; press. Make four units.

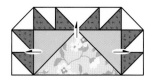

Make 4.

9 Sew a light-green 4⅞" triangle and two light-green 5¼" triangles to a unit from step 8 as shown. Press the seam allowances toward the light-green triangles. Make two. Sew a light-green 4⅞" triangle to the remaining two units from step 8.

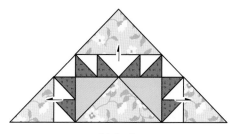

Make 2.

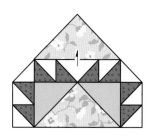

Make 2.

10 Sew one violet 1⅞" triangle and three off-white 1⅞" triangles together as shown. Add a dark green 2⅞" triangle and press. Make 12 units.

Make 12.

11 Sew two violet 1⅞" triangles, two off-white 1⅞" triangles, and two off-white 3¼" triangles together as shown; press. Sew a dark-green 2⅞" triangle to each side; press. Make two.

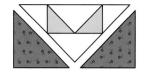 

Make 2.

12 Sew the units from steps 10 and 11 together as shown. Make two rows.

Make 2.

13 Arrange and sew the units from step 9 and the center unit in diagonal rows; press. Sew the rows together.

14 Add the units from step 12 to the top and bottom of the quilt.

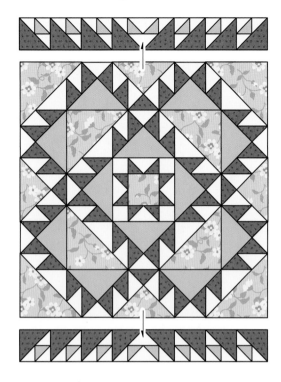

## Finishing the Quilt

1 Layer the quilt top, batting, and backing. Baste the layers together and quilt as desired.

2 Add the violet binding strips and enjoy.

# Amish-Inspired Shoofly

*Shoofly blocks are commonplace in Amish quilts, as are solid colors, both bright and muted. Here, hand-dyed cottons give visual texture to this traditional quilt pattern.*

By Karen Costello Soltys

FINISHED QUILT SIZE: 23¼" x 29½"    FINISHED BLOCK SIZE: 4½" x 4½"

## Materials

*Yardage is based on 42"-wide fabric
unless otherwise noted.*

⅝ yard of dusty turquoise solid for outer border

⅜ yard of dark cinnamon for inner border and
    binding

1 fat quarter of light cinnamon for Shoofly blocks

1 fat quarter of dark blue for Shoofly blocks

1 fat quarter of medium blue for setting triangles

1 fat eighth of dusty blue for setting squares

⅞ yard of fabric for backing

25" x 32" piece of batting

## Cutting

*All measurements include ¼"-wide seam allowances.*

**From the light cinnamon, cut:**

6 squares, 2" x 2"

12 squares, 2⅜" x 2⅜"

**From the dark blue, cut:**

24 squares, 2" x 2"

12 squares, 2⅜" x 2⅜"

**From the dusty blue, cut:**

2 squares, 5" x 5"

**From the medium blue, cut:**

2 squares, 7¾" x 7¾"; cut into quarters diagonally to
    make 8 side triangles (2 will be extra)

2 squares, 4¼" x 4¼"; cut in half diagonally to make
    4 corner triangles

**From the dark cinnamon, cut:**

2 strips, 1½" x 42"

3 strips, 2" x 42"

**From the dusty turquoise, cut:**

4 strips, 4½" x 42"

## Making the Blocks

1 To piece the triangles, you can cut the light-
cinnamon and dark-blue 2⅜" squares in half
diagonally, and then sew a cinnamon triangle to a
blue triangle. Or, you can mark a diagonal line on
the wrong side of the cinnamon squares, layer the
squares right sides together with the blue squares,
and stitch ¼" from the marked line on each side.
Then cut the squares apart on the drawn line. Make
24 triangle squares. Press the seam allowances
toward the dark-blue triangles.

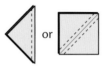 or

Make 24.

2 Lay out one light-cinnamon 2" square, four
dark-blue 2" squares, and four triangle squares
from step 1 in a nine-patch arrangement. Sew the
pieces together in rows, and then sew the rows
together to complete a Shoofly block, pressing
the seam allowances toward the dark-blue fabric.
Repeat to make six blocks.

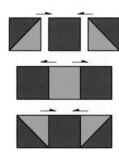 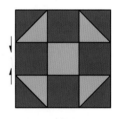

Make 6.

## Assembling the Quilt

1 Lay out the six Shoofly blocks, the two dusty-blue setting squares, and the medium-blue side and corner setting triangles in diagonal rows. Sew the blocks, setting squares, and side triangles together into rows, pressing the seam allowances toward the setting squares and triangles.

2 Sew the rows together, matching seam intersections. Add the corner triangles last and press. The setting triangles were cut a bit oversized for easier cutting and piecing. Trim and square up the quilt top, making sure to leave ¼" beyond the points of all the blocks for seam allowances.

Quilt layout

3 Measure the length of the quilt top. Cut two pieces this length from a dark-cinnamon 1½" strip. Sew them to the sides of the quilt top and press the seam allowances toward the borders. Measure the width of the quilt top. Cut two pieces from the remaining dark-cinnamon border strips and sew them to the top and bottom of the quilt top. Press.

4 Measure, trim, and sew the dusty-turquoise borders to the quilt top in the same manner as for the dark-cinnamon border.

Quilt plan

## Finishing the Quilt

1 Mark any quilting designs on the quilt top.

2 Place the backing right side down on a table or floor, and lay the batting on top, smoothing out any wrinkles. Then add the pressed quilt top, right side up, on top. Hand or pin baste the layers together.

3 Quilt by hand or machine. The quilt shown was machine quilted in the ditch between all blocks and setting pieces, as well as on both sides of the dark-cinnamon border and around all pieces in each Shoofly block. A continuous-line floral design in the plain setting squares and cross-hatching in the outer border completes the design.

4 Using the dark-cinnamon 2"-wide strips, make and attach binding.

# Batik Fun

*Diamonds dance across the surface of the quilt with the careful placement of light, medium, and dark values.*

By Lori Smith of From My Heart to Your Hands
FINISHED QUILT SIZE: 16" x 20"     FINISHED BLOCK SIZE: 2" x 2"

## Materials

*Fat quarters measure approximately 18" x 21".*

1 fat quarter *total* of assorted light batiks for blocks

1 fat quarter *total* of assorted medium batiks for blocks and borders

1 fat quarter *total* of assorted dark batiks for blocks and borders

1 fat quarter of fabric for binding

1 fat quarter of fabric for backing

18" x 22" piece of batting

# Cutting

*All measurements include ¼"-wide seam allowances.*

**From the assorted light batiks, cut:**

48 squares, 1⅞" x 1⅞"; cut in half diagonally to make 96 triangles

**From the assorted medium batiks, cut:**

48 squares, 1½" x 1½"

16 squares, 2⅞" x 2⅞"; cut in half diagonally to make 32 triangles

**From the assorted dark batiks, cut:**

40 squares, 2⅞" x 2⅞"; cut in half diagonally to make 80 triangles

**From the binding fabric, cut:**

4 strips, 1¾" x 20"

# Assembling the Quilt

1 Sew light 1⅞" triangles to two sides of a medium 1½" square as shown; press.

2 Sew the unit from step 1 to a dark 2⅞" triangle; press. The block should measure 2½" x 2½". Make 48 Flying Geese blocks.

Make 32.

3 Sew a medium 2⅞" triangle to a dark 2⅞" triangle; press. Make 32 half-square-triangle units for the borders.

Make 48.

4 Arrange the blocks from step 2 in eight rows of six blocks each. Sew them together in groups of four to make a section. Sew three sections together to make a horizontal row. Make four horizontal

rows and sew the rows together to make the center of the quilt. Press the seam allowances open.

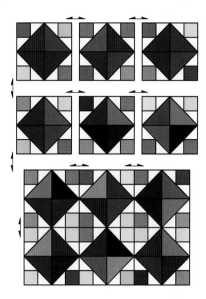

5 Arrange the half-square-triangle units around the center of the quilt, placing the base of the darker triangles along the outer edges. They will create the appearance of a sawtooth border around the quilt. Sew eight units together for each of the four borders. Press the seam allowances open.

6 Sew the borders to the sides of the quilt, and then the top and bottom. Press the seam allowances open.

# Finishing the Quilt

Layer the quilt top, batting, and backing. Baste the layers together and quilt as desired. Add the binding and enjoy.

# Order Coffee Every 60 Minutes in a Coffee Shop

*You'll enjoy sipping your favorite beverage while tucked under this colorful lap quilt.*

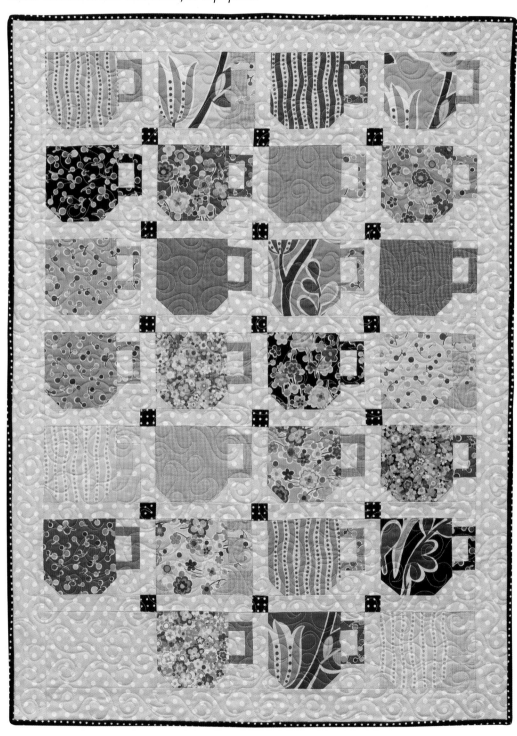

By Mary Etherington and Connie Tesene of Country Threads

FINISHED QUILT SIZE: 31" x 41½"    FINISHED BLOCK SIZE: 4½" x 6"

## Materials

*Yardage is based on 42"-wide fabric. Charm squares are 5" x 5". Instructions are simplified to cut all block backgrounds from the yellow-dotted fabric, but you can cut some from additional contrasting charm squares.*

27 assorted charm squares for coffee cups (28 if you don't want a blank square as shown)

10 charm squares for handles (use duplicates and fabrics similar to coffee-cup squares)

1¼ yards of yellow-dotted fabric for sashing, blank square, background, and border

⅜ yard of black-dotted fabric for cornerstones and binding

1½ yards of fabric for backing

37" x 48" piece of batting

## Cutting

*All measurements include ¼"-wide seam allowances.*

**From each of the charm squares for handles, cut:**

9 rectangles, 1" x 2" (you'll use 81 for 27 blocks, 84 for 28 blocks)

**From the yellow-dotted fabric, cut:**

11 strips, 1½" x 42"; crosscut into:
    54 squares, 1½" x 1½" (56 for 28 blocks)
    27 rectangles, 1½" x 2" (28 for 28 blocks)
    20 rectangles, 1½" x 5" (21 for 28 blocks)
    24 rectangles, 1½" x 6½"

3 strips, 2" x 42"; crosscut into:
    27 rectangles, 1" x 2" (28 for 28 blocks)
    27 squares, 2" x 2" (28 for 28 blocks)

4 strips, 2½" x 42"; crosscut into:
    2 strips, 2½" x 38"
    2 strips, 2½" x 31½"

1 rectangle, 5" x 7½" (you may substitute 1 pieced block and 1 rectangle, 1½" x 5")

**From the black-dotted fabric, cut:**

1 strip, 1½" x 42"; crosscut into 18 squares, 1½" x 1½"

4 strips, 2¼" x 42"

## Creating the Quilt

Each block requires one charm square; three matching or coordinating 1" x 2" rectangles from charm fabric; and two 1½" squares, one 2" square, one 1" x 2" rectangle, and one 1½" x 2" rectangle from the background fabric. The quilt shown has one yellow-dotted square. If you prefer more symmetry, make 28 blocks instead of 27.

1 Sew yellow-dotted 1½" squares to two adjacent corners of the charm square, right sides together and stitching diagonally from corner to corner. Trim excess fabric from the small square and press the seam allowances toward the triangles. Repeat with all the charm squares to make 27 cup units.

2 Match the charm squares with coordinating or matching handle rectangles. Sew a handle 1" x 2" rectangle to a yellow-dotted 1" x 2" rectangle. Sew a matching 1" x 2" rectangle to a yellow-dotted 1½" x 2" rectangle; sew a third matching 1" x 2" rectangle to a yellow-dotted 2" square. Press each unit toward the darker fabric. Sew the three units together as shown. Press. Make 27 handle units.

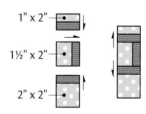

3 Sew a cup unit from step 1 to a coordinating or matching handle unit from step 2 to make a Coffee Cup block. Press toward the coffee-cup unit. Make 27 blocks if you want your quilt to look like the one shown, or make 28 blocks if you don't want an unpieced square.

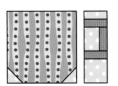 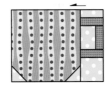

Make 27 or 28.

4 Sew four Coffee Cup blocks in a row, inserting yellow-dotted 1½" x 5" rectangles between the blocks. Press the seam allowances toward the yellow-dotted fabric. Make six rows with four cups in each row. For the seventh row, sew a yellow-dotted 5" x 7½" rectangle to the left side of the row instead of a block and a yellow rectangle.

5 Alternate and sew together four yellow-dotted 1½" x 6" rectangles and three black-dotted squares. Press the seam allowances toward the yellow-dotted fabric. Make six sashing rows.

6 Sew the block and sashing rows together and press the seam allowances toward the sashing rows.

7 Sew the yellow-dotted 2½" x 38" strips to the sides of the quilt and press the seam allowances toward the strips. Sew the yellow-dotted 2½" x 31½" strips to the top and bottom of the quilt and press toward the strips.

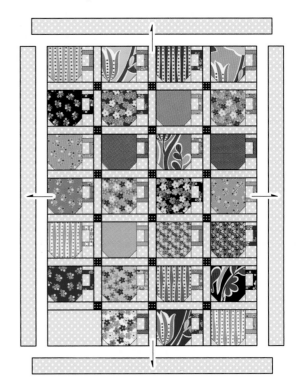

## Finishing the Quilt

Make a quilt back approximately 37" x 48". Layer the quilt top with batting and backing. Baste, and then quilt as desired. Trim the excess batting and backing and bind the quilt with the black-dotted 2¼"-wide strips.

# Twice as Nice

*Using these two different blocks gives the impression of an on-point setting. Everything in this quilt is scrappy—take advantage of it and use up some odds and ends.*

By Ellen Pahl

FINISHED QUILT SIZE: 40½" x 40½"    FINISHED BLOCK SIZE: 5" x 5"

## Materials

*Yardage is based on 42"-wide fabric.*

2⅛ yards *total* of assorted light prints for blocks and border

1 yard *total* of assorted medium to dark prints for blocks

⅜ yard of medium print for binding

2½ yards of fabric for backing

45" x 45" piece of batting

## Cutting

*All measurements include ¼"-wide seam allowances. As you cut, keep the pieces for each block together to make piecing easier.*

### For 1 Turnstile Block (Cut 24 total.)

**From 1 light print, cut:**

2 squares, 3⅜" x 3⅜"; cut in half diagonally to make 4 triangles

1 square, 3¾" x 3¾"; cut into quarters diagonally to make 4 triangles

**From 1 medium or dark print, cut:**

1 square, 3¾" x 3¾"; cut into quarters diagonally to make 4 triangles

### For 1 Spinner Block (Cut 25 total.)

**From 1 light print, cut:**

2 squares, 3⅜" x 3⅜"; cut in half diagonally to make 4 triangles

4 squares, 1¾" x 1¾"

**From 1 medium or dark print, cut:**

4 squares, 2⅛" x 2⅛"; cut in half diagonally to make 8 triangles

### For 1 Half-Spinner Block (Cut 12 total.)

**From 1 light print, cut:**

1 square, 3⅜" x 3⅜"; cut in half diagonally to make 2 triangles

2 squares, 1¾" x 1¾"

**From 1 medium or dark print, cut:**

2 squares, 2⅛" x 2⅛"; cut in half diagonally to make 4 triangles

### For 2 Quarter-Spinner Blocks (Cut 4 total.)

**From 1 light print, cut:**

1 square, 3⅜" x 3⅜"; cut in half diagonally to make 2 triangles

2 squares, 1¾" x 1¾"

**From *each of 2* different medium or dark prints, cut:**

1 square, 2⅛" x 2⅛"; cut in half diagonally to make 2 triangles (4 total)

### For Border and Binding

**From the assorted light prints, cut a total of:**

16 rectangles, 3" x 5½"

**From the medium print for binding, cut:**

5 strips, 2⅛" x 42"

## Making the Turnstile Blocks

1 Using the pieces cut for one block, sew each of the four medium or dark 3¾" triangles to a light-print 3¾" triangle. Press.

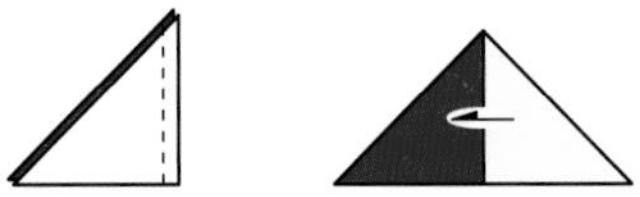

Make 4.

2 Sew each unit from step 1 to a light-print 3⅜" triangle. Press.

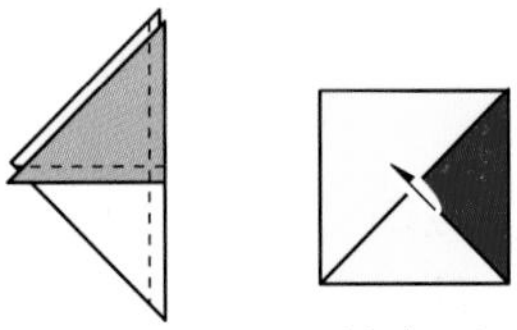

Make 4.

3 Arrange and sew the units from step 2 together as shown to make the block.

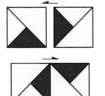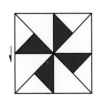

4 Repeat steps 1–3 to make a total of 24 blocks.

## Making the Spinner Blocks

1 Using the pieces cut for one block, sew two medium or dark 2⅛" triangles to adjacent sides of a light-print 1¾" square as shown. Press seam allowances toward the triangles. Repeat to make a total of four units.

Make 4.

2 Sew a unit from step 1 to each of the four light-print 3⅜" triangles. Press.

Make 4.

3 Arrange and sew the units from step 2 together as shown to make the block. Press.

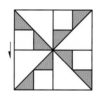

4 Repeat steps 1–3 to make a total of 25 blocks.

5 To make the Half-Spinner blocks, repeat steps 1 and 2 to make two units using the pieces you cut for one block. Arrange and sew the units together as shown to make the half block. Repeat to make a total of 12 half blocks.

Make 12.

6 To make the Quarter-Spinner blocks, repeat steps 1 and 2 using the pieces you cut for one block. Repeat to make a total of four blocks.

Make 4.

## Assembling and Finishing the Quilt

1 Arrange the blocks on a design wall, alternating them as shown in the quilt diagram below. Add the half blocks and 3" x 5½" rectangles along the outer edges. Add a quarter block in each corner. Sew the blocks into rows and press. Sew the rows together; press.

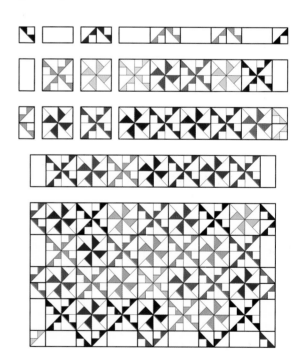

2 Layer, baste, quilt, and add the medium-print binding. The quilt shown is stitched in the ditch horizontally, vertically, and diagonally.

# Box of Chocolates

*Instead of using the same fabric on all sides of the center squares, two different fabrics were used in each block, placed in opposite corners to create an interesting zigzag effect.*

By Karen Costello Soltys

**FINISHED QUILT SIZE: 16½" x 20½"    FINISHED BLOCK SIZE: 4" x 4"**

## Materials

*Yardage is based on 42"-wide fabric unless otherwise noted. Fat eighths measure 9" x 21".*

1 fat eighth *each OR* scraps of 3 cream prints for patchwork

1 fat eighth *each OR* scraps of 3 pink prints for patchwork

1 fat eighth *each OR* scraps of 4 brown prints for patchwork and binding

⅝ yard of fabric for backing*

19" x 23" piece of batting

20 cream buttons, approximately ½" to ⅝" in diameter

*You can use ⅜ yard if you don't mind a seam in your quilt back.*

## Cutting

*All measurements include ¼"-wide seam allowances.*

**From *each* of the pink prints, cut:**
2 strips, 1½" x 21" (6 total)
2 strips, 2½" x 21" (6 total)

**From *3* of the brown prints, cut:**
2 strips, 1½" x 21" (6 total)
2 strips, 2½" x 21" (6 total)

**From *each* of the cream prints, cut:**
7 squares, 2½" x 2½" (21 total; 1 will be extra)

**From the remaining brown print, cut:**
4 binding strips, 2" x 21"

## Making the Blocks

1 Pair a pink 1½"-wide strip with a brown 1½"-wide strip. Sew them together along the long edges. Press the seam allowances toward the brown fabric. Repeat to make a total of six strip sets, pairing the 1½" strips of the same pink and brown fabrics together. Cut the strip sets into 1½"-wide segments (40 total); you'll need 20 matching pairs of segments.

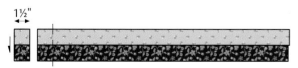

Cut 1½"-wide segments.

2 Sew the pink and brown 2½"-wide strips together in the same manner, again pairing the same fabric combinations. Cut the strip sets into 1½"-wide segments (40 total); you'll need 20 matching pairs of segments.

Cut 1½"-wide segments.

3 For each block, select one cream square and two matching segments from step 1. Sew the segments to opposite sides of the cream square, making sure that the pink squares are diagonally opposite from one another, not directly across. Press the seam allowances toward the segments. Make 20.

Make 20.

4 Sew matching segments from step 2 to each partial block as shown, placing the pink pieces next to the previously attached pink squares. Press both seam allowances in the same direction for ease of matching seams when assembling the quilt top. Make 20 blocks.

Make 20.

## Assembling the Quilt

1 Lay out the blocks in five horizontal rows of four blocks each. Make sure that the pink fabrics are in the upper-left and lower-right corners of all blocks in order to create the diagonal pattern.

Quilt plan

2 When you're satisfied with the placement of colors and fabrics, sew the blocks together into rows. If necessary, rotate the blocks 180° so that adjoining seam allowances are pressed in opposite directions for easier seam alignment.

3 Sew the rows together and press seam allowances in one direction.

## Finishing the Quilt

1 Mark any quilting designs on the quilt top.

2 If necessary, piece the quilt backing and press the seam allowances to one side. Place the backing right side down on a table or floor and lay the batting on top, smoothing out any wrinkles. Then add the pressed quilt top, right side up, on top. Hand or pin baste the layers together.

3 Quilt by hand or machine. The quilt shown was machine quilted with continuous curved lines stitched from one corner of a brown section to the opposite corner, bowing the stitching line to take advantage of the L shape of the fabric pieces. You can quilt along one brown diagonal, turn your quilt a quarter turn, and continue stitching along the pink diagonal for easy no-mark quilting with very little starting and stopping.

4 Using the 2"-wide brown strips, make and attach binding.

5 Sew a button in the center of each light-print square, sewing through all layers to secure it.

# Jacob's Ladder

*This quilt relies on controlled bands of color for its design. Pay careful attention to where the light and dark fabrics are placed.*

By Mary Etherington and Connie Tesene of Country Threads
FINISHED QUILT SIZE: 30" x 30"

## Materials

*Yardage is based on 42"-wide fabric.*

½ yard *total* of assorted light prints for units
½ yard *total* of assorted dark prints for units
¼ yard of tan-striped fabric for border
½ yard of plaid fabric for binding
1 yard of fabric for backing
34" x 34" piece of batting

## Cutting

*All measurements include ¼"-wide seam allowances.*

**From the light prints, cut:**
64 squares, 2" x 2"
16 squares, 3⅞" x 3⅞"; cut in half diagonally to make 32 triangles

**From the dark prints, cut:**

64 squares, 2" x 2"

16 squares, 3⅞" x 3⅞"; cut in half diagonally
   to make 32 triangles

12 squares, 3½" x 3½"

**From the tan-striped fabric, cut:**

8 rectangles, 3½" x 12½"

**From the plaid fabric, cut:**

2½"-wide bias strips to yield 130" of binding

## Making the Units

1 Join light and dark 2" squares to make four-
   patch units.

Make 32.

2 Join light and dark triangles to make half-
   square-triangle units.

Make 32.

## Assembling the Quilt

1 Arrange and sew the units together.

2 Sew dark 3½" squares to the left ends of four
   tan-striped rectangles and to the right ends of
four other tan-striped rectangles. Do not trim the

corner of the rectangles. Press the triangles toward
the corner.

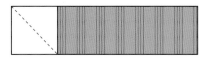

Make 4.

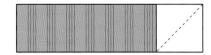

Make 4.

3 Sew the border units together as shown, adding
   dark squares to both ends of the side borders.

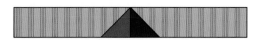

Make 2 for top and bottom borders.

Make 2 for side borders.

4 Sew the top and bottom borders to the quilt
   top; then add the side borders.

## Finishing the Quilt

Layer the quilt top with batting and backing; baste.
Quilt as desired and bind the edges.

# Hopscotch

*Shiny red buttons teamed with rich chocolate brown, warm yellow, and luscious cream prints make for a great game of quilting hopscotch.*

By Cyndi Walker

FINISHED QUILT SIZE: 48½" x 48½"    FINISHED BLOCK SIZE: 8" x 8"

## Materials

*Yardage is based on 42"-wide fabric.*

1⅞ yards *total* of assorted brown prints for blocks and outer border

1¼ yards *total* of assorted cream #1 prints for blocks

⅔ yard of cream #2 print for inner and outer borders

¼ yard *total* of assorted yellow prints for blocks

½ yard of fabric for binding

3½ yards of fabric for backing

58" x 58" piece of batting

12 red buttons, ½" to ⁹⁄₁₆" in diameter

# Cutting

*All measurements include ¼"-wide seam allowances.*

**From the assorted brown prints, cut a *total* of:**

104 squares, 2½" x 2½"

1 strip, 2½" x 42"

2 strips, 1½" x 42"

24 rectangles, 2½" x 8½", in matching pairs*

24 rectangles, 2½" x 4½", in matching pairs*

10 squares, 5¼" x 5¼"; crosscut into quarters diagonally to make 40 triangles

2 squares, 4⅞" x 4⅞"; cut in half diagonally to make 4 triangles

**From the assorted cream #1 prints, cut a *total* of:**

52 squares, 4½" x 4½"

48 squares, 2½" x 2½"

**From the assorted yellow prints, cut a *total* of:**

2 strips, 1½" x 42"

1 strip, 2½" x 42"

**From the cream #2 print, cut:**

5 strips, 2½" x 42"

11 squares, 5¼" x 5½"; cut into quarters diagonally to make 44 triangles

**From the binding fabric, cut:**

6 strips, 2½" x 42"

*Cut these in matching sets of two 2½" x 8½" rectangles and two 2½" x 4½" rectangles.*

## Making the Cross Blocks

1 Mark a light diagonal line on the wrong side of each brown 2½" square. With right sides together, align marked squares with opposite corners of a 4½" cream #1 square as shown. Stitch directly on the marked lines and trim, leaving a ¼" seam allowance; press. Make 52 scrappy units.

Make 52.

2 Arrange four units from step 1 as shown. Sew the units together into rows; press. Sew the rows together to complete the block; press. Make 13 blocks. Each block should measure 8½" x 8½", including seam allowances.

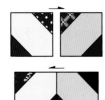 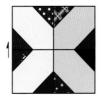

Make 13.

## Making the Snowball Blocks

1 Sew the two yellow 1½"-wide strips and the brown 2½"-wide strip together along their long edges, alternating them as shown to make strip set A; press. Crosscut the strip set into 24 segments, 1½" wide.

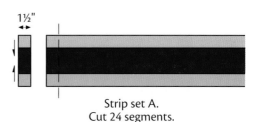

Strip set A.
Cut 24 segments.

2 Sew the two brown 1½"-wide strips and the yellow 2½" strip together along their long edges, alternating them as shown to make strip set B; press. Crosscut the strip set into 12 segments, 2½" wide.

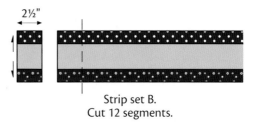

Strip set B.
Cut 12 segments.

3 Arrange two segments from step 1 and one segment from step 2 as shown. Sew the segments together; press. Make 12 scrappy units.

Make 12.

4 Mark a light diagonal line on the wrong side of each 2½" cream #1 square. With right sides together, align marked squares with opposite ends of a brown 2½" x 8½" rectangle as shown. Stitch on the marked lines and trim, leaving a ¼" seam allowance; press. Make 24 units in matching pairs.

Make 24.

5 Arrange one unit from step 3, two matching units from step 4, and two matching brown 2½" x 4½" rectangles as shown. Sew the units and rectangles together into rows; press. Sew the rows together to complete the block; press. Make 12 blocks. Each block should measure 8½" x 8½", including seam allowances.

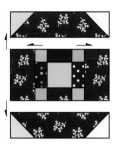
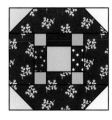

Make 12.

## Assembling the Quilt

1 Arrange the Cross and Snowball blocks into five horizontal rows of five blocks each, alternating them as shown. Sew the blocks together into rows. Press the seam allowances in opposite directions from row to row. Sew the rows together to complete the quilt center; press.

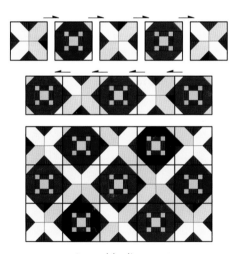

Assembly diagram

2 Sew the 2½"-wide cream #2 strips end to end to make one continuous strip; press. From this strip, cut two 2½" x 40½" inner-border strips and sew them to the sides of the quilt. Press the seam allowances toward the border.

3 From the remaining strip, cut two 2½" x 44½" inner-border strips and sew them to the top and bottom of the quilt; press.

4 With right sides together, sew 10 assorted brown triangles and 11 cream #2 triangles together along their short edges, alternating them as shown; press. Make four outer-border strips.

5 Sew outer-border strips from step 4 to opposite sides of the quilt. Press the seam allowances toward the outer border. Sew the remaining outer-border strips to the top and bottom of the quilt; press. Finish by sewing a brown triangle to each corner of the quilt top. Press the seam allowances toward the corner triangles.

Quilt plan

## Finishing the Quilt

1 Cut and piece the backing fabric so that it measures 10" larger than both the length and width of the quilt top.

2 Layer the quilt top, batting, and backing; baste the layers together.

3 Machine or hand quilt as desired.

4 Use the 2½"-wide strips to prepare the binding; sew the binding to the quilt.

5 Referring to the quilt photo on page 59, sew a red button in the center of each Snowball block with matching thread.

# Maple Sugar Hearts

*A selection of pink and red florals, checks, and stripes*
*brings these hearts to life on a subtle brown background.*

By Karen Costello Soltys

FINISHED QUILT SIZE: 19½" x 23½"

## Materials

*Yardage is based on 42"-wide fabric. Fat quarters measure approximately 18" x 21".*

1 fat quarter of medium-brown print for background

1 fat quarter of light striped fabric for inner border

1 fat quarter of dark-brown print for outer border

Scraps (3½" x 4½") of 20 assorted pink and red florals, checks, and striped fabrics for hearts

1 fat quarter of dark-brown print for binding

⅔ yard of fabric for backing

23" x 27" piece of batting

3½" x 4" piece of template plastic

Fine-point permanent marker

## Cutting

*All measurements include ¼"-wide seam allowances.*

**From the light striped fabric, cut:**

4 strips, 1¼" x 21"

**From the dark-brown print for border, cut:**

4 strips, 3" x 21"

**From the dark-brown print for binding, cut:**

5 strips, 2" x 21"

## Appliquéing the Quilt Top

1 Using the pattern on page 64, trace the heart onto template plastic and cut out exactly on the line. Use your favorite appliqué method to prepare the hearts.

2 Mark placement lines for the hearts on the background fabric. You can mark with a pencil, or simply fold the fabric in half lengthwise and press a crease. This will be the line for the center row of hearts. Mark additional vertical placement lines by measuring 2½" from the center crease, and then fold the fabric along these lines and press.

Continue in this fashion, creasing five vertical placement lines.

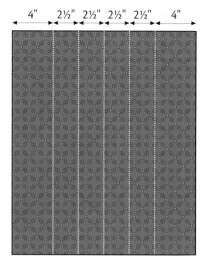

Fold and press
to mark placement lines.

3 Place the first heart along the left placement line, positioning it about 2" from the top of the fabric. Pin or baste, and then appliqué in place using your favorite technique.

4 Place the second heart below the first one so that the bottom point of the first heart is 1" from the inner point at the top of the second heart. Appliqué in place as for the first heart. Continue positioning and appliquéing the row in this manner.

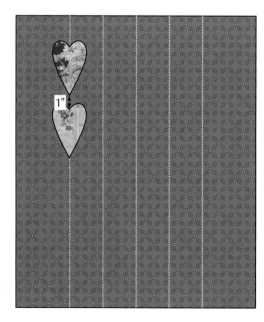

5 For the second row, face the hearts in the opposite direction. Align the vertical center of the hearts with the crease, and align the top and bottom of each heart with the hearts in the first row.

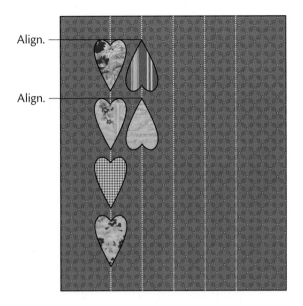

Align.

Align.

6 When all hearts have been appliquéd, press the quilt top from the wrong side. Square up the quilt, measuring 1" from the edges of the hearts to the edge of the fabric.

7 Fold the 1¼" light strips in half lengthwise, wrong sides together. Machine baste a strip to each long side of the quilt using a scant ¼" seam allowance. Then baste the remaining two strips to the short sides of the quilt. Trim the excess fabric.

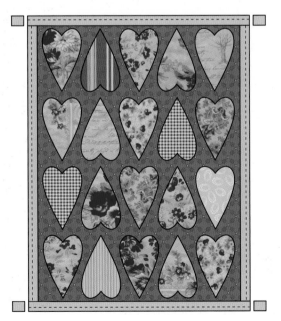

Baste and trim.

8 Measure the length of the quilt top. Trim two of the dark-brown strips to this length. Sew them to the sides of the quilt and press the seam allowances toward the brown borders. The striped strips should lie flat, pressed toward the hearts. In the same manner, measure the width of the quilt and trim the remaining two dark-brown strips to this measurement. Sew them to the top and bottom of the quilt. Press.

## Finishing the Quilt

1 Mark any quilting designs on the quilt top.

2 Place the backing right side down on a table or floor, and lay the batting on top, smoothing out any wrinkles. Then add the pressed quilt top, right side up, on top. Hand or pin baste the layers together.

3 Quilt by hand or machine. The quilt shown was hand quilted, stitched about ¹⁄₁₆" outside each heart. The background was quilted in diagonal lines. The border was quilted with a swag to complement the curves in the hearts.

4 Using the 2"-wide dark-brown strips, make and attach binding.

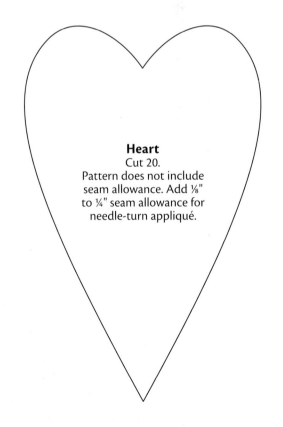

**Heart**
Cut 20.
Pattern does not include seam allowance. Add ⅛" to ¼" seam allowance for needle-turn appliqué.

# Pinwheels in My Garden

*The stylized petals of the appliqué flowers echo the shapes of the Pinwheel blocks, while the alternating blocks within the border create diamond shapes to highlight the Pinwheels.*

By Lori Smith of From My Heart to Your Hands

FINISHED QUILT SIZE: 16" x 20"    FINISHED APPLIQUÉD BLOCK SIZE: 8" x 12"
FINISHED PIECED BLOCK SIZE: 2" x 2"

## Materials

*Fat quarters measure approximately 18" x 21";*
*fat eighths measure 9" x 21".*

1 fat quarter of cream print for appliqué
   background
3 fat eighths *total* of assorted pink prints for blocks
   and appliqués
3 fat eighths *total* of assorted brown prints for
   blocks and appliqués
1 fat quarter *total* of assorted cream prints
   for blocks
1 fat quarter of fabric for binding
1 fat quarter of fabric for backing
18" x 22" piece of batting

## Cutting

*All measurements include ¼"-wide seam allowances.*

**From the fat quarter of cream print, cut:**

1 rectangle, 9" x 13"

**From the assorted brown prints, cut:**

14 squares, 3¼" x 3¼"; cut into quarters diagonally
   to make 56 triangles
28 squares, 1⅞" x 1⅞"; cut in half diagonally to
   make 56 triangles*

**From the assorted cream prints, cut:**

56 squares, 1⅞" x 1⅞"; cut in half diagonally to
   make 112 triangles*

**From the assorted pink prints, cut:**

14 squares, 3¼" x 3¼"; cut into quarters diagonally
   to make 56 triangles
28 squares, 1⅞" x 1⅞"; cut in half diagonally to
   make 56 triangles*

**From the binding fabric, cut:**

4 strips, 1¾" x 20"

*Cut in matching pairs for Pinwheel blocks with
coordinating fabrics.*

## Appliquéing the Center

1 Prepare the appliqué pieces using the patterns
   on page 68. Enlarge the pattern 125%. Cut the
stems on the bias, adding a ³⁄₁₆" seam allowance for
hand appliqué.

2 Fold and lightly press the cream 9" x 13" background rectangle in fourths.

3 Align the dashed lines on the appliqué pattern
   with the creases in the background fabric. Mark
the appliqué pattern on the background fabric.

4 Arrange the appliqué pieces on the background;
   pin and appliqué them in place using your
favorite method.

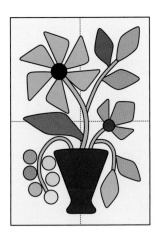

5 Press the appliquéd quilt block from the wrong
   side and trim to 8½" x 12½", keeping the design
centered.

## Assembling the Quilt

1 Select four matching pink 1⅞" triangles and
   four matching cream 1⅞" triangles for each
Pinwheel block. Sew a pink and a cream triangle
together to make a half-square-triangle unit. Make
four. Sew the units together in rows, and then sew
the rows together to make the Pinwheel blocks.
Make 14 pink-and-cream Pinwheel blocks. The
blocks should measure 2½" x 2½".

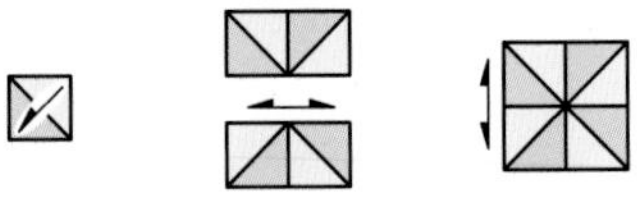

Make 14.

2 Select four brown 1⅞" triangles and four
   cream 1⅞" triangles for each Pinwheel block.
Repeat step 1 to make 14 brown-and-cream
Pinwheel blocks.

Make 14.

3 Working on a design wall, arrange the Pinwheel blocks around the appliquéd quilt center, leaving space for the Hourglass blocks, which will be sewn in step 6. Refer to the quilt diagram below and the quilt photograph on page 65.

4 Place pink 3¼" triangles around the pink Pinwheel blocks. Most of the Pinwheel blocks require three triangles from the same pink fabric around them. Use the remaining pink triangles along the outer and inner edges of the pieced border where only one triangle is required.

5 Repeat step 4 to place the brown 3¼" triangles around the brown Pinwheel blocks.

6 Sew the pink and brown triangles together as shown to make the Hourglass blocks. Make sure that you keep the fabrics in the correct position in each block. The blocks should measure 2½" x 2½". Make 28.

Make 28.

7 Place the Hourglass blocks back on the design wall. Then sew the blocks together in rows. Press the seam allowances open to eliminate bulk.

8 Sew the border rows together and press seam allowances open.

9 Sew the side rows to the appliqué block; press. Sew the top and bottom rows to the quilt.

## Finishing the Quilt

Layer the quilt top, batting, and backing. Baste the layers together and quilt as desired. Add the binding and enjoy.

Enlarge patterns 125%.
Patterns do not include
seam allowances.

# Prairie Baskets

*As the American West was being settled, the hills and prairies were filled with berries of all kinds growing in the wild. Berry picking was a suitable task for the youngest children as well as a favorite pastime for older ones.*

By Kathleen Tracy

FINISHED QUILT SIZE: 17" x 17"    FINISHED BLOCK SIZE: 4" x 4"

## Materials

*Yardage is based on 42"-wide fabric.*

¼ yard of yellow print for blocks and inner border

¼ yard of small-scale indigo print for blocks and
   setting pieces

¼ yard of medium-scale indigo print for
   outer border

¼ yard of dark-blue checked fabric for binding

⅝ yard of fabric for backing

20" x 20" piece of cotton batting

Yellow quilting thread

## Cutting

*All measurements include ¼"-wide seam allowances.*

**From the yellow print, cut:**

12 squares, 1⅞" x 1⅞"; cut *4* squares in half diagonally to make 8 triangles

2 squares, 2⅞" x 2⅞"

2 strips, 1" x 42"

**From the small-scale indigo print, cut:**

8 squares, 1⅞" x 1⅞"

4 squares, 2⅞" x 2⅞"; cut *2* squares in half diagonally to make 4 triangles

8 rectangles, 1½" x 2½"

4 squares, 1½" x 1½"

1 square, 4½" x 4½"

2 squares, 3¾" x 3¾"; cut in half diagonally to make
   4 triangles

1 square, 7" x 7"; cut into quarters diagonally to
   make 4 triangles

**From the medium-scale indigo print, cut:**

2 strips, 2½" x 42"

**From the dark-blue checked fabric, cut:**

2 strips, 2" x 42"

## Assembling the Quilt

1 Draw a diagonal line from corner to corner on
   the wrong side of the eight yellow 1⅞" squares.
Layer each marked square on top of an indigo 1⅞"
square, right sides together. Sew ¼" from the line on
both sides. Cut on the drawn line and press. Make
16 half-square-triangle units.

Make 16.

2 Draw a diagonal line from corner to corner on
   the wrong side of each yellow 2⅞" square. Place
a marked square on top of an indigo 2⅞" square,
right sides together. Sew ¼" from the line on both
sides. Cut on the drawn line and press. Make four
half-square-triangle units.

Make 4.

3 Sew a yellow 1⅞" triangle to the end of an
   indigo 1½" x 2½" rectangle as shown. Make
four of each unit.

Make 4.          Make 4.

4 Arrange and sew one indigo 1½" square, four
   half-square-triangle units from step 1, and one
half-square-triangle unit from step 2 as shown.
Press. Make four.

Make 4.

5 Sew two units from step 3 to a unit from step 4. Add an indigo 2⅞" triangle. Press as shown. Make four Basket blocks.

Make 4.

6 Lay out the Basket blocks, the 4½" indigo square, and the indigo side and corner setting triangles. Sew the blocks and setting pieces together into rows. Press the seam allowances toward the setting pieces.

7 Sew the rows together as shown. Press toward the corner triangles.

8 Measure the length of the quilt through the center. Using a yellow 1" x 42" strip, cut two pieces to the measured length. Sew the pieces to the sides of the quilt top and press toward the border. Measure the width of the quilt through the center, including the borders just added. Using the remaining yellow 1" x 42" strip, cut two pieces to that measurement and sew them to the top and bottom of the quilt top. Press toward the border.

9 Repeat the measuring procedure from step 8 to cut the medium-scale indigo 2½" border strips and sew them to the quilt. Press.

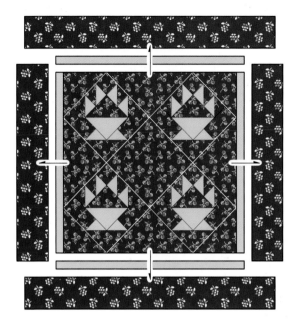

## Finishing the Quilt

1 Layer the quilt top, batting, and backing; baste the layers together.

2 With yellow quilting thread, quilt in the ditch around each block, diagonal lines through the center square, and a straight line through the middle of the border.

3 Attach the blue-checked binding to the quilt.

# Double Hourglass

*The Double Hourglass block used in this quilt is a reminder of how time may have crept by slowly as women during the Civil War waited for news about their husbands, sons, and fathers who had enlisted.*

By Kathleen Tracy; machine quilted by Dawn Larsen

FINISHED QUILT SIZE: 49" x 49"    FINISHED BLOCK SIZE: 6" x 6"

## Materials

*Yardage is based on 42"-wide fabric unless otherwise noted.*

1½ yards of green print for inner and outer borders

⅞ yard of light-green print for alternate blocks and setting triangles

¾ yard *total* of assorted light *OR* shirting prints for block backgrounds

⅓ yard of medium-blue print for middle border

Scraps (3" x 6" pieces) of 16 assorted medium and dark prints for blocks

½ yard of medium-blue print for binding

3½ yards of fabric for backing

55" x 55" piece of cotton batting

## Cutting

*All measurements include ¼"-wide seam allowances.*

**From the assorted light or shirting prints, cut:**

16 sets of 2 matching squares, 2⅞" x 2⅞" (32 total)

16 sets of 5 matching squares, 2½" x 2½" (80 total)

**From each of the 16 assorted medium or dark print scraps, cut:**

2 squares, 2⅞" x 2⅞" (32 total)

**From the light-green print, cut:**

3 squares, 9¾" x 9¾"; cut into quarters diagonally to make 12 side triangles

9 squares, 6½" x 6½"

2 squares, 5⅛" x 5⅛"; cut in half diagonally to make 4 corner triangles

**From the green print, cut on the *lengthwise* grain:**

2 strips, 3½" x 34½"

2 strips, 3½" x 40½"

2 strips, 3½" x 43"

2 strips, 3½" x 49"

**From the medium-blue print for middle border, cut:**

5 strips, 1¾" x 42"

**From the medium-blue print for binding, cut:**

6 strips, 2½" x 42"

## Making the Blocks

For each Double Hourglass block, choose one medium or dark print and one light background print. Some of the light prints may be used more than once. The directions are written for making one block at a time.

1 Draw a diagonal line from corner to corner on the wrong side of two matching light-print 2⅞" squares. Layer the marked squares on top of two matching medium- or dark-print scrap 2⅞" squares, right sides together. Sew ¼" from the line on both sides. Cut on the drawn line and press the seam allowances toward the darker print. Make four half-square-triangle units.

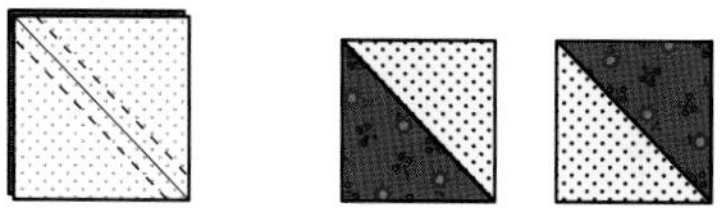

Make 4.

2 Arrange the four half-square-triangle units together with five matching light-print 2½" squares in rows as shown. Sew the rows together to make the Double Hourglass block. Press. Make 16.

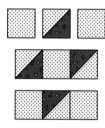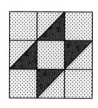

Make 16.

## Assembling the Quilt

1 Referring to the quilt diagram on page 74, lay out the blocks, the light-green 6½" squares, and the light-green 9¾" side setting triangles into diagonal rows. Sew the blocks together and press the seam allowances toward the setting pieces. Sew the rows together, pressing the seam allowances in one

direction. Add the light-green 5⅛" corner triangles and press the seam allowances toward the triangles.

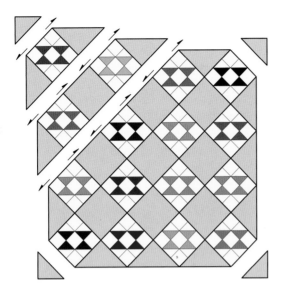

2 Sew the green-print 3½" x 34½" strips to the sides of the quilt top. Press the seam allowances toward the border. Sew the green-print 3½" x 40½" strips to the top and bottom of the quilt. Press.

3 Sew the five medium-blue 1¾" x 42" strips together into one long length. Cut into two strips, 40½" long, and two strips, 43" long. Sew the 40½" strips to the sides of the quilt top. Press the seam allowances toward the blue border. Sew the 43" strips to the top and bottom of the quilt. Press toward the blue border.

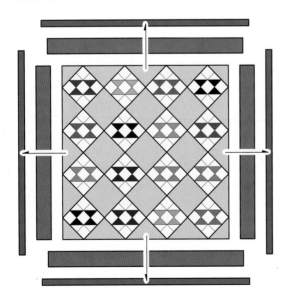

4 Sew the green-print 3½" x 43" strips to the sides of the quilt top. Press the seam allowances toward the border. Sew the green-print 3½" x 49" strips to the top and bottom of the quilt. Press toward the border.

## Finishing the Quilt

1 Layer the quilt top, batting, and backing; baste the layers together.

2 Quilt as desired. This quilt was machine quilted with a feathered-wreath design in the setting blocks, quilted in the ditch along the Double Hourglass blocks, and quilted with a feather motif in the borders.

3 Attach the binding to the quilt.

# Sugarplum Stars

*The stars are merged in this little quilt so that side-by-side stars share the same set of star points. This effect keeps the eye moving across the quilt top.*

By Karen Costello Soltys
FINISHED QUILT SIZE: 20½" x 24½"

## Materials

*Yardage is based on 42"-wide fabric unless otherwise noted. Fat quarters are 18" x 21".*

½ yard of small-scale purple print for star points and binding

1 fat quarter of tan-checked fabric for background

1 fat quarter of purple print for border accent and star centers

1 fat quarter of caramel print for border

Scraps of 5 additional purple prints, plaids, and stripes for star centers

¾ yard of fabric for backing*

23" x 27" piece of batting

*You can use ⅜ yard if you don't mind a seam in your quilt back.*

## Cutting

*All measurements include ¼"-wide seam allowances.*

**From the tan-checked fabric, cut:**

16 squares, 3¼" x 3¼"; cut into quarters diagonally to make 64 triangles (2 will be extra)

20 squares, 2½" x 2½"

**From the small-scale purple print, cut:**

16 squares, 3¼" x 3¼"; cut into quarters diagonally to make 64 triangles (2 will be extra)

3 binding strips, 2" x 42"

**From the purple accent print, cut:**

4 strips, 1" x 21"

2 squares, 2½" x 2½"

**From *each* of the 5 purple scraps, cut:**

2 squares, 2½" x 2½" (10 total)

**From the caramel print, cut:**

4 strips, 3½" x 21"

## Making the Units

The star-point units are made from quarter-square triangles. This allows the finished units to have straight-of-grain edges on the outside of the block, keeping it stable. Unlike half-square triangles, the short edges on these triangles are the bias edges.

1 Sew the tan-checked triangles to the purple triangles with their short edges aligned and tan triangles on top. Trim the dog-ear corners; press the seam allowances toward the purple triangles. Make 62 units, all with the purple triangles on the left.

Make 62.

2 Join pairs of the triangle units, butting the seam intersections. The purple fabric and tan-checked fabric should be adjoining as you sew. Trim the dog-ears and press the units open. Make 31.

Make 31.

## Assembling the Quilt

1 Lay out the units in nine rows of seven units each. In odd-numbered rows (1, 3, 5, 7, and 9), alternate tan-checked squares and triangle units; position the triangle units like bow ties, with the purple triangles on the left and right sides of the units. In the even-numbered rows, alternate the triangle units with the assorted purple 2½" squares.

In these rows, position the triangle units with the purple triangles on the top and bottom.

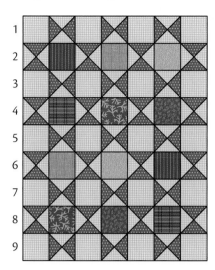

2 Once you're satisfied with the arrangement of the triangle units and purple squares, sew the pieces together into rows. Press the seam allowances toward the tan-checked and purple squares. Sew the rows together, matching seam allowances. Press the seam allowances in one direction.

## Adding the Border

1 Measure the length of your quilt top. Trim two of the caramel strips and two of the purple accent strips to this length. Fold the purple strips in half lengthwise, wrong sides together, and press. Position each purple strip along one edge of a caramel strip and machine baste in place with a narrow (⅛") seam allowance.

2 Reset the stitch length and sew the caramel borders to the sides of the quilt top, making sure to sew the edge with the attached purple accent strip. Press the seam allowances and the purple accent strips toward the borders.

3 Measure the width of the quilt top. Trim the remaining two caramel border strips and purple-accent strips to this length. Prepare the accent strips as before, and then sew the border strips to the top and bottom of the quilt. Again, press the seam allowances and the purple accent strips toward the border.

Quilt plan

## Finishing the Quilt

1 Mark any quilting designs on the quilt top.

2 If necessary, piece the quilt backing and press the seam allowances to one side. Place the backing right side down on a table or floor, and lay the batting on top, smoothing out any wrinkles. Then add the pressed quilt top, right side up, on top. Hand or pin baste the layers together.

3 Quilt by hand or machine. The quilt shown was quilted by hand with Xs through the plain squares and parallel diagonal lines in the border.

4 Using the 2"-wide small-scale purple strips, make and attach binding.

# Flying Bats

*These "bats," made in muted country colors, aren't scary at all! The blocks are surrounded by sashing strips made from simple triangle squares.*

By Mary Etherington and Connie Tesene of Country Threads

**FINISHED QUILT SIZE: 36½" x 47"    FINISHED BLOCK SIZE: 9" x 9"**

# Materials

*Yardage is based on 42"-wide fabric .*

1¾ yards *total* of assorted dark prints #2 for blocks
  and pieced sashing

1½ yards *total* of assorted light prints for blocks and
  pieced sashing

¼ yard *total* of assorted dark prints #1 for blocks

¼ yard of brown-checked fabric for outer border

⅜ yard of fabric for binding

1½ yards of fabric for backing

41" x 51" piece of batting

# Cutting

Cut pieces as indicated in the following chart. You'll have enough pieces to make one block.

| Piece | Fabric | Number of Pieces | Dimensions | Further Cutting |
|---|---|---|---|---|
| #1 | Dark #1 | 1 | 4¼" x 4¼" | Cut into quarters diagonally.* |
| #2 | Light | 1 | 4¼" x 4¼" | Cut into quarters diagonally.* |
| #3 | Light | 2 | 2" x 3½" | |
| #4 | Light | 2 | 2⅜" x 2⅜" | Cut in half diagonally. |
| #5 | Light | 1 | 5¾" x 5¾" | Cut into quarters diagonally. |
| #6 | Dark #2 | 1 | 4¼" x 4¼" | Cut into quarters diagonally.* |
| #7 | Dark #2 | 1 | 5¾" x 5¾" | Cut into quarters diagonally.** |
| #8 | Dark #2 | 2 | 3⅛" x 3⅛" | Cut in half diagonally. |
| #9 | Dark #2 | 2 | 1¼" x 9½" | |
| Borders | Brown-checked fabric | 5 | 2¼" x 42" | |
| Binding | | 5 | 2¼" x 42" | |

*Use only 2 triangles for the block. Reserve the remainder for the pieced border.*

**Use only 2 triangles for the block.*

## Making the Blocks

Referring to the illustration below, make 12 blocks.

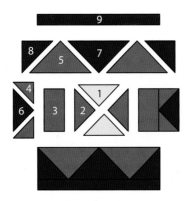

## Assembling the Quilt

1 For the pieced sashing, cut 103 squares, 2⅜" x 2⅜", from assorted light prints and 103 squares, 2⅜" x 2⅜", from assorted dark prints #2. Cut each square in half diagonally to make a total of 206 light triangles and 206 dark triangles.

2 Join the light and dark triangles to make 206 triangle units.

Make 206.

3 Join six units to make a vertical sashing strip. Make 16.

Make 16.

4 Sew three blocks and four sashing strips into a horizontal row, starting and ending each row with a sashing strip. Make four.

5 Make five horizontal sashing strips, joining 22 units for each. Join the rows of blocks and horizontal sashing strips.

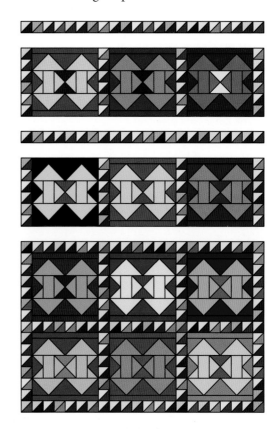

6 Join the brown-checked strips as necessary; cut two border strips, 33½" long, and two strips, 47½" long. Sew the borders to the top, bottom, and sides of the quilt.

## Finishing the Quilt

Layer the quilt top with batting and backing; baste. Quilt as desired and bind the edges.

# Sunny Lanes

*Sunny Lanes is a traditional block made of triangle squares and four-patch units. The color palette for this project is reminiscent of late-1800s quilts, but the techniques are definitely twenty-first century.*

By Karen Costello Soltys

FINISHED QUILT SIZE: 20½" x 20½"     FINISHED BLOCK SIZE: 8" x 8"

## Materials

*Fat quarters measure approximately 18" x 21";
fat eighths measure 9" x 21".*

1 fat quarter of white print for background

1 fat quarter of dark-green print for blocks
   and border

1 fat quarter of medium-green print for blocks
   and binding

1 fat eighth *each OR* scraps of 2 additional green
   prints for blocks

1 fat eighth *each OR* scraps of 4 assorted pink prints
   for blocks

¾ yard of fabric for backing*

23" x 23" piece of batting

*You can use ⅜ yard if you don't mind a seam in
your quilt back.*

## Cutting

*All measurements include ¼"-wide seam allowances.*

**From *each* of the 4 pink prints, cut:**

2 strips, 1½" x 21"; crosscut into 16 squares,
   1½" x 1½" (64 total)

**From the white print, cut:**

3 strips, 2⅞" x 21"; crosscut into 16 squares,
   2⅞" x 2⅞"

5 strips, 1½" x 21"; crosscut into 64 squares,
   1½" x 1½"

**From the dark-green print, cut:**

4 strips, 2½" x 21"

4 squares, 2⅞" x 2⅞"

**From the medium-green print, cut:**

5 strips, 2" x 21"

4 squares, 2⅞" x 2⅞"

**From *each* of the remaining 2 green prints, cut:**

4 squares, 2⅞" x 2⅞" (8 total)

## Making the Blocks

1 Select two matching pink squares and two white squares and arrange them into a four-patch unit as shown. Sew the squares into pairs and press the seam allowances toward the pink squares. Sew the pairs together, matching the seam intersections. Press. Repeat to make a total of 32 four-patch units.

Make 32.

2 To piece the triangles, you can either cut all the white and green squares in half diagonally, and then sew a green triangle to a white triangle, or you can mark a diagonal line on the wrong side of each white square, layer the square right sides together with a green square, and stitch ¼" from the marked line on each side. Then cut the squares apart on the line. You will have 32 triangle squares. For either method, trim the dog-ear corners and press the seam allowances to one side.

Make 32.

3 To assemble one block, select eight triangle squares and eight four-patch units. Be sure to mix up the fabrics so your quilt will have a subtly scrappy look. Lay out the units in four sections of four units each, making sure to arrange them as shown so that the diagonal path will be apparent. Sew the units together into sections, press the seam allowances toward the four patches, and then

sew the sections together. Press. Repeat to make four blocks.

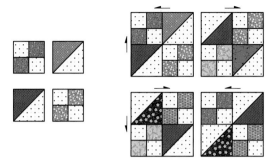

Make 4.

## Assembling the Quilt

1 Lay out the four blocks as shown, rotating them so that the green-and-white triangle squares form a diamond-shaped pathway around the quilt.

2 Sew the blocks together in pairs, and then sew the pairs together, matching all seam intersections. Press.

Quilt layout

3 Measure the length of the quilt top and trim two of the dark-green strips to this length. Sew the borders to opposite sides of the quilt and press the seam allowances toward the borders. Measure the width of the quilt top, including the borders, and trim the remaining two dark-green strips to this length. Sew the borders to the top and bottom of the quilt and press.

## Finishing the Quilt

1 Mark any quilting designs on the quilt top.

2 If necessary, piece the quilt backing and press the seam allowances to one side. Place the backing right side down on a table or floor, and lay the batting on top, smoothing out any wrinkles. Then add the pressed quilt top, right side up, on top. Hand or pin baste the layers together.

3 Quilt by hand or machine. The quilt shown was hand quilted ¼" inside all of the green triangles and diagonally through the center of each four-patch unit using ¼"-wide quilter's masking tape as a guideline. The white triangles were stitched with parallel diagonal lines and the border with small tulips that alternate direction.

4 Using the 2"-wide medium-green strips, make and attach binding.

# Be Mine

*Made for either your sweetheart or a baby, this playful little quilt is sure to brighten anyone's day!*

By Sara Diepersloot; quilted by Deborah Rasmussen

FINISHED QUILT SIZE: 43½" x 43½"   FINISHED BLOCK SIZE: 8" x 8"

## Materials

*Yardage is based on 42"-wide fabric unless otherwise noted.*

1⅓ yards of valentine print for blocks and outer border

⅔ yard of red print for sashing and binding

½ yard of white-and-red polka-dot print for blocks

⅜ yard of green print for blocks and inner border

⅓ yard of light-blue print for blocks

¼ yard of lavender print for blocks and sashing squares

2⅞ yards of fabric for backing

52" x 52" piece of batting

# Cutting

*All measurements include ¼"-wide seam allowances.*

**From the green print, cut:**

1 strip, 2½" x 42"

3 strips, 2" x 42"

**From the lavender print, cut:**

1 strip, 2½" x 42"

1 strip, 1½" x 42"; crosscut into 16 squares, 1½" x 1½"

**From the light-blue print, cut:**

3 strips, 2½" x 42"; crosscut into 40 squares, 2½" x 2½"

**From the white-and-red polka-dot print, cut:**

5 strips, 2½" x 42"; crosscut into 20 rectangles, 2½" x 4½", and 20 squares, 2½" x 2½"

**From the valentine print, cut:**

1 strip, 8½" x 42"; crosscut into 4 squares, 8½" x 8½"

5 strips, 6½" x 42"

**From the red print, cut:**

6 strips, 1½" x 42"; crosscut into 24 pieces, 1½" x 8½"

5 strips, 2¼" x 42"

# Making the Blocks

1 Sew the green and lavender 2½" x 42" strips together to make a strip set. Press the seam allowances toward the green. Crosscut the strip set into 10 segments, 2½" wide.

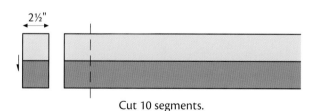

Cut 10 segments.

2 Sew two 2½" segments together to make a four-patch unit. Make five units.

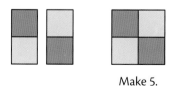

Make 5.

3 Draw a diagonal line from corner to corner on the wrong side of the light-blue 2½" squares. Lay a square on one end of a polka-dot 2½" x 4½" rectangle, right sides together. Sew on the drawn line. Trim the excess ¼" from the stitching line. Press the seam allowances toward the triangle. Repeat on the other end of the rectangle, orienting the diagonal line in the opposite direction. Make 20 of these star-point units.

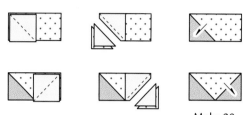

Make 20.

4 Arrange the polka-dot 2½" squares, the star-point units, and the four-patch units as shown. Join the units into rows, and then sew the rows together to make the block. Make five blocks.

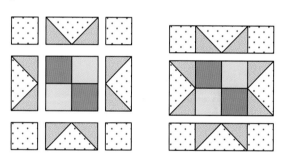

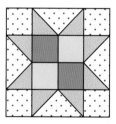

Make 5.

# Assembling the Quilt

1 Sew three red-print sashing pieces together with four lavender sashing squares. Press the seam allowances toward the sashing. Make four sashing rows.

Make 4.

2 Arrange the pieced blocks and valentine-print squares in rows along with the red-print sashing pieces as shown in the quilt diagram. Join into rows. Press the seam allowances toward the sashing pieces. Sew the rows together with the sashing rows. Press.

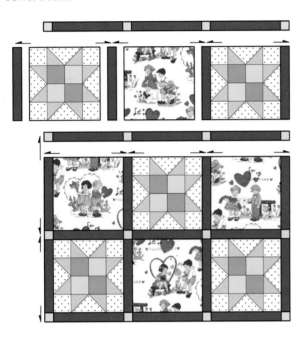

3 Add the green inner border and the valentine-print outer border.

## Finishing the Quilt

1 Layer the quilt top with batting and backing and quilt as desired. This sweet valentine quilt has a flowing heart design quilted in red thread for a dramatic look.

2 Bind the edges of the quilt using the red strips.

# Pink Dogwood

*The dogwood symbolizes durability and undiminished love. Display this wall hanging to enjoy springtime all year long, or make it for a cherished family member as a symbol of your love.*

By Nancy Mahoney

FINISHED QUILT SIZE: 43½" x 43½"    FINISHED BLOCK SIZE: 9" x 9"

## Materials

*Yardage is based on 42"-wide fabric unless otherwise noted. Fat eighths measure 9" x 21".*

1⅛ yards of green floral for sashing, first and fourth borders, and binding

1 yard of cream solid for block backgrounds

½ yard of light-pink plaid for second border

⅓ yard of dark-pink print for third border

1 fat eighth of gold print for flower center appliqués

9" x 9" square *each* of 9 assorted pink prints for flower appliqués

3 yards of fabric for backing

50" x 50" piece of batting

2¼ yards of 16"-wide lightweight fusible web (optional)

## Cutting

*Cut all strips across the width of the fabric. All measurements include ¼"-wide seam allowances.*

**From the cream solid, cut:**

3 strips, 10" x 42"; crosscut into 9 squares, 10" x 10"

**From the green floral, cut:**

8 strips, 2" x 42"; crosscut into:
  2 strips, 2" x 33⅓"
  4 strips, 2" x 30½"
  6 strips, 2" x 9½"
5 strips, 2" x 42"
5 strips, 1½" x 42"

**From the light-pink plaid, cut:**

4 strips, 3½" x 42"

**From the dark-pink print, cut:**

5 strips, 1½" x 42

## Appliquéing the Blocks

1 Using the patterns on page 90 and your preferred method, prepare nine pink flowers and nine gold flower centers.

2 Center a pink flower, and then a gold flower center on each cream 10" square and appliqué them in place. Make nine blocks. Trim each block to measure 9½" square.

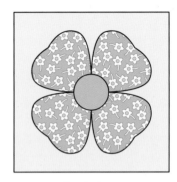

Appliqué placement

## Assembling the Quilt

1 Sew three blocks and two green-floral 2" x 9½" strips together as shown. Press the seam allowances toward the sashing strips. Make three block rows.

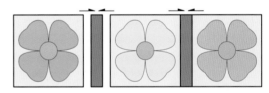

Make 3.

2 Sew the block rows and two of the green-floral 2" x 30½" strips together as shown. Press the seam allowances toward the sashing strips. Sew the remaining green-floral 30½"-long strips to opposite sides of the quilt center for the first border. Then sew the green-floral 33½"-long strips to the top and bottom edges of the quilt top. Press the seam allowances toward the border strips.

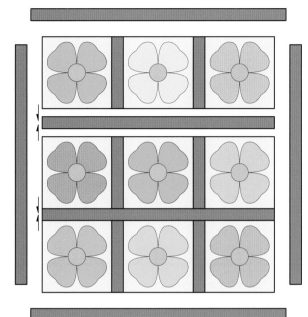

3 Measure, cut, and sew the light-pink 3½"-wide strips, joining them to the sides, and then to the top and bottom edges of the quilt top. Press the seam allowances toward the just-added border strips.

4 Sew the dark-pink 1½"-wide strips together end to end to make a long strip. Measure and cut; then sew the strips to the quilt top. Press the seam allowances toward the just-added border strips.

5 Sew the green-floral 1½"-wide strips together end to end to make a long strip. Measure and cut; then sew the strips to the quilt top. Press the seam allowances toward the just-added border strips.

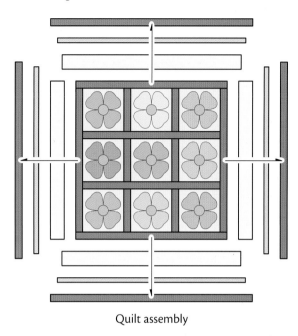

Quilt assembly

## Finishing the Quilt

Layer the quilt top with batting and backing. Hand or machine quilt as desired. Trim the batting and backing even with the quilt top. Using the green-floral 2"-wide strips, make and attach the binding.

Patterns do not include
seam allowances.

**Flower**
Make 9 from assorted pink prints.

**Flower center**
Make 9 from gold print.

# Five-Cent Fairy Garden

*This cheery little quilt is adorable as a candle mat or table topper.*
*Use a nickel for perfectly shaped berries and flower centers.*

By Kim Diehl

FINISHED QUILT SIZE: 21½" x 21½"

## Materials

*Yardage is based on 42"-wide fabric*
*unless otherwise noted.*

½ yard of medium or dark homespun for inner
   border and binding

40 assorted homespun squares, 1½" x 1½", for
   quilt center

30 assorted homespun rectangles, 1½" x 2½", for
   quilt center

4 assorted tan homespun rectangles, 5½" x 11½",
   for outer border

4 assorted tan homespun squares, 5½" x 5½", for
   outer border

Assorted homespun scraps for appliqué

Assorted green homespun scraps for appliqué

¾ yard of fabric for backing

27" x 27" piece of batting

1 nickel for appliqué template

⅜" bias bar

## Cutting

*All strips are cut across the width of the fabric unless*
*otherwise noted. All measurements include ¼"-wide*
*seam allowances. Patterns are on page 93.*

**From the ½ yard of medium or dark**
**homespun, cut:**

2 strips, 1" x 10½"

2 strips, 1" x 11½"

6 strips, 2½" x 18"

**From the assorted homespun scraps, cut:**

4 using pattern A

4 using pattern D

4 using pattern E

4 using pattern G

4 using pattern H

24 circles traced with a nickel

**From the assorted green homespun scraps, cut:**

16 using pattern B

8 using pattern C

4 using pattern F

8 bias strips, 1½" x 10"

## Piecing the Candle-Mat Center

Lay out 40 assorted homespun 1½" squares and 30 assorted homespun 1½" x 2½" rectangles to form four rows of squares and three rows of rectangles, with 10 pieces in each row. Join the pieces in each row. Press the seam allowances of each row in alternating directions. Join the rows and press the seam allowances in one direction. The pieced candle-mat center should measure 10½" square.

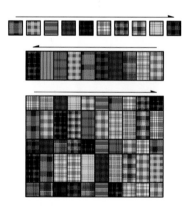

## Adding the Borders

1 Join medium or dark homespun 1" x 10½" strips to the right and left sides of the candle-mat center. Press the seam allowances toward the strips. Join 1" x 11½" strips to the top and bottom of the candle-mat center. Press the seam allowances toward the strips.

2 Join assorted tan 5½" x 11½" rectangles to the right and left sides of the quilt top. Press the seam allowances toward the dark inner-border strips.

3 Join an assorted tan 5½" x 5½" square to each short end of the two remaining tan homespun rectangles to form a strip. Press the seam allowances toward the squares.

4 Join the pieced border strips to the top and bottom of the quilt top. Press the seam allowances toward the dark inner-border strips.

## Appliquéing the Borders

Using the patterns on page 93, prepare appliqués.

1 With *wrong* sides together, fold each 1½" x 10" green homespun strip in half lengthwise and stitch a scant ¼" in from the long raw edges to form a tube; trim to ⅛". Insert the bias bar into the tube and slide it along as you press the stem, making sure the seam is centered and lies flat. Fold under the raw edge at one end about ¼" and use a fabric glue stick to anchor it in place.

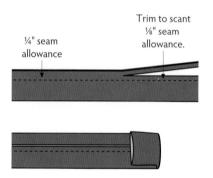

¼" seam allowance

Trim to scant ⅛" seam allowance.

2 Using the quilt photo on page 91 as a guide, lay out the appliqués and prepared stems. Begin stitching with pattern C. Then proceed to the 10" stems. As the remaining appliqués are stitched in place, they will cover the unfinished ends of the stems positioned in the corners.

# Finishing the Candle Mat

Layer the quilt top, batting, and backing. Quilt the layers together. The featured quilt was hand quilted with diagonal lines through the center squares and rectangles to form kite shapes. The borders were echo quilted to emphasize the appliqués. Use the six 2½" x 18" strips to bind the quilt.

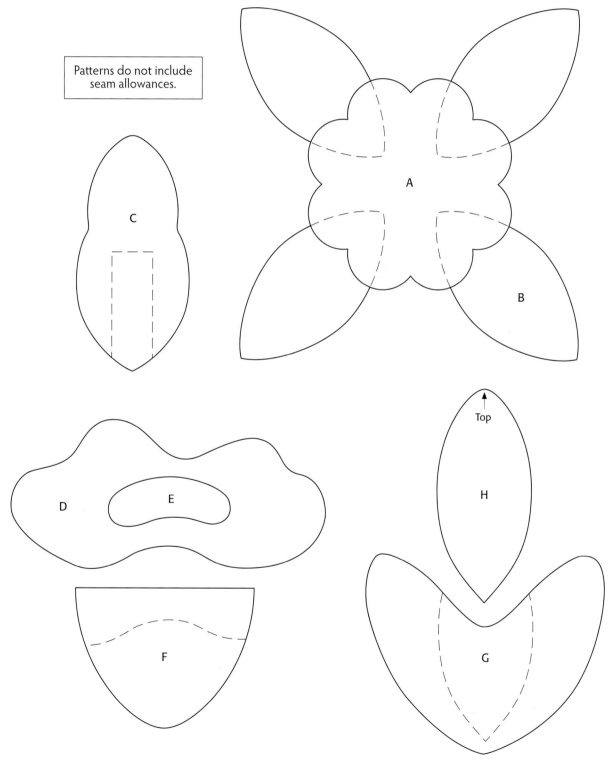

Patterns do not include seam allowances.

# Scrap Squares

*This little doll quilt is a perfect example of an easy way to use up some of your scraps or charm packs. It's so quick—make one for yourself and one for a friend!*

By Kathleen Tracy

FINISHED QUILT SIZE: 17½" x 22¾"    FINISHED BLOCK SIZE: 4" x 4"

## Materials

*Yardage is based on 42"-wide fabric unless otherwise noted. Charm squares are 5" x 5".*

¼ yard of light shirting print for sashing

12 different charm squares *OR* scraps for blocks

⅛ yard *total* of assorted medium or dark print scraps, at least 1¾" x 1¾", for sashing squares

¼ yard of red print for binding

¾ yard of fabric for backing

22" x 27" piece of thin cotton batting

## Cutting

*All measurements include ¼"-wide seam allowances.*

**From each assorted charm square or scrap, cut:**

1 square, 4½" x 4½" (12 total)

**From the light shirting print, cut:**

4 strips, 1¾" x 42"; crosscut into 31 rectangles, 1¾" x 4½"

**From the assorted medium or dark print scraps, cut:**

20 squares, 1¾" x 1¾"

**From the red print, cut:**

3 strips, 2" x 42"

## Assembling the Quilt

1. Sew three 4½" squares together with four light 1¾" x 4½" sashing rectangles to make a row. Press seam allowances toward the squares. Make four rows.

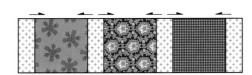

Make 4.

2. Sew three light sashing rectangles together with four medium or dark 1¾" squares to make a sashing row. Press the seam allowances toward the squares. Make five rows.

Make 5.

3. Sew the rows together as shown.

## Finishing the Quilt

1. Layer the quilt top, batting, and backing, and pin or baste the layers together.

2. Quilt as desired. This quilt was machine quilted with a simple diagonal crosshatch pattern using brown thread.

3. Attach the binding to the quilt.

# Underground Railroad

*Quilt patterns such as the Underground Railroad may represent the network of safe houses for slaves on their journey to freedom during the years before the Civil War.*

By Kathleen Tracy

**FINISHED QUILT SIZE: 19" x 25"    FINISHED BLOCK SIZE: 6" x 6"**

## Materials

*Yardage is based on 42"-wide fabric.*

¼ yard of deep-blue reproduction print for blocks

¼ yard of gold reproduction print for blocks

¼ yard of dark-red checked fabric for inner border

¼ yard of medium-blue fabric for outer border

¼ yard *total* of assorted scraps of light and dark reproduction prints for blocks

¼ yard of brown fabric for binding

⅞ yard of fabric for backing

22" x 28" piece of batting

## Cutting

*All measurements include ¼"-wide seam allowances.*

**From the assorted light and dark reproduction prints, cut:**

48 squares, 2" x 2"

**From the deep-blue reproduction print, cut:**

6 squares, 3⅞" x 3⅞"

**From the gold reproduction print, cut:**

6 squares, 3⅞" x 3⅞"

**From the dark-red checked fabric, cut:**

2 strips, 1¼" x 42"; crosscut into 2 pieces, 1¼" x 12½", and 2 pieces, 1¼" x 20"

**From the medium-blue fabric, cut:**

2 strips, 3" x 42"; crosscut into 2 pieces, 3" x 20", and 2 pieces, 3" x 19"

**From the brown fabric, cut:**

3 strips, 2" x 42"

## Assembling the Quilt

1 Randomly sew the light and dark 2" squares together into 12 four-patch units as shown, pressing the seam allowances of each pair in opposite directions. When joining pairs to make a four-patch unit, press the seam allowances in either direction.

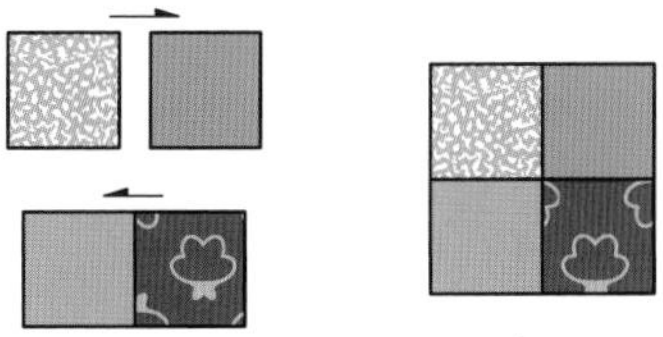

Make 12.

2 Layer each deep-blue 3⅞" square with a gold 3⅞" square, right sides together and with the lighter square on top. Draw a diagonal line across each light square. Stitch ¼" from the line on both sides and cut on the drawn line. Press the seam allowances toward the blue fabric.

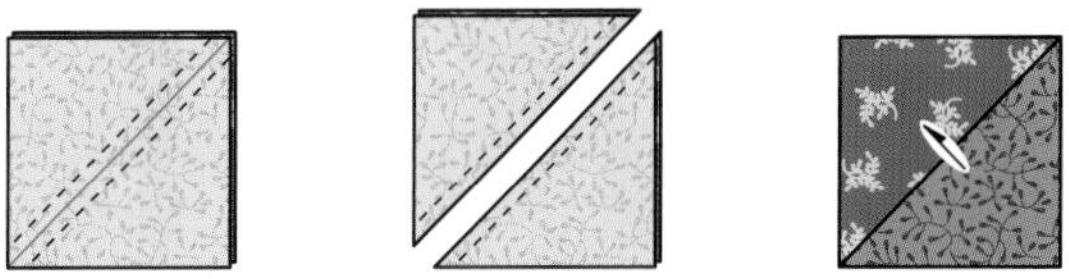

Make 12.

3 Sew two triangle squares and two four-patch units together as shown, pressing the seam allowances toward the four-patch unit. When joining the pairs, press the seam allowances in either direction.

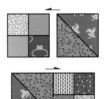 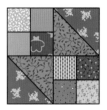

Make 6.

4 Arrange the blocks in three rows of two blocks each as shown to make the quilt center. Sew the blocks together into rows, and press the seam allowances in opposite directions from row to row. Sew the rows together, and press the seam allowances in one direction.

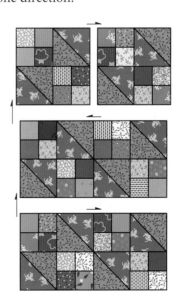

5 Sew the two red-checked 12½" pieces to the top and bottom of the quilt center, pressing the seam allowances toward the red pieces. Sew the two red-checked 20" pieces to the sides; press.

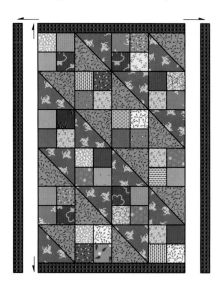

6 Sew the two medium-blue 20" pieces to the sides of the quilt top, pressing the seam allowances toward the outer border. Sew the two medium-blue 19" pieces to the top and bottom of the quilt top; press.

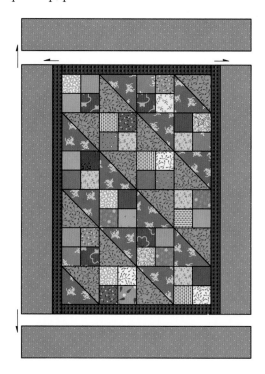

## Finishing the Quilt

1 Layer the quilt top, batting, and backing, and baste the layers together.

2 Quilt an X through the center of each block and quilt in the ditch around the inside and outside edges of the inner border. Quilt through the middle of the outer border.

3 Attach the binding to the quilt.

# Sweet Pea

*What little girl wouldn't love this sweet little quilt for her dolls? Fusible appliqué is easy and durable, making it a good choice for a doll quilt that will be played with frequently.*

By Karen Costello Soltys

FINISHED QUILT SIZE: 18" x 25"     FINISHED BLOCK SIZE: 6½" x 6½"

## Materials

*Fat quarters measure approximately 18" x 21"; fat eighths measure 9" x 21".*

1 fat quarter *each* of a small-scale and a medium-scale yellow print for blocks and sashing

1 fat quarter of light-blue print for quarter circles and sashing squares

1 fat eighth *each OR* scraps of pink print and green print for floral appliqués

1 fat quarter of light-blue tone-on-tone print for border

1 fat quarter of pink-floral print for binding

⅝ yard of fabric for backing

20" x 27" piece of batting

½ yard of lightweight fusible web

Blue, pink, and green thread to match appliqué
fabrics

## Preparing the Appliqué Shapes

Using the patterns on page 101, trace six large circles, 24 small circles, and 48 leaves onto the paper side of fusible web. Fuse the large circles onto the blue print, the small circles onto the pink print, and the leaves onto the green print.

## Cutting

*All measurements include ¼"-wide seam allowances.*

**From the light-blue print, cut:**

6 large circles, prepared with fusible web

2 squares, 1" x 1"

**From the small-scale yellow print, cut:**

6 squares, 5" x 5"

7 strips, 1" x 7"

**From the medium-scale yellow print, cut:**

12 squares, 4¼" x 4¼"; crosscut in half diagonally to
make 24 triangles

**From the pink print, cut:**

24 small circles, prepared with fusible web

**From the green print, cut:**

48 leaves, prepared with fusible web

**From the light-blue tone-on-tone print, cut:**

4 strips, 2½" x 21"

**From the pink-floral print, cut:**

5 binding strips, 2" x 21"

## Making the Blocks

1 After cutting out the large blue circles on the drawn lines, fold each circle in half and crease. Cut the circles in half on the creases. Then fold the semicircles in half again, crease, and cut into quarter circles.

Cut circles
into quarters.

2 Fuse a quarter circle onto each corner of a small-scale yellow 5" square, aligning the cut edges in the corners of the block. Machine blanket stitch the curved edges in place using blue thread. Repeat for all six blocks.

Fuse and blanket
stitch into place.

3 Sew medium-scale yellow triangles to opposite sides of an appliquéd block. Press the seam allowances toward the triangles. Sew the remaining triangles to the two remaining sides of the block and press in the same manner. Repeat to make six blocks. Trim and square up the blocks to 7" x 7".

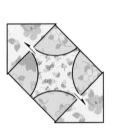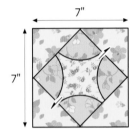

Make 6.

4 Place one pink circle and two leaves in each corner triangle, taking care to position the pieces so that they will not extend into the outer ¼" seam allowance of the block. When satisfied with the placement, fuse in place. Machine blanket stitch around each shape with coordinating thread. Repeat for all six blocks.

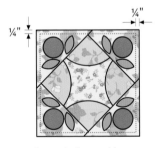

Fuse circles and leaves
¼" from block edges.

## Assembling the Quilt

1 Lay out the quilt blocks in three rows of two blocks each. Place small-scale yellow 1" x 7" sashing strips between the blocks and light-blue 1" squares between the horizontal sashing strips.

2 Sew the block and sashing pieces into rows, and then sew the rows together, pressing all seam allowances toward the sashing strips.

3 Measure the length of the quilt top. Trim two of the blue tone-on-tone border strips to this length and sew them to the sides of the quilt top. Press seam allowances toward the borders. Measure the width of the quilt top. Trim the remaining two border strips to this length and sew them to the top and bottom of the quilt in the same manner.

## Finishing the Quilt

1 If desired, mark any quilting designs on the quilt top.

2 Place the backing right side down on a table or floor and lay the batting on top, smoothing out any wrinkles. Then add the pressed quilt top, right side up, on top. Hand or pin baste the layers together.

3 Quilt by hand or machine. The quilt shown was machine quilted in the ditch of the seams and about 1/8" or less from the appliquéd pieces—the quarter circles, flower circles, and leaves.

4 Using the 2"-wide pink-floral strips, make and attach binding.

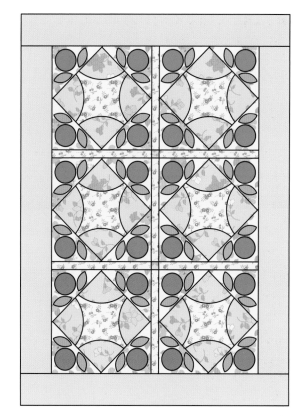

Quilt plan

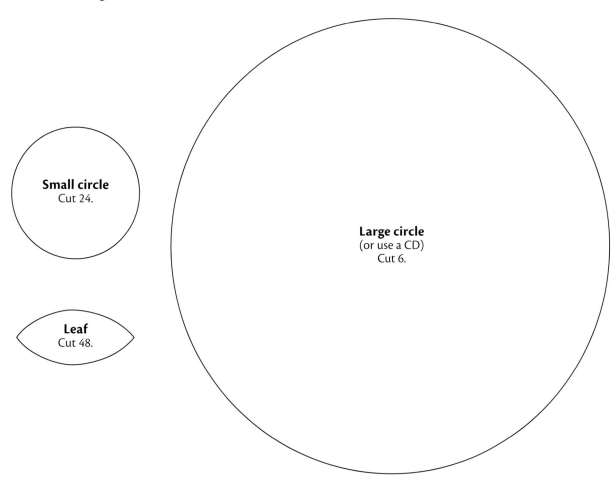

**Small circle**
Cut 24.

**Large circle**
(or use a CD)
Cut 6.

**Leaf**
Cut 48.

# Feedsack Flower Garden

*Americans faced trying times in the 1930s, yet the quilts created during this period were remarkably optimistic, featuring pastels, bright colors, and light backgrounds.*

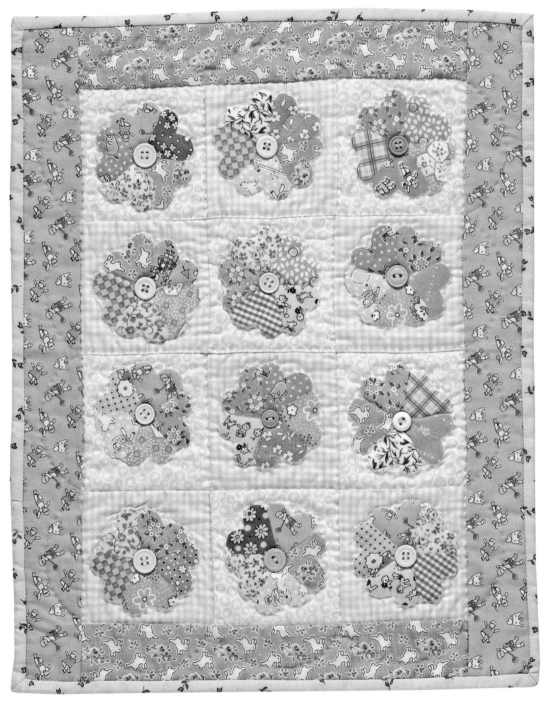

By Kathleen Tracy

**FINISHED QUILT SIZE: 14" x 17½"    FINISHED BLOCK SIZE: 3½" x 3½"**

## Materials

*Yardage is based on 42"-wide fabric unless otherwise noted.*

¼ yard of pink-and-white checked fabric for block backgrounds

¼ yard of light-pink print for block backgrounds

¼ yard *total* of assorted pastel 1930s reproduction scraps for blocks

⅛ yard of green 1930s reproduction print for borders

⅛ yard of medium-pink 1930s reproduction print for borders

¼ yard of yellow print for binding

⅝ yard of fabric for backing

17" x 21" piece of batting

¼ yard of lightweight fusible web

12 assorted pastel buttons, ¼" to ⅜" in diameter

## Cutting

*All measurements include ¼"-wide seam allowances.*

**From the pink-and-white checked fabric, cut:**
6 squares, 4" x 4"

**From the light-pink print, cut:**
6 squares, 4" x 4"

**From the medium-pink, cut:**
1 strip, 2" x 42"; crosscut into 2 pieces, 2" x 11"

**From the green 1930s reproduction print, cut:**
1 strip, 2" x 42"; crosscut into 2 pieces, 2" x 17½"

**From the yellow print, cut:**
2 strips, 2" x 42"

## Assembling the Quilt

1 Trace 60 hearts from the pattern below right onto the fusible web. Cut out the pieces and remove the paper backing. Fuse the shapes to the wrong sides of the assorted pastel reproduction fabrics following the manufacturer's directions for the fusible web. Cut out the hearts.

2 Mark a dot at the center of each 4" square. Use five hearts, each from a different fabric, to make the flowers. Place the hearts on a square, positioning the points at the dot. The edges of the hearts will overlap. Fuse the hearts in place leaving the edges unfinished, or blanket stitch around the edges by machine or by hand.

Make 12.

3 Sew the blocks into four rows of three blocks each, alternating pink-checked blocks and light-pink blocks as shown. Press.

4 Sew the medium-pink 11" pieces to the top and bottom of the quilt, pressing the seam allowances toward the borders. Sew the green 17½" pieces to the sides of the quilt; press.

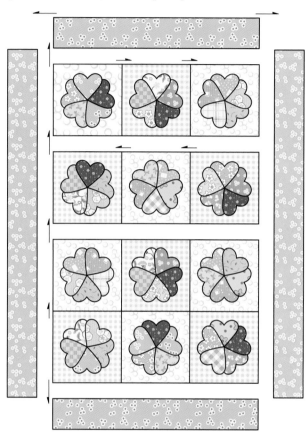

## Finishing the Quilt

1 Layer the quilt top, batting, and backing, and baste the layers together.

2 Quilt ¹⁄₁₆" from the fused heart flowers and in the ditch around each block. Using a small lid or cup and a quilting pen or white pencil, trace a scalloped design from one block to the next in the green and pink borders. Quilt on the curved lines. Sew a button to the center of each heart flower.

3 Attach the binding to the quilt.

**Heart**
Cut 60.

# Civil War Scraps

*You can't have too many scraps, and they certainly come in handy for making this little quilt.*

By Kathleen Tracy

**FINISHED QUILT SIZE: 17½" x 22"    FINISHED BLOCK SIZE: 6" x 6"**

## Materials

*Yardage is based on 42"-wide fabric unless otherwise noted.*

⅛ yard *total* of 5 assorted medium and dark Civil War reproduction prints for blocks

⅛ yard *total* of 5 assorted light prints for four-patch units

⅛ yard *total* of 5 assorted light prints for block backgrounds

⅛ yard *total* of 5 assorted medium-blue prints for four-patch units

⅓ yard *OR* 1 fat quarter of dark-blue print for setting triangles

⅛ yard of green print for borders

5 pieces, 3" x 3", of red, blue, or green Civil War reproduction prints for block centers

¼ yard of red print for binding

¼ yard of blue print for binding

⅝ yard of fabric for backing

22" x 26" piece of thin cotton batting

## Cutting

*All measurements include ¼"-wide seam allowances.*

**From *each* of the 5 assorted light prints for block backgrounds, cut:**
2 squares, 2⅞" x 2⅞" (10 total)

**From *each* of the 5 assorted medium and dark reproduction prints, cut:**
2 squares, 2⅞" x 2⅞" (10 total)

**From *each* of the 5 red, blue, or green reproduction prints, cut:**
1 square, 2½" x 2½" (5 total)

**From *each* of the 5 assorted light prints for four-patch units, cut:**
8 squares, 1½" x 1½" (40 total)

**From *each* of the 5 assorted medium-blue prints, cut:**
8 squares, 1½" x 1½" (40 total)

**From the dark-blue print, cut:**
1 square, 9¾" x 9¾"; cut into quarters diagonally to make 4 triangles
2 squares, 5⅛" x 5⅛"; cut in half diagonally to make 4 triangles

**From the green print, cut:**
2 strips, 2¾" x 17½"

**From the red print for binding, cut:**
2 strips, 2" x 23"

**From the blue print for binding, cut:**
2 strips, 2" x 19"

## Making the Blocks

1 Select two matching light 2⅞" squares and two matching medium or dark 2⅞" squares. Layer the light and dark squares right sides together. Draw a diagonal line from corner to corner on the wrong side of each light square. Stitch ¼" from the line on both sides and cut on the drawn line. Press the seam allowances toward the darker fabric. Make four half-square-triangle units.

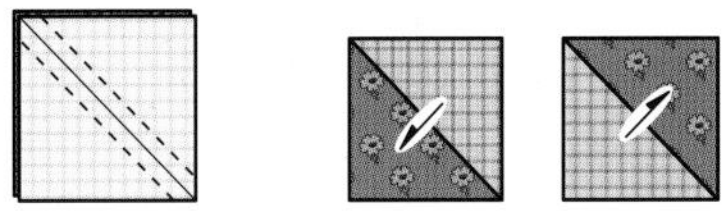

Make 4.

2 Sew two matching light 1½" squares and two matching medium-blue 1½" squares together as shown. Make four matching four-patch units.

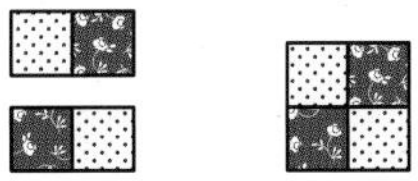

Make 4.

3 Assemble a block by sewing the half-square-triangle units, the four-patch units, and a reproduction 2½" square into rows as shown. Press. Sew the rows together. Make a total of five blocks.

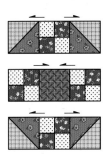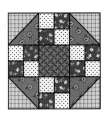

Make 5.

## Assembling the Quilt

1 Lay out the finished blocks and the dark-blue side setting triangles in diagonal rows. Sew the blocks into rows and press the seam allowances toward the setting pieces. Sew the rows together as shown, pressing the seam allowances in opposite directions. Add the dark-blue corner triangles and press the seam allowances toward the triangles.

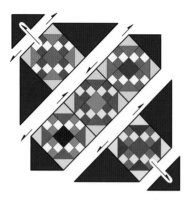

2 Add the green strips to the top and bottom of the quilt top. Press the seam allowances toward the border.

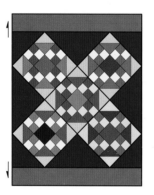

## Finishing the Quilt

1 Layer the quilt top, batting, and backing; baste the layers together.

2 Quilt as desired. This quilt was hand quilted with a simple design in the center square of the center block and in the ditch along the other blocks, and a crosshatch design in the blue triangles and horizontal lines along the borders.

3 Bind the sides of the quilt with the red strips. Then use the blue strips to bind the top and bottom edges, tucking under the ends to align with the edges of the quilt and to hide the raw edges.

# Don't Play with Table Utensils

*But didn't your little brother or cousin look cute with a spoon balanced on the end of his nose? Almost as cute as this little wall quilt or table runner!*

By Mary Etherington and Connie Tesene of Country Threads

**FINISHED QUILT SIZE:** 13¼" x 26¼"  **FINISHED BLOCK SIZE:** 4⅜" x 4⅜"

## Materials

*Yardage is based on 42"-wide fabric unless otherwise noted. Charm squares are 5" x 5".*

17 assorted light-value charm squares
17 assorted dark-value red and blue charm squares
¼ yard of blue print for binding
½ yard of fabric for backing
18" x 30" piece of batting

## Cutting

*All measurements include ¼"-wide seam allowances.*

**From each charm square, cut:**
4 strips, 1⅛" x 5" (136 total)*
**From the blue print, cut:**
3 strips, 2¼" x 42"
*Keep strips of the same fabric together.*

## Creating the Quilt

Each block is made from one light and one dark fabric.

1 Sew four dark 1⅛" x 5" strips alternated with three light 1⅛" x 5" strips. You'll have one light strip left over. Press the seam allowances toward the dark strips. Make 17 blocks.

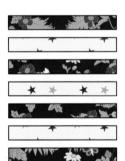

Make 17.

2 Measure the average height of the blocks. They should be about 4⅞". Trim the width of the blocks to match the height so the blocks are square (4⅞" x 4⅞").

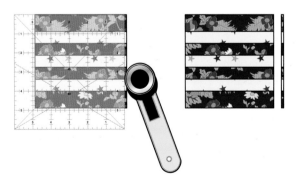

3 Sew seven of the remaining light-value strips together to make one block and trim it to the size of the other blocks.

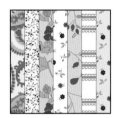

4 Arrange the blocks in six rows of three blocks each, rotating the blocks to run horizontally and vertically. Sew together in rows, pressing the seam allowances in opposite directions from row to row. Sew the rows together and press.

## Finishing the Quilt

Make a quilt back approximately 18" x 30". Layer the quilt top with batting and backing. Baste; quilt as desired. Trim the excess batting and backing and bind the quilt with the blue 2¼"-wide strips.

# Midnight Star

*Choosing a striped fabric, like the one used here for the inner border, gives a lot of movement to a quilt. Star blocks combine with Double Snowball blocks for a lovely quilted treat.*

By Mary Hickey; pieced by Mary Hickey and Pat Blodgett; machine quilted by Dawn Kelly

FINISHED QUILT SIZE: 41½" x 41½"    FINISHED BLOCK SIZE: 6" x 6"

## Materials

*Yardage is based on 42"-wide fabric unless otherwise noted.*

1⅜ yards of red floral for outer border

1 yard *total* of assorted beige fabrics for Star blocks and Double Snowball blocks

¼ yard *each* of 4 assorted small-scale red fabrics for Star blocks

¼ yard *each* of 3 assorted light-green fabrics for Double Snowball blocks

¼ yard of medium-green striped fabric for Star blocks and inner border

¼ yard of mottled-green fabric for Double Snowball blocks

⅛ yard *each* of 2 assorted medium-green fabrics for Star blocks

⅛ yard *total OR* scraps no smaller than 4" x 8" of 4 assorted large-scale red fabrics for Star blocks

½ yard of dark-red fabric for binding

2⅞ yards of fabric for backing

45" x 45" piece of batting

## Cutting

*All measurements include ¼"-wide seam allowances. Cut all strips across the width of fabric (selvage to selvage) unless instructed otherwise.*

**From *each* of the 4 assorted small-scale red fabrics, cut:**

3 strips (12 total), 2" x 21"; crosscut into 104 squares, 2" x 2"

1 rectangle, 1½" x 10" (4 total)

2 rectangles, 1½" x 5" (8 total)

**From the assorted beige fabrics, cut a *total* of:**

5 strips, 3½" x 42"; crosscut into 48 squares, 3½" x 3½"

5 strips, 2" x 42"; crosscut into 52 rectangles, 2" x 3½"

8 rectangles, 1½" x 10"

4 rectangles, 1½" x 5"

**From *each* of the 4 assorted large-scale red fabrics, cut:**

2 squares, 3½" x 3½" (8 total)

**From *each* of the 2 medium-green fabrics, cut:**

1 strip (2 total), 2" x 42"; crosscut into 40 squares, 2" x 2"

**From the medium-green striped fabric, cut:**

4 strips, 1½" x 42"

12 squares, 2" x 2"

**From *each* of the 3 assorted light-green fabrics, cut:**

4 squares, 6½" x 6½" (12 total)

**From the mottled-green fabric, cut:**

3 strips, 2" x 42"; crosscut into 48 squares, 2" x 2"

**From the *lengthwise grain* of the red floral, cut:**

4 strips, 5" x 44"

**From the dark-red fabric, cut:**

5 strips, 2½" x 42"

## Making the Star Blocks

1 Draw a diagonal line from corner to corner on the wrong side of each red 2" square. Align a marked square on one end of each beige 2" x 3½"

rectangle, right sides together. Stitch on the marked line. Trim ¼" from the stitching line. Flip the red triangle up and press toward the square. Repeat on the opposite end of the beige rectangle, positioning the matching marked square as shown. Make four matching units for each block (52 total).

Make 52.

2 Sew matching beige 1½" x 10" rectangles to both long sides of an assorted red 1½" x 10" rectangle to make strip set A. Make one strip set from each red (four total). Cut a total of 10 segments, 1½" wide.

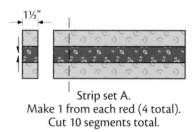

Strip set A.
Make 1 from each red (4 total).
Cut 10 segments total.

3 Using the same combination of fabrics that you used for the A strip sets, sew assorted red 1½" x 5" rectangles to both long sides of a beige 1½" x 5" rectangle to make strip set B. Make one strip set from each red (four total). Cut a total of five segments, 1½" wide.

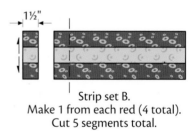

Strip set B.
Make 1 from each red (4 total).
Cut 5 segments total.

4 Using A and B segments from the same combination of fabrics, arrange two strip set A segments and one strip set B segment as shown. Sew the segments together to make a nine-patch unit. Make five.

Make 5.

**5** Arrange and sew four matching units from step 1, four matching medium-green or medium-green striped 2" squares, and either an assorted red 3½" square *or* a nine-patch unit from step 4 together as shown to make a block. Make the number of blocks indicated for each combination.

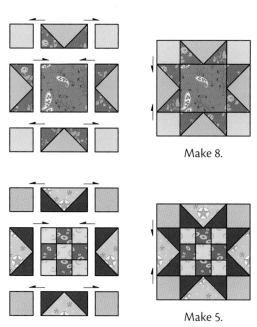

Make 8.

Make 5.

## Making the Double Snowball Blocks

**1** Draw a diagonal line from corner to corner on the wrong side of each beige 3½" square. With right sides together, place marked squares on opposite corners of each light-green 6½" square as shown. Stitch on the marked line. Trim ¼" from the stitching line. Flip open the triangles on the large square and press toward the beige triangles. Repeat for the remaining corners of each square, positioning the marked squares as shown. Make 12.

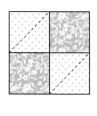

Make 12.

**2** Draw a diagonal line from corner to corner on the wrong side of each mottled-green 2" square. Place a marked square on each corner of the squares from step 1. Stitch on the marked lines. Trim ¼" from the stitching line. Flip open the triangles and press the seam allowances toward the green triangles to complete one Double Snowball block. Make 12 blocks.

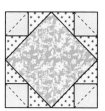
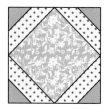

Make 12.

## Assembling the Quilt

**1** Arrange the blocks into five horizontal rows of five blocks each, alternating the Star and Double Snowball blocks in each row and from row to row.

**2** Sew the blocks in each row together; press the seam allowances toward the Double Snowball blocks. Sew the rows together, pressing the seam allowances all in one direction.

**3** Measure, cut, and sew the green-striped 1½"-wide inner-border strips, and then the red-floral 5"-wide outer-border strips to the quilt top.

## Finishing the Quilt

**1** Layer the quilt top with batting and backing. Baste the layers together.

**2** Hand or machine quilt as desired. The quilt shown was machine quilted with a small medallion in the centers of the Double Snowball blocks, curving lines and in-the-ditch quilting in the Star blocks, and a beautiful swirl design in the borders.

**3** Trim the batting and backing fabric so the edges are even with the quilt top.

**4** Use the dark-red 2½"-wide strips to make the binding. Sew the binding to the quilt.

# Pretty Poinsettias

*The flowers are quilted with gold metallic thread, adding glitz to the project. Gold beads stitched to the center of each flower give the quilt an extra dimension of texture and elegance.*

By Cheryl Almgren Taylor

FINISHED QUILT SIZE: 37½" x 37½"    FINISHED BLOCK SIZE: 8" x 8"

## Materials

*Yardage is based on 42"-wide fabric.*

⅞ yard of white print for block backgrounds

⅞ yard of red-and-gold dot print for inner border and bias binding

⅝ yard of holly print for outer border

⅝ yard of green-and-white dot print for sashing

⅜ yard *total* of 4 assorted red prints that read as solid for poinsettia appliqués

⅜ yard *total* of 4 assorted red-and-gold metallic prints for poinsettia appliqués

¼ yard *total* of 2 different green prints for poinsettia leaf appliqués

⅛ yard of red-and-gold print for sashing squares

1¼ yards of fabric for backing

41½" x 41½" square of batting

¾ yard of 22"-wide lightweight paper-backed fusible web

54 gold metallic beads, 4 mm

Gold metallic thread for quilting (optional)

# Cutting

*All measurements include ¼"-wide seam allowances.*

**From the white print, cut:**

9 squares, 9" x 9"

**From the green-and-white dot print, cut:**

24 rectangles, 1¾" x 8½"

**From the red-and-gold print, cut:**

16 squares, 1¾" x 1¾", centering a gold motif in
each square

**From the red-and-gold dot print, cut:**

4 strips, 1¼" x 42"

160" of 2½"-wide bias binding

**From the holly print, cut:**

4 strips, 3¾" x 42"

# Making the Appliqué Blocks

1 Prepare the appliqué pieces on page 114 from
the fabrics indicated. You might want to use a
red fabric and a red-and-gold fabric in each block
for a scrappy look, alternating where you use the
red-and-gold fabric (either in the upper or lower
bracts). Do the same for the green leaf prints if
desired.

2 Referring to the placement guide, center and
arrange the pieces for one block on a white
square in the order indicated. Follow the manufacturer's instructions to fuse the shapes in place.
Repeat to make a total of nine blocks.

Placement guide

3 Finish the raw edges of each appliqué piece
using a blanket stitch, zigzag stitch, or
satin stitch.

4 Square up the completed blocks to 8½" x 8½",
keeping the designs centered.

# Assembling the Quilt

1 Alternately join four green-and-white
1¾" x 8½" sashing strips and three blocks
to make a block row. Repeat to make a total of
three rows. Press the seam allowances toward the
sashing strips.

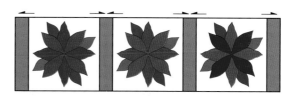

Make 3.

2 To make the sashing rows, alternately join four
red-and-gold 1¾" squares and three green-and-
white 1¾" x 8½" sashing strips. Repeat to make a
total of four rows. Press the seam allowances toward
the sashing strips.

Make 4.

3 Refer to the quilt assembly diagram to alternately sew the sashing and block rows together.
Press the seam allowances toward the sashing rows.

4 Measure and add the red-and-gold dot 1¼"-
wide inner border first, and then add the holly
print 3¾"-wide outer border.

Quilt assembly

## Finishing the Quilt

1 Prepare the backing so that it is 4" longer and 4" wider than the quilt top.

2 Layer the backing, batting, and quilt top; baste together.

3 Quilt as desired. Metallic threads add Christmas sparkle to the quilt.

4 When the quilting is complete, square up the quilt sandwich and attach the bias binding.

5 Hand stitch six gold beads to the center of each flower. When attaching the beads, stitch into the batting but not all the way through the backing fabric. This will firmly attach the beads but keep the back of your quilt looking nice.

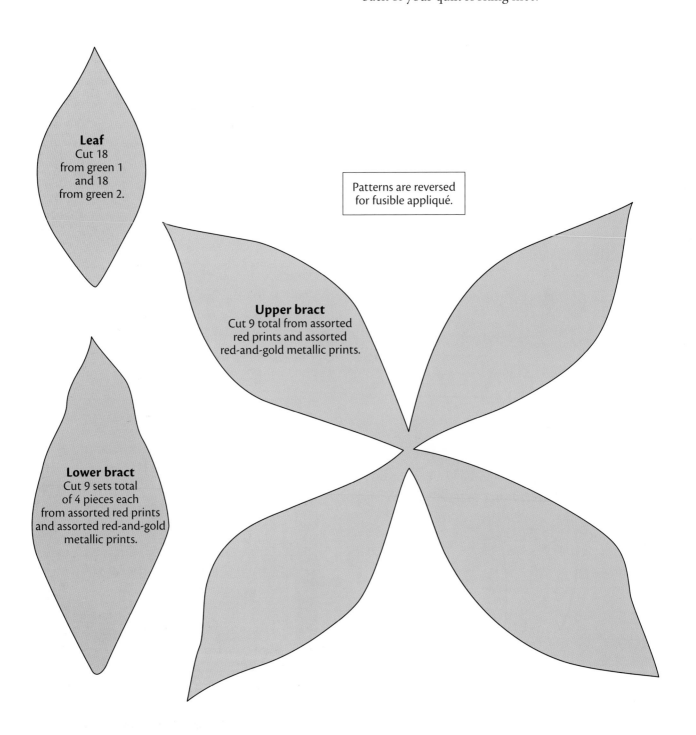

**Leaf**
Cut 18
from green 1
and 18
from green 2.

Patterns are reversed
for fusible appliqué.

**Upper bract**
Cut 9 total from assorted
red prints and assorted
red-and-gold metallic prints.

**Lower bract**
Cut 9 sets total
of 4 pieces each
from assorted red prints
and assorted red-and-gold
metallic prints.

# Christmas Lanterns

*Although Margaret used her collection of Christmas prints for this quilt, she also added other complementary red, green, and beige prints.*

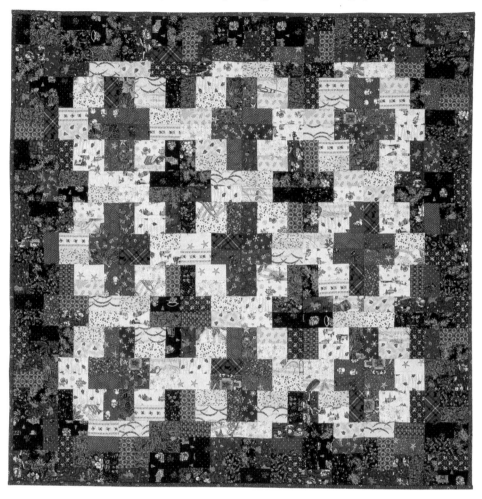

By Margaret Rolfe; quilted by Beth Reid
FINISHED QUILT SIZE: 45" x 45"    FINISHED BLOCK SIZE: 6" x 6"

## Materials

*Yardage is based on 42"-wide fabric.*

1¼ yards *total* of assorted green Christmas prints for blocks and border

¾ yard *total* of assorted beige Christmas prints for blocks

¾ yard *total* of assorted red Christmas prints for blocks and border

½ yard of red print for blocks and binding

2¼ yards of fabric for backing

49" x 49" piece of batting

## Cutting

*All measurements include ¼"-wide seam allowances.*

**From the red print, cut:**

5 strips, 2½" x 42"

**From the assorted red prints, including remaining red print for binding, cut a *total* of:**

97 rectangles, 2" x 3½"

**From the assorted green prints, cut a *total* of:**

209 rectangles, 2" x 3½"

**From the assorted beige prints, cut a *total* of:**

144 rectangles, 2" x 3½"

## Making the Blocks

You'll need a total of 36 pieced blocks. Avoid duplicating prints within the blocks and units.

1 For block 1, arrange two green, four beige, and two red rectangles as shown. Sew the rectangles together; press. Make 18 of block 1.

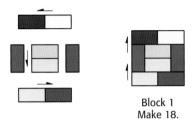

Block 1
Make 18.

2 For block 2, arrange two green, four beige, and two red rectangles as shown. Sew and press as for block 1. Make 18 of block 2.

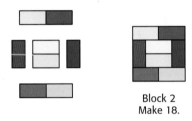

Block 2
Make 18.

## Assembling the Quilt

1 Arrange the blocks in six horizontal rows of six blocks each, alternating and rotating the blocks as shown.

2 Sew the blocks together into rows. Press the seam allowances in opposite directions from row to row.

3 Pin and sew the rows together; press.

4 Sew the remaining green and red rectangles to make the units shown. Press as indicated. Make 29 of unit A and 25 of unit B.

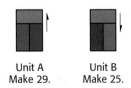

Unit A
Make 29.

Unit B
Make 25.

5 Arrange eight of unit A and seven of unit B in a row to make the left border as shown. Sew the units together and press the seam allowances to one side. Label the border. Repeat to arrange, sew, and press nine of unit A and six of unit B to make the right border as shown. Label the border.

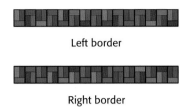

Left border

Right border

6 Arrange six each of units A and B in a row to make the top border as shown. Sew the units together and press the seam allowances to one side. Label the border. Repeat to arrange, sew, and press six each of units A and B to make the bottom border as shown. Label the border.

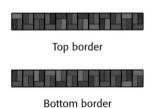

Top border

Bottom border

7 Sew the borders from step 6 to the top and bottom of the quilt; press the seam allowances toward the borders. Repeat to sew the borders from step 5 to the appropriate sides of the quilt top; press toward the borders.

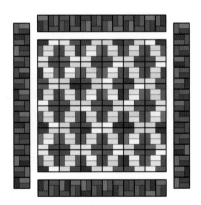

Assembly diagram

## Finishing the Quilt

1 Divide the backing fabric crosswise into two equal panels of approximately 49" each. Join the panels to make a single large backing panel.

2 Center and layer the quilt top and batting over the backing; baste, and then quilt as desired.

3 Use the red 2½"-wide strips to make the binding. Sew the binding to the quilt.

# Nine Patch Nostalgia

*The traditional Nine Patch block honors our quilting heritage; it's simple, yet many beautiful designs can be created with it.*

By Lori Smith of From My Heart to Your Hands

FINISHED QUILT SIZE: 16" x 20"    FINISHED BLOCK SIZE: 3" x 3"

## Materials

*Fat quarters measure approximately 18" x 21"; fat eighths measure 9" x 21".*

1 fat quarter of red print for blocks
1 fat quarter of medium-green fabric for setting triangles
1 fat eighth of medium plaid for alternate blocks
1 fat eighth of dark plaid for border
1 fat eighth of off-white print for blocks
1 fat eighth of light-green fabric for alternate blocks
1 fat quarter of fabric for binding
1 fat quarter of fabric for backing
18" x 22" piece of batting

## Cutting

*All measurements include ¼"-wide seam allowances.*

**From the red print, cut:**
60 squares, 1½" x 1½"

117

**From the off-white print, cut:**

48 squares, 1½" x 1½"

**From the light-green fabric, cut:**

3 squares, 3⅞" x 3⅞"; cut in half diagonally to make 6 triangles

1 square, 4¼" x 4¼"; cut into quarters diagonally to make 4 triangles

**From the medium-green fabric, cut:**

2 squares, 3" x 3"; cut in half diagonally to make 4 triangles

3 squares, 5½" x 5½"; cut into quarters diagonally to make 12 triangles (2 will be extra)

**From the medium plaid, cut:**

2 squares, 3" x 3"; cut in half diagonally to make 4 triangles

1 square, 5½" x 5½"; cut into quarters diagonally to make 4 triangles (2 will be extra)

**From the dark plaid, cut:**

2 strips, 2⅛" x 20½"

2 strips, 2" x 13¼"

**From the binding fabric, cut:**

4 strips, 1¾" x 20"

## Making the Blocks

1 Sew four off-white squares and five red squares together as shown to make a Nine Patch block. Make 12 blocks.

Make 12.

2 Sew a light-green 4¼" triangle to a medium-plaid 3" triangle along the short edges; press. Sew this unit to a light-green 3⅞" triangle. Make two. Repeat to make two more units, changing the orientation of the smaller triangles.

Make 2 of each.

3 Sew a light-green 3⅞" triangle to a medium-plaid 5½" triangle to make a half-square-triangle unit. Press the seam allowances toward the plaid triangle. Make two half-square-triangle units.  Make 2.

## Assembling the Quilt

1 Arrange the Nine Patch blocks, the medium-green triangles, and the units from steps 2 and 3 of "Making the Blocks" in diagonal rows as shown in the assembly diagram.

2 Sew the blocks and units into rows, pressing the seam allowances as shown. Sew the rows together and press the seam allowances in one direction.

3 Sew the dark-plaid 2" x 13¼" border strips to the top and bottom of the quilt. Press toward the border strips. Add the dark-plaid 2⅛" x 20½" border strips to the sides of the quilt.

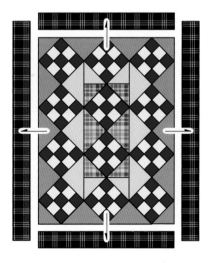

## Finishing the Quilt

Layer the quilt with backing and batting. Baste the layers together and quilt as desired. Add the binding and enjoy.

# Bear's Paw

*The traditional Bear's Paw block looks good in any color.*

By Kathleen Tracy

**FINISHED QUILT SIZE: 19¼" x 19¼"     FINISHED BLOCK SIZE: 12¼" x 12¼"**

## Materials

*Yardage is based on 42"-wide fabric unless otherwise noted.*

⅛ yard *each OR* scraps of 6 to 12 medium prints for block

¼ yard of brown print for block center and outer border

⅛ yard *each* of 2 different black prints for block

⅛ yard of blue-checked fabric for inner border

Scraps of 6 to 12 light prints for block

¼ yard of maroon print for binding

¾ yard of fabric for backing

23" x 23" piece of cotton batting

## Cutting

*All measurements include ¼"-wide seam allowances.*

**From the light prints, cut:**

8 squares, 2⅝" x 2⅝"

4 matching squares, 2¼" x 2¼"

**From *each* of 4 medium prints, cut:**

1 square, 4" x 4" (4 squares total)

**From the remaining scraps of medium prints, cut:**

8 squares, 2⅝" x 2⅝"

**From *each* of the 2 black prints, cut:**

1 strip, 2¼" x 12" (2 strips total); crosscut into 2 pieces, 2¼" x 5¾" (4 pieces total)

**From the brown print, cut:**

1 square, 2¼" x 2¼"

2 strips, 3" x 42"; crosscut into 2 pieces, 3" x 14¼", and 2 pieces, 3" x 19¼"

**From the blue-checked fabric, cut:**

2 strips, 1¼" x 40"; crosscut into 2 pieces, 1¼" x 12¾", and 2 pieces, 1¼" x 14¼"

**From the maroon print, cut:**

3 strips, 2" x 42"

## Assembling the Quilt

1 Draw a diagonal line from corner to corner on the wrong side of each light 2⅝" square. Layer a marked square on top of a medium 2⅝" square, right sides together. Stitch ¼" from the line on both sides and cut on the drawn line. Press toward the darker fabric. Make 16 half-square-triangle units.

Make 16.

2 Sew the half-square-triangle units together in pairs as shown. Press. Make four of each.

Make 4.  Make 4.

3 Sew one of the units from step 2 to the top of a medium 4" square, pressing as shown. Make four.

Make 4.

4 Sew a light 2¼" square to each of the remaining units from step 2 as shown. Press toward the light square.

Make 4.

5 Sew a unit from step 4 to one side of a unit from step 3 as shown. Press. Make four paw units.

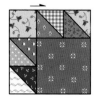

Make 4.

6 Sew pairs of paw units from step 5 together with two matching black 2¼" x 5¾" pieces as shown. Press the seam allowances toward the black print. Sew the two remaining black pieces to opposite sides of the brown 2¼" square. Press toward the black print.

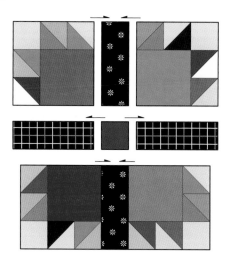

7 Sew the rows together to make the Bear's Paw block. Press.

8 Sew the blue-checked 1¼" x 12¾" strips to the sides of the quilt top, pressing the seam allowances toward the border. Sew the blue-checked 1¼" x 14¼" strips to the top and bottom of the quilt and press.

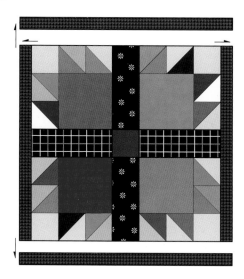

9 Sew the brown 3" x 14¼" strips to the sides of the quilt top, pressing the seam allowances toward the outer border. Sew the brown 3" x 19¼" strips to the top and bottom of the quilt top and press.

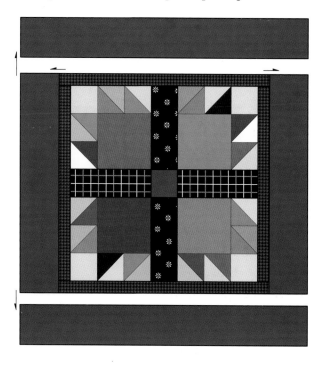

## Finishing the Quilt

1 Layer the quilt top, batting, and backing; baste the layers together.

2 Quilt a large X in each sashing strip and quilt in the ditch around each patch. Quilt diagonal lines through the block squares and at the border corners, and quilt straight lines at regular intervals across the width of the borders.

3 Attach the maroon-print binding to the quilt.

# Better to Be Overdressed
# Than Underdressed

*Spiffy little Bow Tie blocks dress up this quilt,
but its country flair gives it a down-home feel.*

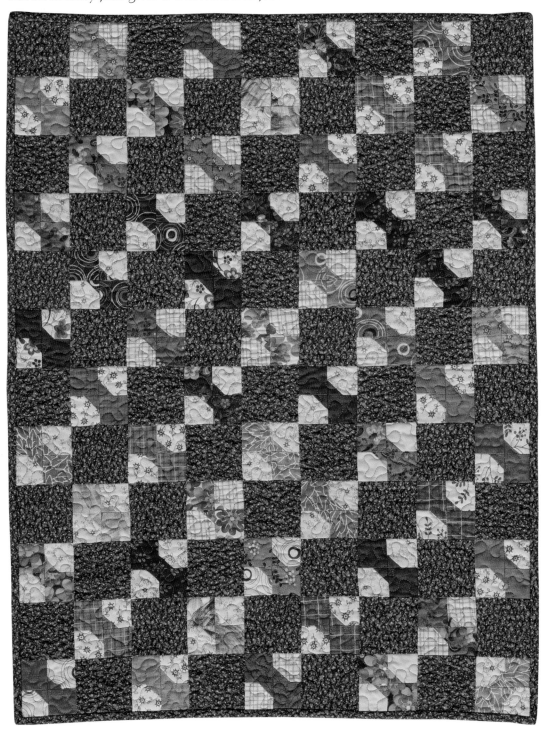

By Mary Etherington and Connie Tesene of Country Threads

FINISHED QUILT SIZE: 22½" x 30"     FINISHED BLOCK SIZE: 2½" x 2½"

## Materials

*Yardage is based on 42"-wide fabric unless otherwise noted. Charm squares are 5" x 5".*

27 assorted dark-value charm squares for Bow Tie blocks

27 assorted light-value charm squares for Bow Tie blocks

⅞ yard of dark-purple print for unpieced blocks and binding

⅞ yard of fabric for backing

28" x 36" piece of batting

## Cutting

*All measurements include ¼"-wide seam allowances.*

**From *each* of the assorted dark-value charm squares, cut:**

4 squares, 1¾" x 1¾" (108 total)*

4 squares, 1⅛" x 1⅛" (108 total)*

**From *each* of the assorted light-value charm squares, cut:**

4 squares, 1¾" x 1¾" (108 total)*

**From the dark-purple print, cut:**

5 strips, 3" x 42"; crosscut into 54 squares, 3" x 3"

4 strips, 2¼" x 42"

*\*Keep squares of the same fabric together.*

## Creating the Quilt

Each Bow Tie block is made from four matching dark-value and two matching light-value squares.

1 Place a dark 1⅛" square on the corner of a light 1¾" square, right sides together. Stitch diagonally from corner to corner on the dark square; trim the outside corner of the small square and press toward the corner. Repeat with a second set of matching dark- and light-value squares.

Make 2.

2 Arrange the two units from step 1 with two matching dark-value 1¾" charm squares and sew the units together to make a Bow Tie block.

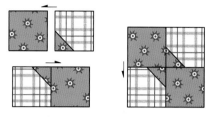

3 Repeat steps 1 and 2 to make 54 Bow Tie blocks.

4 Alternate the Bow Tie blocks and dark-purple 3" squares in 12 rows of nine blocks and squares in each row. Sew the rows together and press.

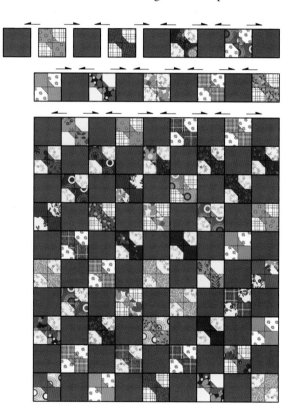

## Finishing the Quilt

Make a quilt back approximately 26" x 36". Layer the quilt top with batting and backing. Baste, and then quilt as desired. Trim the excess batting and backing and bind the quilt with the dark-purple 2¼"-wide strips.

# Plaid Coins

*Chinese Coins is a favorite pattern that combines narrow bits of scraps into long strips. All the strips are cut 1½" wide, so dig into your scrap bag to use up leftovers, or start with a group of fabrics you like and cut new strips.*

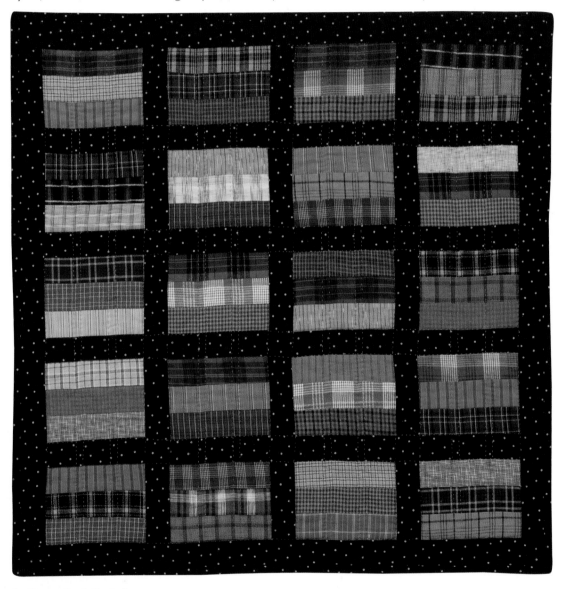

By Karen Costello Soltys
FINISHED QUILT SIZE: 21½" x 21½"

## Materials

*Yardage is based on 42"-wide fabric unless otherwise noted.*

½ yard of black print for sashing, border, and binding

Plaid scraps *OR* fat eighths*

¾ yard of fabric for backing

24" x 24" piece of batting

*\*Karen used 33 different scrap fabrics, but you can use fewer.*

## Cutting

*All measurements include ¼"-wide seam allowances.*

**From the plaid scraps, cut:**

60 pieces, 1½" x 4½"

**From the black print, cut:**

6 strips, 1½" x 42"; crosscut into:

    2 strips, 1½" x 21½"

    5 strips, 1½" x 19½"

    16 pieces, 1½" x 4½"

3 strips, 2" x 42"

## Assembling the Quilt

1   Lay out the plaid pieces in groups of three, separated by the short black pieces. You'll need 15 plaid pieces and 4 black pieces for each of the four vertical strips. Rearrange the pieces until you're satisfied with the color placement.

2   Sew the pieces together into vertical strips. Press all seam allowances in one direction.

3   Sew a black 19½" strip to the right edge of each plaid strip. Then sew the sections together. Add the remaining black 19½" strip to the left edge of the quilt top. Press all seam allowances toward the black strips.

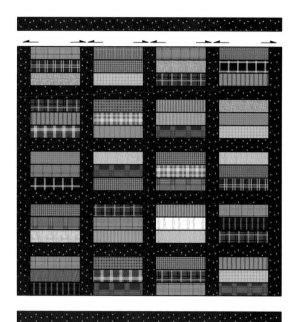

4   Join the black 21½" strips to the top and bottom of the quilt top. Press the seam allowances toward the black borders.

## Finishing the Quilt

1   Mark any quilting designs on the quilt top.

2   Place the backing right side down on a table or floor and lay the batting on top, smoothing out any wrinkles. Then add the pressed quilt top, right side up, on top. Hand or pin baste the layers together.

3   Quilt by hand or machine. The quilt shown was hand quilted in the ditch along all the black sashing and border pieces. In addition, two sets of vertical lines were quilted through each column of plaid fabrics by stitching on either side of ¼"-wide masking tape.

4   Using the black 2"-wide strips, make and attach binding.

# Friendship Star

*The Friendship Star block is filled with sentiment. Make a keepsake quilt to commemorate the special relationships in your life.*

By Kathleen Tracy

**FINISHED QUILT SIZE: 20½" x 25"   FINISHED BLOCK SIZE: 4½" x 4½"**

## Materials

*Yardage is based on 42"-wide fabric unless otherwise noted.*

⅛ yard *each* of 12 different light prints for star backgrounds

⅛ yard *each* of 12 different medium prints for star points

⅓ yard of blue floral for outer border

¼ yard of pink print for inner border

Scraps of 12 different medium prints for star centers

¼ yard of brown print for binding

¾ yard of fabric for backing

24" x 28" piece of cotton batting

## Cutting

*All measurements include ¼"-wide seam allowances.*

**From *each* of the 12 light prints, cut:**

2 squares, 2⅜" x 2⅜" (24 total)

4 squares, 2" x 2" (48 total)

**From *each* of the 12 medium prints for star points, cut:**

2 squares, 2⅜" x 2⅜" (24 total)

**From *each* of the 12 medium prints for star centers, cut:**

1 square, 2" x 2" (12 total)

**From the pink print, cut:**

2 strips, 1¼" x 42"; crosscut into 2 pieces, 1¼" x 15½", and 2 pieces, 1¼" x 18½"

**From the blue floral, cut:**

2 strips, 3" x 42"; crosscut into 2 pieces, 3" x 20", and 2 pieces, 3" x 20½"

**From the brown print, cut:**

3 strips, 2" x 42"

## Assembling the Quilt

It's easiest to make this quilt one block at a time, selecting four 2" squares and two 2⅜" squares from the same light print and two 2⅜" squares from the same medium print. That way, the star points and the background will be consistent within each block.

1 Draw a diagonal line from corner to corner on the wrong side of each light 2⅜" square. Layer each marked square on top of a medium 2⅜" square, right sides together. Stitch ¼" from the line on both sides and cut on the drawn line. Press the seam allowances toward the darker fabric. Make a total of 48 half-square-triangle units.

Make 48 in matching sets of 4.

2 Sew four matching units from step 1, four matching light 2" squares, and a 2" square of a contrasting medium print together as shown to make a Friendship Star block. Press the seam allowances as shown. Repeat to make 12 blocks.

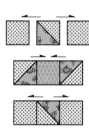 

Make 12.

3 Sew the blocks together into four rows of three blocks each. Press the seam allowances in the opposite direction from row to row. Sew the rows together and press the seam allowances in one direction.

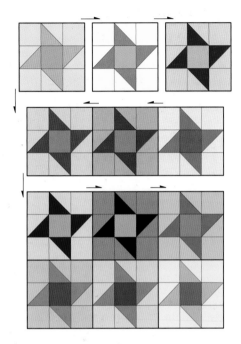

4 Sew the pink 1¼" x 18½" strips to the sides of the quilt top, pressing the seam allowances toward the border. Sew the pink 1¼" x 15½" strips to the top and bottom of the quilt top and press.

5 Sew the blue-floral 3" x 20" strips to the sides of the quilt top, pressing the seam allowances toward the outer border. Sew the blue-floral 3" x 20½" strips to the top and bottom of the quilt top and press.

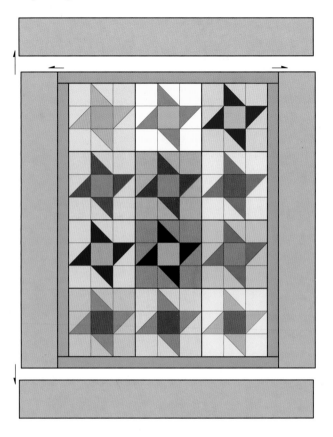

## Finishing the Quilt

1 Layer the quilt top, batting, and backing, and baste the layers together.

2 Quilt an X through the center of each block.

3 Attach the brown-print binding to the quilt.

# Say "Please"

*Choose charm squares with fabrics you really love; then play with the circles and layout, experimenting with different arrangements. If someone wants to borrow your quilt, they have to say "please."*

By Mary Etherington and Connie Tesene of Country Threads

FINISHED QUILT SIZE: 32½" x 32½"    FINISHED BLOCK SIZE: 4½" x 4½"

## Materials

*Fat quarters measure approximately 18" x 21"; charm squares are 5" x 5".*

25 charm squares for center squares*

17 squares, 4" x 4", for circles (you may substitute 5" charm squares)*

1 fat quarter *each* of light, medium, and dark fabric for border (3 fat quarters total)

¼ yard of gold tone-on-tone fabric for binding

1 yard of fabric for backing

36" x 36" piece of batting

½ yard of 17"-wide fusible web

*You can substitute 5 assorted 5" x 42" strips (or fat quarters) for backgrounds and 6 assorted 4" x 13" scraps for circles. Cut a total of 25 background squares, 5" x 5".*

## Cutting

*All measurements include ¼"-wide seam allowances.*

**From the fat quarter of light fabric, cut:**

3 strips, 5½" x 20"; crosscut into 20 rectangles, 2¾" x 5½"

**From the fat quarter of medium fabric, cut:**

3 strips, 5½" x 20"; crosscut into 20 rectangles, 2¾" x 5½"

**From the fat quarter of dark fabric, cut:**

4 corner squares, 5½" x 5½"

**From the gold tone-on-tone fabric, cut:**

4 strips, 1½" x 42"

## Assembling the Quilt

1 Arrange the 5" squares into five rows of five squares each.

2 Using fusible web, the 4" squares, and the patterns on page 131, prepare five large circles and 12 small circles for appliqué. Arrange the circles on the 5" squares until you like how they look. Fuse the circles to the squares.

3 Sew the squares into rows. Press the seam allowances in opposite directions from row to row. Sew the rows together and press.

4 With your sewing machine, zigzag or blanket stitch around each circle.

5 To make a border, sew 10 rectangles together as shown, alternating the light and medium fabrics. Make four borders.

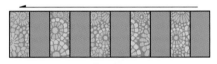

Border.
Make 4.

6 Sew two borders to opposite sides of the quilt top. Press toward the quilt center.

7 Sew a dark 5½" square to each end of the two remaining borders. Sew these borders to the top and bottom of the quilt top.

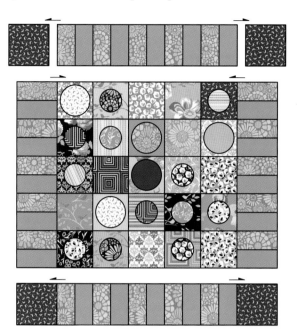

## Finishing the Quilt

Layer the quilt top with batting and backing; baste. Quilt as desired. Sew the gold 1½"-wide strips together end to end to make one long strip. Use this strip to bind your quilt.

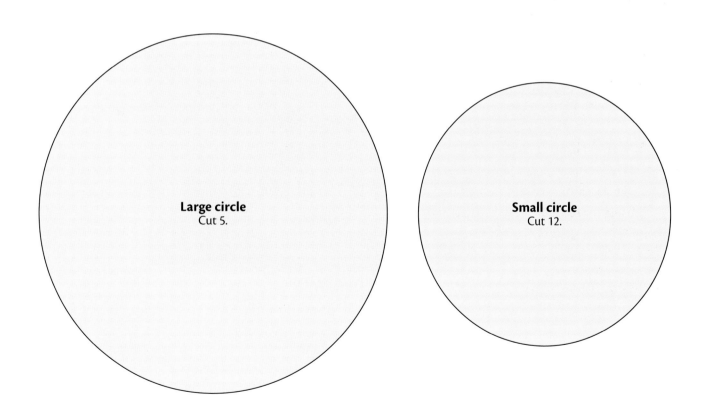

**Large circle**
Cut 5.

**Small circle**
Cut 12.

# Sherbet Parfait

*Mix yummy fabrics and simple blocks together and you'll get delicious results! This pattern combines a 6" Snowball block with the basic Nine Patch block in a diagonal setting.*

By Tammy Kelly; machine quilted by Cydne Walker

**FINISHED QUILT SIZE: 39" x 47½"**   **FINISHED BLOCK SIZE: 6" x 6"**

## Materials

*Yardage is based on 42"-wide fabric.*

⅞ yard of pink-striped fabric for Snowball blocks and border-corner Pinwheel blocks

¼ yard *each* of 3 assorted pink prints for Nine Patch blocks and border

¼ yard *each* of 3 assorted purple prints for Nine Patch blocks and border

⅝ yard of yellow fabric for Nine Patch blocks and setting triangles

½ yard of dark-pink fabric for Snowball blocks and border-corner Pinwheel blocks

⅛ yard of lime-green print for Nine Patch blocks

⅛ yard of orange-and-pink print for Nine Patch blocks

½ yard of purple fabric for binding

2⅞ yards of fabric for backing

45" x 54" piece of batting

## Cutting

*All measurements include ¼"-wide seam allowances.*

**From the dark pink, cut:**

5 strips, 2½" x 42"; crosscut into 80 squares, 2½" x 2½"

**From the pink-striped fabric, cut:**

4 strips, 6½" x 42"; crosscut into 20 squares, 6½" x 6½"

**From *each* of the 3 assorted pink prints, cut:**

1 strip, 2½" x 42" (3 total)

**From the remainder of *each of 2* of the assorted pink prints, cut:**

2 pieces, 3" x 11⅛" (4 total)

2 pieces, 3" x 9" (4 total)

**From *each* of the 3 assorted purple prints, cut:**

1 strip, 2½" x 42" (3 total)

**From the remainder of *each of 2* of the assorted purple prints, cut:**

2 pieces, 3" x 11⅛" (4 total)

2 pieces, 3" x 9" (4 total)

**From the lime-green print, cut:**

1 strip, 2½" x 42"

**From the orange-and-pink print, cut:**

1 strip, 2½" x 42"

**From the yellow fabric, cut:**

1 strip, 2½" x 42"

4 squares, 9¾" x 9¾"; cut into quarters diagonally to make 16 side triangles (2 will be extra)

2 squares, 5⅛" x 5⅛"; cut in half diagonally to make 4 corner triangles

**From the purple fabric, cut:**

5 strips, 2½" x 42"

## Making the Blocks

1 To make the Snowball blocks, press the dark-pink 2½" squares in half diagonally, wrong sides together. Open each square and align one on each corner of a pink-striped square as shown. Sew on the fold line of each corner square. Trim ¼" from the seam, using a rotary cutter and ruler to cut accurately. Set aside the cut-away triangle pairs for making the border-corner blocks, keeping the pairs together. Press open the attached triangle in each

corner to complete the Snowball block. The block should measure 6½" square. Repeat to make a total of 20 blocks.

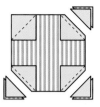

Make 20.

2 To make the Nine Patch blocks, sew together the pink, purple, lime-green, orange-and-pink, and yellow 2½" x 42" strips as shown to make strip sets A, B, and C. Press the seam allowances in the directions indicated for each strip set. The strip sets should measure 6½" wide. Crosscut each strip set into 12 segments, 2½" wide.

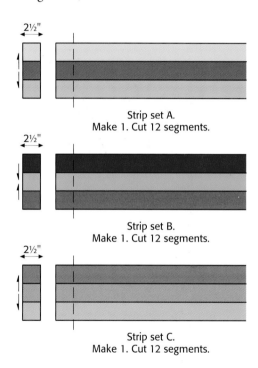

2½"

Strip set A.
Make 1. Cut 12 segments.

2½"

Strip set B.
Make 1. Cut 12 segments.

2½"

Strip set C.
Make 1. Cut 12 segments.

3 Lay out one segment from each strip set into three vertical rows as shown. Sew the segments together. Press the seam allowances away from the center segment to complete a Nine Patch block. The block should measure 6½" square. Repeat to make a total of 12 blocks.

Make 12.

## Assembling the Quilt Center

1 Lay out the blocks and yellow side setting triangles in diagonal rows.

2 Sew together the blocks and side triangles in each row. Press the seam allowances toward the Nine Patch blocks and side triangles.

3 Sew the rows together, adding the yellow corner triangles last. Press the seam allowances in one direction. Press the entire quilt center.

4 Square up the quilt center, trimming the edges ¼" from the block corners as needed. The pieced quilt center should measure 34½" x 43".

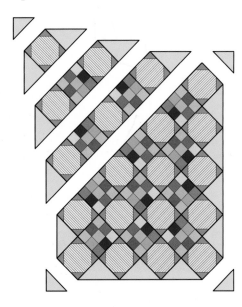

## Assembling the Border-Corner Blocks

1 Select 16 pairs of triangles that were set aside after trimming the corners of the Snowball blocks.

2 Sew the pairs of triangles together to make 16 half-square-triangle units. Press the seam allowances toward the dark-pink fabric. Use a ruler and rotary cutter to trim each unit to 1¾" square.

3 Sew together two half-square-triangle units to make a pair. Make eight pairs. Press the seam allowances in one direction. Join two pairs as shown to make a Pinwheel block. Press the seam allowances in one direction. Repeat to make a total of four Pinwheel blocks.

Make 8.        Make 4.

## Assembling and Adding the Borders

1 To make the side borders, sew together two purple and pink 3" x 11⅛" pieces end to end, alternating colors. Repeat to make a total of two side border strips. Sew the borders to the quilt center. Press the seam allowances toward the borders.

2 To make the top and bottom borders, sew together two purple and pink 3" x 9" pieces end to end, alternating colors. Repeat to make a total of two strips. Sew Pinwheel blocks to both ends of each strip. Sew the borders to the quilt center as shown. Press the seam allowances toward the borders.

Quilt assembly

## Finishing the Quilt

1 Layer the quilt top with the batting and backing. Baste the layers together.

2 Hand or machine quilt as desired.

3 Prepare and sew the purple binding to the quilt.

# Going in Circles

*This quilt is a happy reminder of summertime meals of fresh corn on the cob and strawberry pie—served on cheerful Fiestaware.*

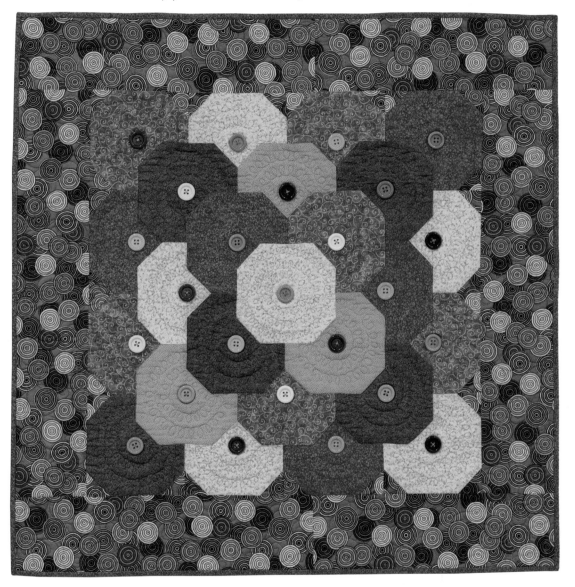

By Loraine Manwaring

FINISHED QUILT SIZE: 44½" x 44½"

## Materials

*Yardage is based on 42"-wide fabric.*

1¼ yards of large-scale multicolored print for border

⅞ yard of red print for blocks and binding

½ yard of green print for blocks

½ yard of blue print for blocks

⅜ yard of yellow print for blocks

¼ yard of orange print for blocks

2¼ yards of fabric for backing

50" x 50" piece of batting

25 buttons, 1⅛" in diameter, in colors to match block fabrics

## Cutting

*All measurements include ¼"-wide seam allowances.*

**From the yellow print, cut:**

1 strip, 8½" x 42"; crosscut into:
   1 square, 8½" x 8½"
   5 rectangles, 4½" x 8½"

1 square, 4½" x 4½"

1 strip, 2½" x 42"; crosscut into 9 squares, 2½" x 2½"

**From the red print, cut:**

2 strips, 4½" x 42"; crosscut into:
   5 rectangles, 4½" x 8½"
   2 squares, 4½" x 4½"

1 strip, 2½" x 42"; crosscut into 8 squares, 2½" x 2½"

5 strips, 2¾" x 42"

**From the green print, cut:**

2 strips, 4½" x 42"; crosscut into:
   6 rectangles, 4½" x 8½"
   2 squares, 4½" x 4½"

1 strip, 2½" x 42"; crosscut into 10 squares, 2½" x 2½"

**From the blue print, cut:**

2 strips, 4½" x 42"; crosscut into:
   5 rectangles, 4½" x 8½"
   5 squares, 4½" x 4½"

1 strip, 2½" x 42"; crosscut into 5 squares, 2½" x 2½"

**From the orange print, cut:**

1 strip, 4½" x 42"; crosscut into:
   3 rectangles, 4½" x 8½"
   2 squares, 4½" x 4½"

1 strip, 2½" x 42"; crosscut into 4 squares, 2½" x 2½"

**From the large-scale multicolored print, cut:**

2 strips, 2½" x 42"; crosscut into 28 squares, 2½" x 2½"

5 strips, 6½" x 42"

## Making the Units

1 Draw a diagonal line from corner to corner on the wrong side of each 2½" square.

2 On the yellow 8½" square, position a red 2½" square on the upper-left corner, a green 2½" square on the upper-right corner, a blue 2½" square on the lower-left corner, and an orange 2½" square on the lower-right corner, with right sides together. Stitch on the diagonal lines. Trim ¼" from the stitching lines; press the triangles and the seam allowances toward the corners.

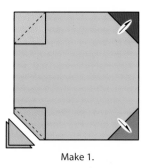

Make 1.

3 In the same manner, place the 2½" squares on opposite upper corners of the 4½" x 8½" rectangles to make units in the color combinations shown.

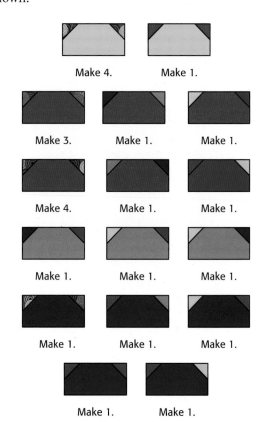

Make 4.    Make 1.

Make 3.    Make 1.    Make 1.

Make 4.    Make 1.    Make 1.

Make 1.    Make 1.    Make 1.

Make 1.    Make 1.    Make 1.

Make 1.    Make 1.

4 Using the same technique, place the 2½" squares on the upper-left corner of the 4½" squares to make a total of 12 units in the color combinations shown.

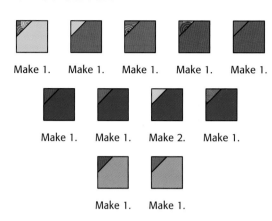

Make 1.   Make 1.   Make 1.   Make 1.   Make 1.

Make 1.   Make 1.   Make 2.   Make 1.

Make 1.   Make 1.

## Assembling the Quilt

1 To make the center section, arrange and sew the appropriate units together as shown. Press the seam allowances as indicated.

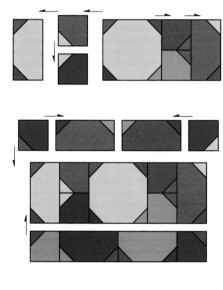

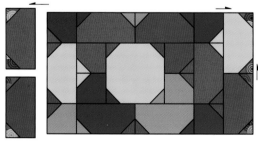

2 Arrange and sew the remaining units together to make the top and bottom sections as shown.

Press the seam allowances as indicated. Sew the sections together. Press.

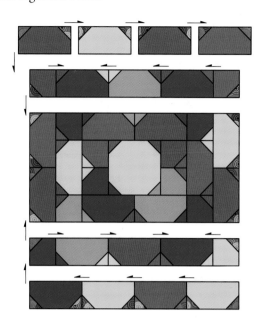

3 Add the multicolored strips to the quilt top.

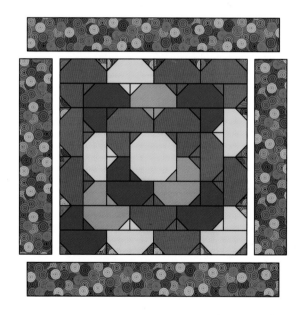

## Finishing the Quilt

1 Layer the quilt top with batting and backing; baste the layers together.

2 Hand or machine quilt as desired.

3 Use the red 2¾"-wide strips to bind the quilt.

4 Refer to the photo on page 135 to embellish your quilt with the buttons.

# Leaf Chain

*This cute little quilt is perfect for fall decorating.*
*Use it to top a table or add color to a wall or door.*

By Cathy Wierzbicki

FINISHED QUILT SIZE: 44½" x 44½"   FINISHED BLOCK SIZE: 8" x 8"

## Materials

*Yardage is based on 42"-wide fabric.*

1 yard of light fabric for blocks

⅝ yard *total* of assorted dark fabrics for blocks

¾ yard of focus print for outer border

½ yard of contrasting fabric for inner border

½ yard of fabric for binding

2⅞ yards of fabric for backing

50" x 50" piece of batting

# Cutting

*All measurements include ¼"-wide seam allowances.*

**From the light fabric, cut:**

2 strips, 4½" x 42"; crosscut into 16 squares,
    4½" x 4½" (G)

2 strips, 2⅞" x 42"; crosscut into 16 squares,
    2⅞" x 2⅞". Cut squares in half diagonally to yield
    32 triangles (C).

6 strips, 2½" x 42"; crosscut into:
    48 squares, 2½" x 2½" (B)
    16 rectangles, 2½" x 6½" (E)

**From the assorted dark fabrics, cut:**

8 squares *total*, 4½" x 4½" (A)

8 pairs of matching squares, 2⅞" x 2⅞" (16 total).
    Cut squares in half diagonally to yield *8 sets of 4*
    matching triangles (32 total) (C).

40 squares, 2½" x 2½" (F)

**From the contrasting fabric, cut:**

4 strips, 2½" x 42"

From the focus fabric, cut:

5 strips, 4½" x 42"

**From the binding fabric, cut:**

5 strips, 2½" x 42"

## Making the Leaf Blocks

1 With right sides together, align a B square on
  one corner of each A square as shown. Sew,
trim, and press as shown. Make eight.

Make 8.

2 Sew a C half-square triangle and a D half-
  square triangle together as shown; press. Make
32 in matching sets of four.

Make 32
in matching
sets of 4.

3 Sew two matching units from step 2 together as
  shown; press. Make eight of each.

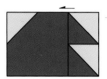

Make 8 of each.

4 Sew a unit from step 3 to the right edge of a
  matching unit from step 1 as shown; press.
Make eight.

Make 8.

5 Sew a B square to the right edge of each
  remaining unit from step 3; press. Make eight.
Sew a matching unit to the bottom edge of each
unit from step 4; press.

Make 8.

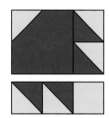 

6 Sew an E rectangle to the right edge of each
  unit from step 5; press. Make eight.

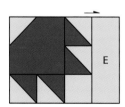

Make 8.

7 Sew an E rectangle to an F square as shown; press. Sew to the bottom edge of each unit from step 6; press. Make eight Leaf blocks.

Make 8.

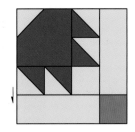
Make 8.

## Making the Chain Blocks

1 Arrange two B squares and two scrappy F squares as shown. Sew the squares together into rows; press. Sew the rows together; press. Make 16.

Make 16.

2 Arrange two units from step 1 and two G squares as shown. Sew the units and squares together into rows; press. Sew the rows together; press. Make eight Chain blocks.

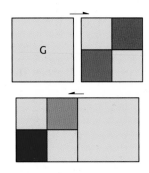
Make 8.

## Assembling the Quilt

1 Arrange the Leaf and Chain blocks in four horizontal rows of four blocks each as shown in the assembly diagram. Sew the blocks into rows; press. Sew the rows together; press.

2 Trim two contrasting 2½"-wide strips to measure 2½" x 32½" and sew them to the sides of the table topper; press. Trim the remaining contrasting strips to measure 2½" x 36½" and sew them to the top and bottom; press.

3 Sew the focus-print 4½"-wide strips end to end to make one continuous strip. From this long strip, cut two strips, 4½" x 36½", for the side borders, and two strips, 4½" x 44½", for the top and bottom borders. Sew the appropriate borders to the sides, and then to the top and bottom of the quilt top. Press the seam allowances toward the border.

Assembly diagram

## Finishing the Quilt

1 Layer the backing, batting, and quilt top; baste.

2 Hand or machine quilt as desired.

3 Use the 2½"-wide strips to bind the edges.

# Tumbling Leaves

*Autumn is in the air with the geese flying south and vibrant leaves tumbling to the ground. Enjoy the crisp air and stitch up this small quilt to welcome the season.*

By Lori Smith of From My Heart to Your Hands

FINISHED QUILT SIZE: 16" x 20"    FINISHED BLOCK SIZE: 4½" x 4½"

## Materials

*Fat quarters measure approximately 18" x 21";*
*fat eighths measure 9" x 21".*

8 fat eighths of assorted brown, orange, yellow, and
　green prints for blocks and appliqués
1 fat quarter of brown print for blocks and border
1 fat quarter of off-white print for block
　backgrounds
1 fat quarter of fabric for binding
1 fat quarter of fabric for backing
18" x 22" piece of batting

## Cutting

*All measurements include ¼"-wide seam allowances.*

**From the off-white print, cut:**

18 squares, 2" x 2"
27 squares, 2⅜" x 2⅜"; cut in half diagonally to
　make 54 triangles

**From *each* of the 8 assorted brown, orange,
yellow, and green prints, cut:**

2 squares, 2⅜" x 2⅜"; cut in half diagonally to make
　4 triangles (32 total)
3 squares, 2" x 2" (24 total)
1 bias strip, ¾" x 3" (8 total)

**From the brown print, cut:**

2 squares, 2⅜" x 2⅜"; cut in half diagonally to make
　4 triangles
3 squares, 2" x 2"
1 bias strip, ¾" x 3"
1 strip, 3" x 20½"
1 strip, 4" x 14"

**From the leftovers of the 8 assorted brown,
orange, yellow, and green prints, cut a *total* of:**

3 squares, 4¼" x 4¼"; cut into quarters diagonally to
　make 12 triangles (1 will be extra)

**From the binding fabric, cut:**

4 strips, 1¾" x 20"

## Making the Blocks

1 Choose four 2⅜" triangles, three 2" squares, and
one 3" bias strip of the same assorted fabric.
Sew the assorted triangles to the off-white triangles
to make four half-square-triangle units.

2 Appliqué the bias strip to one off-white 2"
square along the diagonal as shown to make the
stem. Trim the ends even with the square.

Trim.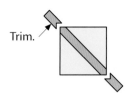

3 Arrange the units from step 1, the three 2"
squares, the appliquéd stem block, and an
off-white 2" square in three horizontal rows as
shown to make a Maple Leaf block. Sew the units
into rows; press. Sew the rows together. The block
should measure 5" x 5".

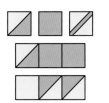

4 Repeat steps 1–3 using the pieces cut from the
assorted fat eighths and the brown fat quarter
to make a total of nine Maple Leaf blocks.

## Assembling the Quilt

1 Sew an off-white 2⅜" triangle to each side of an assorted 4¼" triangle as shown to make a flying-geese unit. Repeat to make nine flying-geese units, and then sew them together to make a row.

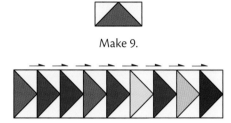

Make 9.

2 Arrange the Maple Leaf blocks in three horizontal rows of three blocks each. Position them in alternate directions as shown. Sew the blocks into rows and sew the rows together. Sew the flying-geese row to the top of the quilt.

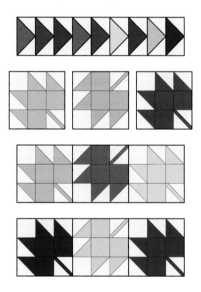

3 Sew the brown 4" x 14" border strip to the bottom of the quilt; press. Sew the brown 3" x 20½" border strip to the left side; press.

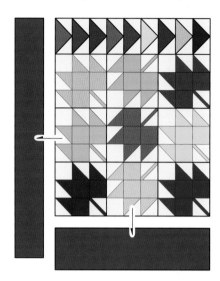

4 Prepare the pumpkin and sunflower appliqués using the patterns on page 144. Cut the sunflower stem on the bias wide enough that it will finish ⅝" wide. Arrange the pieces on the quilt and appliqué them in place using your favorite method. Appliqué two assorted 4¼" triangles in the upper-left corner.

## Finishing the Quilt

Layer the quilt top, batting, and backing. Baste the layers together and quilt as desired. Add the binding and enjoy.

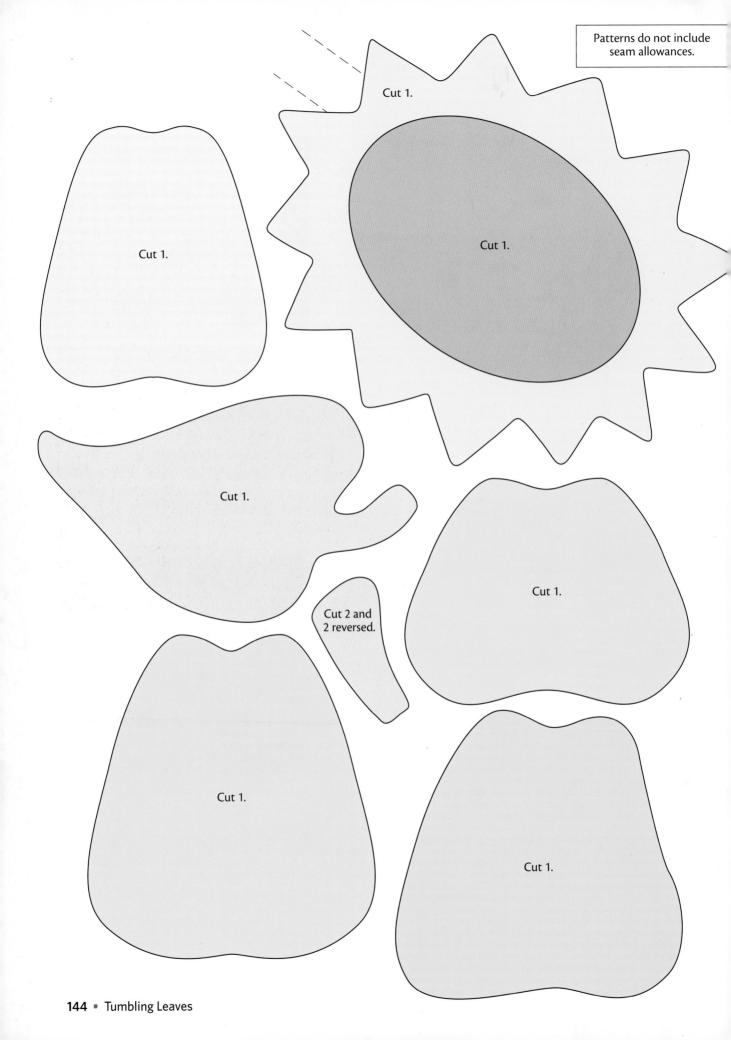

Cut 1.

Cut 1.

Patterns do not include
seam allowances.

Cut 1.

Cut 1.

Cut 1.

Cut 2 and
2 reversed.

Cut 1.

Cut 1.

Cut 1.

# Little Forest

*This magic little forest has trees with dots, checks, and even leaves, but the best trees have buttons. This quilt is fast and fun, and will be a joy for many years to come.*

By Mary Hickey; pieced by Judy Pollard; machine quilted by Dawn Kelly

**FINISHED QUILT SIZE: 39" x 27"   FINISHED BLOCK SIZE: 6" x 6"**

## Materials

*Yardage is based on 42"-wide fabric unless otherwise noted.*

⅛ yard *each* of 8 assorted green fabrics for Tree blocks

⅞ yard of beige fabric for block backgrounds

⅞ yard of dark-green fabric for outer border and binding

¼ yard of dark-red fabric for inner border

¼ yard of medium-green fabric for Chain blocks

7 scraps, no smaller than 4" x 4", of assorted red fabrics for Chain blocks

Scraps of assorted brown fabrics for Tree blocks

1⅓ yards of fabric for backing

31" x 43" piece of batting

Red star, heart, and round buttons (optional)

## Cutting

*All measurements include ¼"-wide seam allowances.*

**From the beige fabric, cut:**

2 strips, 2½" x 42"; crosscut into 28 squares, 2½" x 2½"

3 strips, 2¼" x 42"; crosscut into 48 squares, 2¼" x 2¼"

2 strips, 2¼" x 42"; crosscut into 16 rectangles, 1¾" x 2¼", and 16 rectangles, 1" x 2¼"

3 strips, 1½" x 42"

2 strips, 1¼" x 42"; crosscut into 16 rectangles, 1¼" x 3"

**From *each* of the 8 assorted green fabrics, cut:**
1 rectangle, 2¼" x 4" (8 total)
1 rectangle, 2¼ x 5½" (8 total)
1 rectangle, 2¼" x 6½" (8 total)
**From the brown scraps, cut:**
8 rectangles, 1¼" x 1½"
**From the medium-green fabric, cut:**
3 strips, 1½" x 42"
**From *each* of the red scraps, cut:**
1 square, 2½" x 2½" (7 total)
**From the dark-red fabric, cut:**
4 strips, 1½" x 42"
**From the dark-green fabric, cut:**
4 strips, 3¾" x 42"
4 strips, 2½" x 42"

## Making the Tree Blocks

1 Draw a diagonal line from corner to corner on the wrong side of each beige 2¼" square. Place a marked square on one end of each green 2¼" x 4" rectangle as shown. Stitch on the marked lines. Trim ¼" from the stitching line. Flip open the triangle and press the seam allowances toward the green rectangle. Repeat on the opposite end of the green rectangle. Repeat to sew a marked square on each end of the green 2¼" x 5½" and 2¼" x 6½" rectangles as shown. Be sure to position the marked squares as shown on each unit. Keep each tree-unit size together.

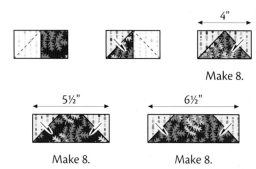

Make 8.

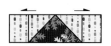 

Make 8. Make 8.

2 Stitch one 4" unit from step 1 between two beige 1¾" x 2¼" rectangles; press. Make eight. Stitch one 5½" unit from step 1 between two beige 1" x 2¼" rectangles; press. Make eight.

Make 8. Make 8.

3 Stitch one brown 1¼" x 1½" rectangle between two beige 1¼" x 3" rectangles as shown. Make eight trunk units.

Make 8.

4 Each Tree block is made from one green fabric. Arrange and sew one of each unit together to make one Tree block. Repeat to make eight blocks.

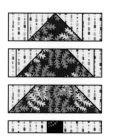 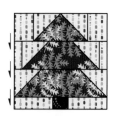

Make 8.

## Making the Chain Blocks

1 Stitch a beige 1½" x 42" strip to one long side of each medium-green 1½" x 42" strip to make a strip set. Make three. Crosscut the strip sets into 56 segments, 1½" wide.

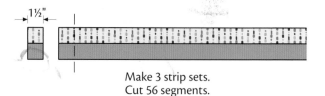

Make 3 strip sets.
Cut 56 segments.

2 Stitch two segments together as shown to make a four-patch unit. Make 28.

Make 28.

3 Sew one red 2½" square between two beige 2½" squares; press. Make seven.

Make 7.

4 Stitch four units from step 2, one unit from step 3, and two beige 2½" squares together as shown to make one block. Make seven Chain blocks.

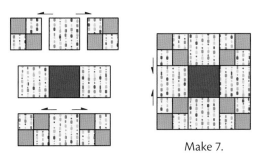

Make 7.

## Assembling the Quilt

1 Arrange the blocks in three rows of five blocks each, alternating the Tree and Chain blocks in each row and from row to row.

2 Stitch the blocks in each row together; press toward the Chain blocks. Stitch the rows together; press the seam allowances in one direction.

3 Measure, cut, and sew the dark-red 1½"-wide inner-border strips, and then the dark-green 3¾"-wide outer-border strips to the quilt top.

## Finishing the Quilt

1 Layer the quilt top with batting and backing. Baste the layers together.

2 Hand or machine quilt as desired. The quilt shown was machine quilted with branches in the blocks, windy swirls in the background, and arcs in the borders.

3 Trim the batting and backing fabric so the edges are even with the quilt top. Use the dark-green 2½"-wide strips to make the binding. Sew the binding to the quilt. Stitch buttons to the trees as desired.

Assembly diagram

# Inspiration Point

*Talk about easy! Using the quilt-as-you-go technique, you can start this
project after breakfast and be ready to bind the edges by lunchtime.*

By Ann Kisro
FINISHED QUILT SIZE: 40" x 40"

## Materials

*Yardage is based on 42"-wide fabric.*

¾ yard of red print for wide borders

⅝ yard of holly print for medium borders

⅝ yard of cardinal print for center square and
corner triangles

⅜ yard of green print for narrow borders

½ yard of fabric for binding

1½ yards of fabric for backing

48" x 48" piece of fusible or regular batting

# Cutting

*All measurements include ¼"-wide seam allowances.*

**From the cardinal print, cut:**

1 strip, 15⅛" x 42"; crosscut into:

    2 squares, 15⅛" x 15⅛"*

    1 square, 8½" x 8½"**

**From the green print, cut:**

5 strips, 1½" x 42"; crosscut into:

    2 strips, 1½" x 8½"

    2 strips, 1½" x 10½"

    2 strips, 1½" x 28½"

    2 strips, 1½" x 30½"

**From the holly print, cut:**

6 strips, 2½" x 42"; crosscut into:

    2 strips, 2½" x 10½"

    2 strips, 2½" x 14½"

    2 strips, 2½" x 30½"

    2 strips, 2½" x 34½"

**From the red print, cut:**

6 strips, 3½" x 42"; crosscut into:

    2 strips, 3½" x 14½"

    2 strips, 3½" x 20½"

    2 strips, 3½" x 34½"

    2 strips, 3½" x 40½"

**From the binding fabric, cut:**

5 strips, 2¼" x 42"

*\*If you're using a nondirectional print, cut each square in half diagonally to make 4 triangles. If you're using a directional print, lay both squares right side up so the print reads correctly as it faces you. Cut one square in half diagonally from the upper-left corner to the lower-right corner; cut the remaining square from the lower-left corner to the upper-right corner.*

*\*\*If you're using a directional print, fussy cut the square so that when it's standing on its point, rather than on a flat side, the motif is straight.*

# Assembling the Quilt

1 Piece the backing fabric to create a 48" x 48" square.

2 Baste the batting to your backing. If you're using fusible batting, follow the manufacturer's instructions to adhere the batting to the wrong side of the backing. Mark the horizontal and vertical centerlines on the batting.

3 Place the cardinal-print 8½" square, right side up, in the center of the batting, lining up the points of the square with the centerlines. Pin the square in place, inserting the pins so they're perpendicular to the square edges.

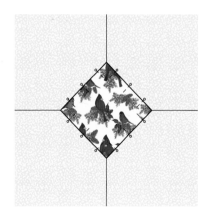

4 With right sides together, place green 1½" x 8½" strips on opposite sides of the center square as shown. Pin the strips in place and sew through all of the layers. Press the strips outward.

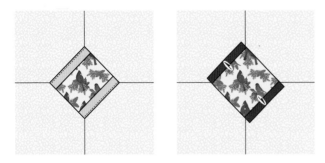

5 Sew green 1½" x 10½" strips to the remaining sides of the square; press the strips outward.

6 Repeat steps 4 and 5 with the holly 2½" x 10½" and 2½" x 14½" strips, and then the red 3½" x 14½" and 3½" x 20½" strips. The pieced center should now measure 20½" x 20½".

7 Sew a cardinal-print triangle to each side of the quilt center as shown, taking care to position the triangles so they are all facing the same direction. The quilt center should now measure 28½" x 28½".

8 Repeat steps 4 and 5 to add the green 1½" x 28½" and 1½" x 30½" strips; the holly 2½" x 30½" and 2½" x 34½" strips; and the red 3½" x 34½" and 3½" x 40½" strips.

## Finishing the Quilt

Press the completed top and trim off the excess batting and backing even with the edges. Bind the edges with the 2¼"-wide binding strips.

# Christmas Weather Vane

*The simple Weather Vane and Chain blocks combined make this a dynamic quilt. The combination forms layers of graphic design that look intricate but are really quite easy to make.*

By Mary Hickey; machine quilted by Dawn Kelly

FINISHED QUILT SIZE: 38½" x 38½"    FINISHED BLOCK SIZE: 10" x 10"

## Materials

*Yardage is based on 42"-wide fabric.*

1⅛ yards *total* of assorted white fabrics for block backgrounds

⅝ yard *total* of assorted green fabrics for Chain blocks, Weather Vane blocks, and inner border

½ yard of red-and-white dot fabric for outer border

½ yard of red-and-white checked fabric for Weather Vane blocks and binding

¼ yard of dark-red fabric for Weather Vane blocks

2⅜ yards of fabric for backing*

43" x 43" piece of batting

*\*If backing fabric is 42" wide after washing, you can use a single width of 1⅜ yards.*

## Cutting

*All measurements include ¼"-wide seam allowances. Cut all strips across the width of fabric (selvage to selvage).*

**From the assorted white fabrics, cut a *total* of:**

2 strips, 4½" x 42"; crosscut into 2 rectangles, 4½" x 15", and 8 rectangles, 2½" x 4½"

2 strips, 4¼" x 42"; crosscut into 2 rectangles, 4¼" x 20", and 10 rectangles, 3" x 4¼"

4 strips, 3" x 42"; crosscut *2 of the strips* into 16 squares, 3" x 3"

1 strip, 2½" x 42"; crosscut into 16 squares, 2½" x 2½"

2 strips, 1¾" x 42"

**From the dark-red fabric, cut:**

2 strips, 3" x 42"; crosscut into 16 squares, 3" x 3"

**From the red-and-white checked fabric, cut:**

6 strips, 2½" x 42"; crosscut *1 of the strips* into 16 squares, 2½" x 2½"

**From the assorted green fabrics, cut a total of:**

3 strips, 1¾" x 42"

4 strips, 1½" x 42"

1 rectangle, 3" x 20"

1 rectangle, 2½" x 15"

**From the red-and-white dot fabric, cut:**

4 strips, 3½" x 42"

# Making the Weather Vane Blocks

1 Draw a diagonal line from corner to corner on the wrong side of each white 3" square. Place each marked square on a dark-red square, right sides together. Stitch ¼" from the marked line on both sides. Cut the squares apart on the marked line. Press the seam allowances toward the red. Make 32 half-square-triangle units. Trim the squares to 2½" x 2½".

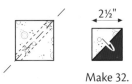

Make 32.

2 Arrange and sew two half-square-triangle units from step 1, one red-and-white checked square, and one white 2½" square together as shown; press. Make 16.

Make 16.

3 Stitch the green 2½" x 15" rectangle between the two white 4¼" x 15" rectangles to make a strip set as shown. Crosscut the strip set into four segments, 2½" wide.

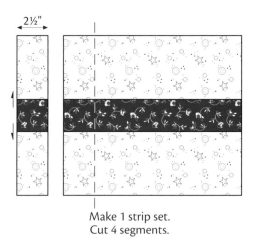

Make 1 strip set.
Cut 4 segments.

4 Arrange and sew four units from step 2, one segment from step 3, and two white 2½" x 4½" rectangles as shown; press. Make four Weather Vane blocks.

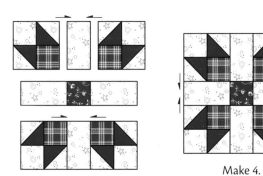

Make 4.

# Making the Chain Blocks

1 Stitch a green 1¾" x 42" strip to one long side of each white 3" x 42" strip to make a strip set; press. Make two. Crosscut the strip sets into 40 segments, 1¾" wide.

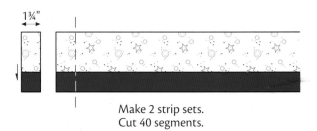

Make 2 strip sets.
Cut 40 segments.

**2** Sew the remaining green 1¾" x 42" strip between the two white 1¾" x 42" strips; press. Crosscut the strip set into 20 segments, 1¾" wide.

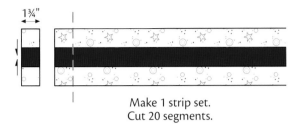

Make 1 strip set.
Cut 20 segments.

**3** Sew one segment from step 2 between two segments from step 1 as shown; press. Make 20 units.

Make 20.

**4** Sew the green 3" x 20" rectangle between two white 4¼" x 20" rectangles to make a strip set; press. Crosscut the strip set into five segments, 3" wide.

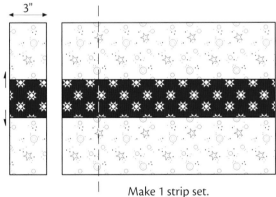

Make 1 strip set.
Cut 5 segments.

**5** Stitch four units from step 3, one segment from step 4, and two white 3" x 4¼" rectangles together as shown; press. Make five Chain blocks.

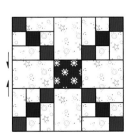

Make 5.

# Assembling the Quilt

**1** Arrange the blocks in three rows of three blocks each, alternating the Weather Vane blocks and Chain blocks in each row and from row to row.

**2** Stitch the blocks together in rows; press toward the Chain blocks. Sew the rows together, pressing the seam allowances in one direction.

**3** Measure, cut, and sew the green 1½"-wide inner-border strips, and then the red-and-white dot 3½"-wide outer-border strips to the quilt top.

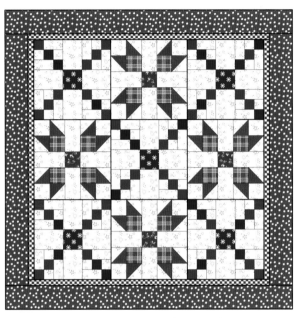

Assembly diagram

# Finishing the Quilt

**1** Layer the quilt top with batting and backing. Baste the layers together.

**2** Hand or machine quilt as desired. The quilt shown was machine quilted with arcs in the blocks, swirls in the background, and a jaunty tree design in the borders.

**3** Trim the batting and backing fabric so the edges are even with the quilt top.

**4** Use the red-and-white checked 2½"-wide strips to make the binding. Sew the binding to the quilt.

# Break Off One Bite-Sized
# Piece of Roll at a Time

*Nine Patch blocks with light fabrics in the corners join to make a woven design.*
*But it looks as though someone's taken a big bite out of the corner of the quilt!*

By Mary Etherington and Connie Tesene of Country Threads

**FINISHED QUILT SIZE: 30" x 42"**    **FINISHED BLOCK SIZE: 6" x 6"**

## Materials

*Yardage is based on 42"-wide fabric unless otherwise noted. Charm squares are 5" x 5".*

34 assorted light-brown OR white charm squares for blocks*

34 assorted dark-value charm squares for blocks*

9 assorted dark-red charm squares for blocks*

½ yard of dark-blue print for unpieced block and binding

1½ yards of fabric for backing

36" x 48" piece of batting

*You can substitute 2½" x 42" strips for the charm squares. You'll need 9 light-value strips, 9 dark-value strips, and 3 red strips.*

## Cutting

*All measurements include ¼"-wide seam allowances.*

**From each charm square, cut:**

4 squares, 2½" x 2½" (136 dark, 136 light, and 36 red total)*

**From the dark-blue print, cut:**

1 square, 6½" x 6½"

4 strips, 2¼" x 42"

*Keep squares of the same fabric together.*

## Creating the Quilt

Each block is made from four matching light-value squares, four matching dark-value squares, and one red square.

1 Arrange four matching light-value squares, four matching dark-value squares, and one red square into a Nine Patch block with the red in the center and the light-value squares in the corners. Sew the squares together and press as shown. Make 34 blocks. You'll have two red squares left over.

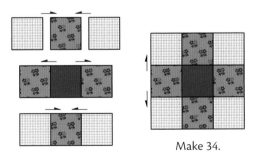

Make 34.

2 Arrange the blocks in seven rows of five blocks each. In one corner of the quilt, place the dark-blue 6½" square. Sew the blocks into rows and press the seam allowances in opposite directions. Sew the rows together and press.

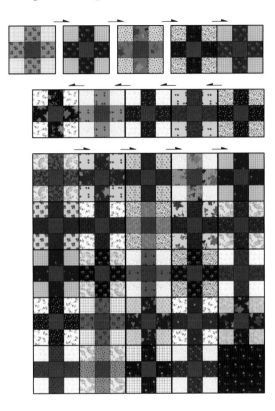

## Finishing the Quilt

Make a quilt back approximately 36" x 48". Layer the quilt top with batting and backing. Baste, and then quilt as desired. Trim the excess batting and backing and bind the quilt with the dark-blue 2¼"-wide strips.

# Follow the Red Brick Road

*Shelly used a quick and accurate technique similar to Seminole piecing to create this Stacked Bricks quilt. She selected prints in shades of red, but this pattern would also look great if made with a variety of colors.*

By Shelly Burge

FINISHED QUILT SIZE: 21" x 23¾"

# Materials

*Yardage is based on 42"-wide fabric.*

¼ yard *total* of assorted tan prints for background

⅓ yard *total* of 13 red prints for bricks

⅝ yard of black striped fabric for sashing and
  inner border*

⅓ yard of red print for outer border

¼ yard of black print for binding

¾ yard of fabric for backing

23" x 26" piece of batting

*If you want to use the same fabric for the binding,
there's enough yardage to cut lengthwise-grain
binding strips.*

# Cutting

*All measurements include ¼"-wide seam allowances.*

**From the assorted tan prints, cut:**

26 strips, 1" x 10"

**From *each* of the 13 red prints, cut:**

1 strip, 3" x 10" (13 total)

**From the *lengthwise grain* of the black striped
fabric, cut:***

2 strips, 1¼" x 18½"

4 strips, 1¼" x 18"

2 strips, 1¼" x 16½"

*Adjust the width as needed, according to the repeat
of the stripe.*

**From the *crosswise grain* of the red print, cut:**

2 strips, 3½" x 18½"

2 strips, 3½" x 21"

**From the *crosswise grain* of the black print, cut:**

3 strips, 1¼" x 32" (or cut 5 lengthwise strips, each
  1¼" x 22", from the black striped fabric)

# Assembling the Quilt

1 Sew two tan strips to each red strip. Make 13
  strip units. Press the seam allowances toward
the tan prints.

2 Cut nine segments, each 1" wide, from each strip
  unit for a total of 117 segments (7 are extra).

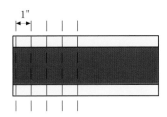

3 To make a stacked-brick unit that angles to the
  right, join 22 segments, offsetting each by ½" as
shown. For the row to angle to the right, the bottom
brick should feed under the needle *first* as you stitch
the units together on your machine. Press all seam
allowances in the same direction, being careful not
to stretch the rows. Make three stacked-brick units
that angle to the right.

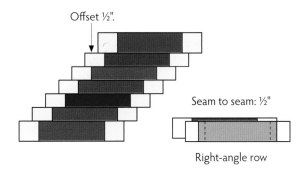

Offset ½".

Seam to seam: ½"

Right-angle row

4 Make two stacked-brick units that angle to the
  left by positioning the top brick to feed under
the needle first. Use 22 segments for each unit and
offset each segment by ½".

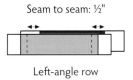

Seam to seam: ½"

Left-angle row

5 Place a ruler across the approximate middle of
  a stacked-brick unit, from inner point to inner
point at a 90° angle, and rotary cut. (It might seem
scary to make this cut, but take a deep breath and
go for it.)

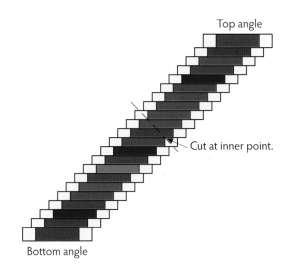

Top angle

Cut at inner point.

Bottom angle

6 Sew the top of the stacked brick unit to the bottom as shown, then press. Cut and join the remaining units.

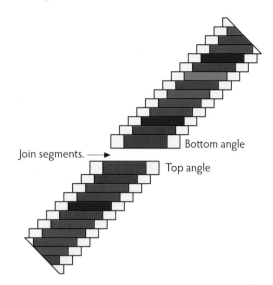

Join segments. →

Bottom angle

Top angle

7 Trim the sides of each stacked-brick unit, leaving a ¼" seam allowance. Each unit should measure 2⅝" x 17".

8 Trim each black striped 18"-long sashing strip to match the length of your brick unit. Fold each sashing strip and brick unit in half and mark the centers with pins. Arrange the units as shown. Join the units, matching the centers and the top and bottom edges.

9 Sew the black striped inner-border strips to the quilt top and miter the corners.

10 Sew the red-print outer-border strips to the quilt top.

## Finishing the Quilt

Layer the quilt top with batting and backing; baste. Quilt as desired. Bind the edges with the black strips to finish.

# Star Medallion

*During World War I, quilters liked to use reds, whites, and blues in patterns that proudly displayed patriotism in unconventional and creative ways.*

By Kathleen Tracy

FINISHED QUILT SIZE: 15½" x 15½"     FINISHED BLOCK SIZE: 5" x 5"

## Materials

*Yardage is based on 42"-wide fabric.*

½ yard *total* of 5 different light-tan prints for blocks

¼ yard *total* of 6 different red prints for blocks

¼ yard *total* of 7 different blue prints for blocks

¼ yard of blue fabric for binding

½ yard of fabric for backing

19" x 19" piece of batting

## Cutting

*All measurements include ¼"-wide seam allowances.*

**From *each of 2* of the red prints, cut:**

1 square, 3" x 3" (2 total)

**From *each of 3* of the red prints, cut:**

8 squares, 1¾" x 1¾" (24 total)

**From the *remaining* red print, cut:**

4 strips, 2⅛" x 5½"

**From *each of 3* of the blue prints, cut:**

1 square, 3" x 3" (3 total)

**From *each of 2* of the blue prints, cut:**

8 squares, 1¾" x 1¾" (16 total)

**From *each of the 2 remaining* blue prints, cut:**

2 strips, 2⅛" x 5½" (4 total)

**From *each of 3* of the light-tan prints, cut:**

4 squares, 1¾" x 1¾" (12 total)

4 rectangles, 1¾" x 3" (12 total)

**From *1 of the remaining* light-tan prints, cut:**

8 squares, 1¾" x 1¾"

8 rectangles, 1¾" x 3"

**From the *remaining* light-tan print, cut:**

4 strips, 2⅛" x 5½"

**From the blue fabric for binding, cut:**

2 strips, 2" x 42"

## Assembling the Quilt

Three of the Star blocks are made up of one blue 3" square, four matching light-tan 1¾" x 3" rectangles, four matching 1¾" squares of the same light tan as the rectangles, and eight matching red 1¾" squares. Two of the Star blocks are made up of one red 3" square, four matching light-tan 1¾" x 3" rectangles, four matching 1¾" squares of the same light tan as the rectangles, and eight matching blue 1¾" squares. The top-right and lower-left Star blocks have the same light-tan background.

1 Lay out the sets of fabrics for each block in advance. Draw a diagonal line across each red and blue 1¾" square on the wrong side of the fabric.

2 To make each block, place one 1¾" square on top of one end of a 1¾" x 3" rectangle, right sides together. Sew on the line and trim to a ¼" seam allowance. Press the triangle toward the corner. Place another square on the other end of the rectangle, right sides together, and stitch on the drawn line. Be sure the diagonal line is oriented in the opposite direction from the first piece. Trim to a ¼" seam allowance and press the triangle toward the corner. Make a total of four flying-geese units.

Make 4.

3 Sew a light-tan square to each end of two of the flying-geese units and press the seam allowances toward the squares. Sew a flying-geese unit to each side of the 3" square and press the seam allowances toward the square. Sew these rows together and press the seam allowances toward the center row. Repeat steps 2 and 3 to make five Star blocks.

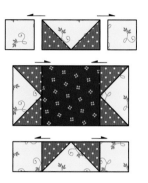

Make 5.

4 Sew the red, blue, and light-tan 2⅛" x 5½" strips together to make a total of four units. Press the seam allowances in one direction toward the red strips. Trim these blocks to 5½" x 5½".

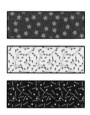

Make 4.

5 Sew the Star blocks and the striped units together into three rows as shown, placing the blue strips closest to the center star. The blue strips of the same fabric are on opposite sides of the center Star block. Press the seam allowances of each row toward the striped block. Sew the rows together and press toward the middle row.

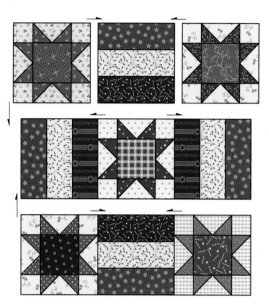

## Finishing the Quilt

1 Layer the quilt top, batting, and backing, and baste the layers together.

2 Quilt an X through the center of each Star block and quilt in the ditch around each star. Quilt through the middle of each blue and tan stripe.

3 Attach the blue binding to the quilt.

# Amish Sparklers

*Solid colors really "pop" when combined with a black background.*
*Use your favorite bright colors to make this cheerful quilt.*

By Cathy Wierzbicki

FINISHED QUILT SIZE: 46½" x 46½"    FINISHED BLOCK SIZE: 16" x 16"

## Materials

*Yardage is based on 42"-wide fabric unless otherwise noted.*

1⅜ yards of dark solid for blocks and outer border

¾ yard *total* of bright solids for blocks and inner corner squares

⅔ yard of teal solid for sashing, inner border, and outer-border corner squares

½ yard of fabric for binding

2⅞ yards of fabric for backing

52" x 52" piece of batting

## Cutting

*All measurements include ¼"-wide seam allowances.*

**From the bright solids, cut:**

96 squares, 2⅞" x 2⅞"; cut squares in half diagonally to yield 192 triangles (A)

5 matching squares (dark red), 2½" x 2½"

**From the dark solid, cut:**

24 squares, 4⅞" x 4⅞"; cut squares in half diagonally to yield 48 triangles (B)

4 strips, 4½" x 38½"

16 squares, 4½" x 4½" (C)

**From the teal solid, cut:**

4 strips, 2½" x 16½" (D)

4 strips, 2½" x 34½"

4 squares, 4½" x 4½" (F)

**From the binding fabric, cut:**

5 strips, 2½" x 42"

## Making the Blocks

1 Sew two assorted A half-square triangles together as shown; press. Sew assorted A half-square triangles to two adjacent sides of the unit; press. Make 48.

Make 48.

2 Sew a B half-square triangle to each unit from step 1 as shown; press. Make 48.

Make 48.

3 Arrange 12 units from step 2 and four C squares as shown. Sew the units and squares together into rows; press. Sew the rows together to complete the block; press. Make four.

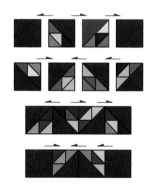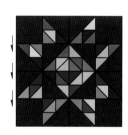

Make 4.

## Assembling the Quilt

1 Sew a D strip between two blocks as shown; press. Make two.

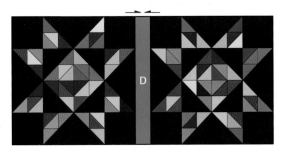

Make 2.

2 Sew an E square between the remaining D strips as shown; press. Sew this strip between the two rows from step 1; press.

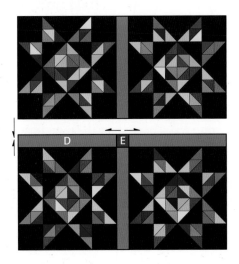

3 Referring to the assembly diagram, sew teal 2½" x 34½" inner-border strips to the top and bottom of the quilt. Press the seam allowances toward the strips. Sew a remaining E square to each end of each remaining teal 2½" x 34½" strip; press. Make two and sew them to the sides; press.

4 Repeat step 3, using the F squares and the dark 4½" x 38½" strips to add the outer borders. Press the seam allowances toward the outer border.

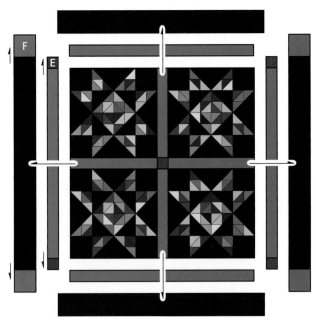

Assembly diagram

## Finishing the Quilt

1 Layer the backing, batting, and quilt top; baste.

2 Hand or machine quilt as desired.

3 Use the 2½"-wide strips to bind the quilt edges.

# Broken Dishes

*The Broken Dishes pattern was one of the most popular designs of pioneers heading West. Roads were often bumpy, and breakable items such as dishes and glassware were wrapped in quilts to safeguard them.*

By Kathleen Tracy

**FINISHED QUILT SIZE: 18" x 18"    FINISHED BLOCK SIZE: 4" x 4"**

## Materials

*Yardage is based on 42"-wide fabric unless otherwise noted.*

⅛ yard *each OR* scraps of 8 to 10 assorted blue, pink, and light prints for blocks

¼ yard of red-checked fabric for outer border

⅛ yard of medium-blue print for inner border

Scraps of 2 red prints for blocks

¼ yard of dark-blue print for binding

⅔ yard of fabric for backing

21" x 25" piece of cotton batting

## Cutting

*All measurements include ¼"-wide seam allowances.*

**From the assorted light prints, cut:**
15 squares, 2⅞" x 2⅞"

**From the assorted pink prints, cut:**
9 squares, 2⅞" x 2⅞"

**From the assorted blue prints, cut:**
20 squares, 2⅞" x 2⅞"

**From the red scraps, cut:**
4 squares, 2⅞" x 2⅞"

**From the medium-blue print, cut:**
2 strips, 1¼" x 42"; crosscut into 2 pieces, 1¼" x 12½", and 2 pieces, 1¼" x 18"

**From the red-checked fabric, cut:**
2 strips, 2½" x 42"; crosscut into 4 pieces, 2½" x 18"

**From the dark-blue print, cut:**
2 strips, 2" x 42"

## Assembling the Quilt

1 Draw a diagonal line from corner to corner on the wrong side of each light-print and pink-print 2⅞" square. At random, layer a marked square on top of a blue or red 2⅞" square, right sides together. Stitch ¼" from the line on both sides and cut on the drawn line. Press the seam allowances toward the darker fabric. Make 48.

Make 48.

2 Arrange four half-square-triangle units into a block, balancing color and value; use at least two matching units, or two that are very similar, in each block. Sew the units together and press as shown. Repeat to make 12 Broken Dishes blocks.

Make 12.

3 Sew the blocks together into four rows of three blocks each. Press the seam allowances in opposite directions from row to row. Sew the rows together and press the seam allowances in one direction.

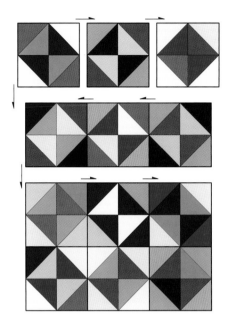

4 Sew the blue 1¼" x 12½" strips to the top and bottom of the quilt top, pressing the seam allowances toward the border. Sew the blue 1¼" x 18" strips to the sides of the quilt top and press.

5 Sew two of the red-checked 2½" x 18" strips to the sides of the quilt top, pressing the seam allowances toward the outer border. Sew the two remaining red-checked strips to the top and bottom of the quilt top and press.

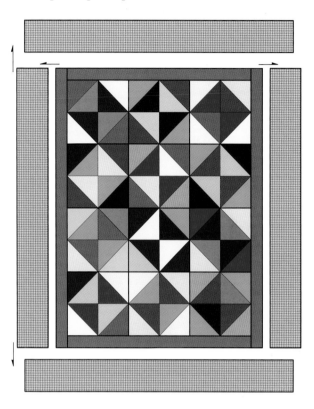

## Finishing the Quilt

1 Layer the quilt top, batting, and backing; baste the layers together

2 Quilt in the ditch around each triangle and block, or as desired.

3 Attach the dark-blue binding strips to the quilt.

# Prairie Points

*Simple blocks, set on point, really sparkle with the addition of scrappy prairie points. If you've never made prairie points before, this little quilt is the perfect opportunity to experiment!*

By Kathleen Tracy

FINISHED QUILT SIZE: 24" x 30"    FINISHED BLOCK SIZE: 4" x 4"

## Materials

*Yardage is based on 42"-wide fabric unless otherwise noted.*

1 yard *total* of assorted light, medium, and dark scraps for blocks and prairie points

½ yard *total* of 2 different light-tan prints for setting pieces

½ yard of light-blue print for border

⅛ yard *total* of assorted medium-blue print scraps for blocks

¼ yard of red print for binding

1 yard of fabric for backing

28" x 34" piece of cotton batting

## Cutting

*All measurements include ¼"-wide seam allowances.*

**From the assorted light scraps, cut:**

48 rectangles, 1½" x 2½" (12 sets of 4 matching rectangles)

**From the assorted medium scraps, cut:**

24 squares, 1½" x 1½"

**From the assorted dark scraps, cut:**

24 squares, 1½" x 1½"

**From the assorted medium and dark scraps, cut:**

38 squares, 3" x 3"

**From the assorted medium-blue print scraps, cut:**

48 squares, 1½" x 1½"

**From the 2 different light-tan prints, cut:**

6 squares, 4½" x 4½"

3 squares, 7" x 7"; cut into quarters diagonally to make 12 side triangles (2 will be extra)

2 squares, 3¾" x 3¾"; cut in half diagonally to make 4 corner triangles

**From the light-blue print, cut:**

2 strips, 3¾" x 23"

2 strips, 3¾" x 24"

**From the red print, cut:**

3 strips, 2" x 42"

## Making the Blocks

1 For each block, sew a medium 1½" square together with a dark 1½" square. Press toward the dark fabric. Make two. Join two units to make a four-patch unit as shown. Make 12 four-patch units.

Make 12.

2 Sew two matching light 1½" x 2½" rectangles to the sides of a four-patch unit. Press the seam allowances toward the four-patch unit. Sew a medium-blue 1½" square to the short ends of two matching light 1½" x 2½" rectangles. Press the seam allowances toward the blue fabric. Sew these to the top and bottom of the unit. Press toward the four-patch unit. Make 12 blocks.

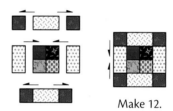

Make 12.

## Assembling the Quilt

1 Lay out the blocks, the light-tan 4½" setting squares, and the light-tan side and corner setting triangles in diagonal rows. Sew the blocks, setting squares, and side triangles into rows, pressing the seam allowances toward the setting squares and triangles.

2 Sew the rows together, matching seam intersections. Add the light-tan corner triangles
and press toward the triangles. If necessary, trim
and square up the quilt top, making sure to leave
¼" beyond the points of all the blocks for seam
allowances.

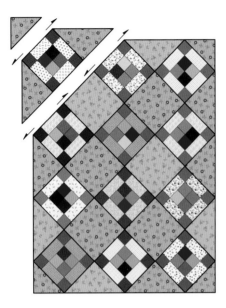

## Making the Prairie Points

1 To make a prairie point, fold a 3" scrap
square in half diagonally. Press. Fold the triangle in half diagonally again and press. Make 38
prairie points.

Make 38.

2 Place the prairie points evenly around the raw
edge of the right side of the quilt as shown,
tucking each one into the fold of the one next to
it. Place 8 prairie points on the top edge, 8 on the
bottom, and 11 along each side. Pin in place and
machine baste the points a scant ¼" all around.

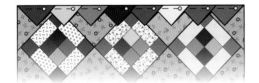

## Adding the Border

With the prairie points basted in place, sew the
light-blue 3¾" x 23" strips to the sides of the quilt
top. Press the seam allowances toward the border.
Sew the light-blue 3¾" x 24" strips to the top and
bottom of the quilt top and press toward the border.
Give the prairie points an extra shot of steam to
make them lie flat.

## Finishing the Quilt

1 Layer the quilt top, batting, and backing; baste
the layers together.

2 Quilt as desired. The quilt shown was quilted
in the ditch around each block, with a flower in
the tan blocks, an X in the Nine Patch blocks, and
an outline around the triangles.

3 Attach the binding to the quilt.

# Crosses Mourning

*This little mourning quilt serves as a memorial to the many pioneer men, women, and children who died on the trail West.*

By Kathleen Tracy

**FINISHED QUILT SIZE: 25½" x 25½"     FINISHED BLOCK SIZE: 5" x 5"**

## Materials

*Yardage is based on 42"-wide fabric unless otherwise noted.*

⅛ yard *each OR* scraps of 9 black prints for blocks
⅛ yard *each OR* scraps of 9 light prints for blocks
⅜ yard of dark-floral print for outer border
¼ yard of dark print for sashing and inner border
Scraps of 9 medium prints for blocks
¼ yard of black print for binding
⅞ yard of fabric for backing
29" x 29" piece of cotton batting

## Cutting

*All measurements include ¼"-wide seam allowances.*

**From *each* of the 9 light prints, cut:**
2 squares, 2⅞" x 2⅞" (18 total)

**From *each* of the 9 black prints for blocks, cut:**
2 squares, 2⅞" x 2⅞" (18 total)
5 squares, 1½" x 1½" (45 total)

**From *1* black print, cut:**
4 squares, 1½" x 1½"

**From *each* of the 9 medium prints, cut:**
4 squares, 1½" x 1½" (36 total)

**From the dark print, cut:**
4 strips, 1½" x 42"; crosscut into:
 12 pieces, 1½" x 5½"
 2 pieces, 1½" x 17½"
 2 pieces, 1½" x 19½"

**From the dark-floral print, cut:**
3 strips, 3½" x 42"; crosscut into 2 pieces,
 3½" x 19½", and 2 pieces, 3½" x 25½"

**From the black print for binding, cut:**
3 strips, 1½" x 42"

## Assembling the Quilt

Each block consists of one light print, one medium print, and three different black prints. It's easiest if you select fabric for each block before you begin stitching the blocks together.

1 Draw a diagonal line from corner to corner on the wrong side of each light-print 2⅞" square. Layer two matching marked squares on top of two matching black-print 2⅞" squares, right sides together. Stitch ¼" from the line on both sides

and cut on the drawn line. Press the seam allowances toward the darker fabric. Make 36 half-square-triangle units, four each from the nine different prints.

Make 36 in matching sets of 4.

2 Sew four matching black-print 1½" squares and four matching medium-print 1½" squares together into pairs. Press toward the darker fabric. Make 36.

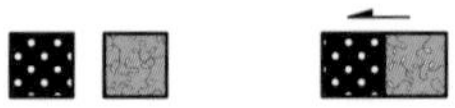

Make 36 in matching sets of 4.

3 Sew two matching units from step 2 together with four matching half-square-triangle units from step 1. Make nine pairs. Be sure to pair step 1 and step 2 units that feature a different black print.

Make 9 pairs.

4 Sew two matching units from step 2 together with a 1½" square of a different black print as shown, pressing the seam allowances toward the black squares.

Make 9.

5 Sew two matching units from step 3 together with the matching unit from step 4 to make the Cross block. Press the seam allowances as shown. Make nine blocks.

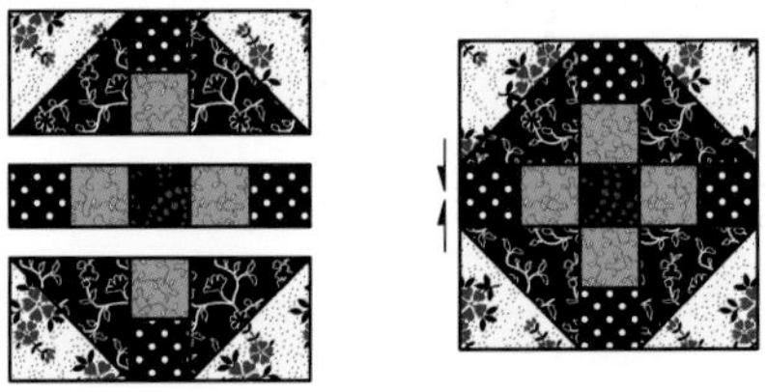

Make 9.

6 Sew three blocks together with two dark-print 1½" x 5½" sashing pieces to make a row. Press toward the sashing. Make three rows.

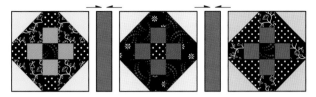

Make 3 rows.

7 Sew three dark-print 1½" x 5½" sashing pieces together with two black-print 1½" squares to make a sashing row. Press toward the sashing. Make two.

Make 2.

8 Sew the block rows and the sashing rows together, pressing the seam allowances toward the sashing rows.

9 Add the dark-print 1½" x 17½" strips to the sides of the quilt top, pressing toward the border. Sew the dark-print 1½" x 19½" strips to the top and bottom of the quilt top. Press the seam allowances toward the border.

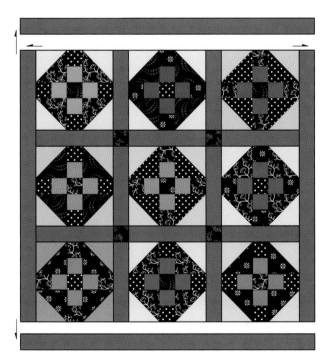

10 Sew the dark-floral 3½" x 19½" strips to the sides of the quilt top. Press the seam allowances toward the outer border. Add the dark-floral 3½" x 25½" strips to the top and bottom of the quilt top and press toward the outer border.

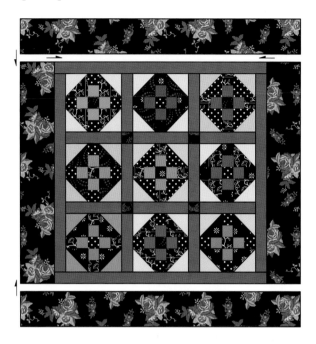

## Finishing the Quilt

1 Layer the quilt top, batting, and backing, and baste the layers together.

2 Quilt in the ditch around each block; quilt a cross within the crosses. Quilt in the borders as desired.

3 Attach the black-print binding to the quilt.

# Whirlwind

*Most, but not all, of the fabrics in this quilt are Japanese; feel free to mix in other types of fabric. Sometimes variety makes things more interesting!*

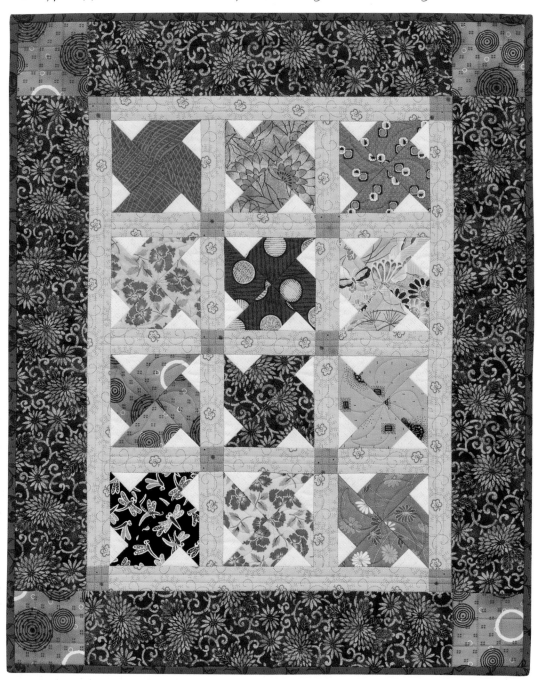

By Ellen Pahl

**FINISHED QUILT SIZE:** 21" x 25½"  **FINISHED BLOCK SIZE:** 3½" x 3½"

## Materials

*Yardage is based on 42"-wide fabric unless otherwise noted.*

12 pieces, 14" x 14" *each,* of assorted prints for blocks and outer-border corner squares

¼ yard of purple floral for outer border

¼ yard of light-taupe print for sashing and inner border

1 fat quarter of white print for blocks

2" x 18" piece of taupe print for sashing and inner-border squares

¼ yard of dark print for binding

⅞ yard of fabric for backing

26" x 31" piece of batting

Freezer paper *OR* half-square ruler

## Cutting

*All measurements include ¼"-wide seam allowances.*

**From *each* of the assorted prints, cut:**

1 bias strip, 2" x 18" (12 total)*

**From the white print, cut:**

6 bias strips, 1¾" x 18"*

**From the light-taupe print, cut:**

4 strips, 1½" x 42"; crosscut into:

    17 rectangles, 1½" x 4"

    2 strips, 1½" x 13"

    2 strips, 1½" x 17½"

**From the taupe print, cut:**

10 squares, 1½" x 1½"

**From the purple floral, cut:**

2 strips, 3½" x 19½"

2 strips, 3½" x 15"

**From *1* of the assorted prints, cut:**

4 squares, 3½" x 3½"

**From the dark print for binding, cut:**

3 strips, 2⅛" x 42"

*Cutting the strips on the bias will result in blocks with straight-grain edges.*

## Making the Blocks

1 Sew an assorted-print bias strip to each long edge of a white bias strip. Press.

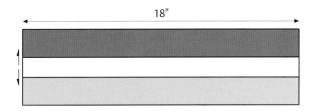

2 If you're using freezer paper, trace the cutting-guide pattern on page 176 onto the dull side of a piece of freezer paper at least eight times; cut out the freezer-paper templates. Press eight templates, shiny side down, to the strip set from step 1 as shown, aligning the dashed line on the template with the appropriate seam. Cut out four along the bottom edge and four along the top edge. If you're using a half-square ruler, align the dashed yellow line at the top of the ruler with the upper seam line. Cut eight triangles from the strip set, four along the top and four along the bottom.

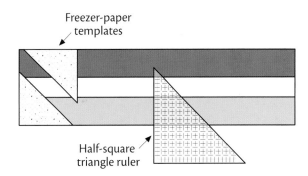

Freezer-paper templates

Half-square triangle ruler

3 Gently remove the tiny triangle of the second fabric color from the point of each piece.

4 Sew each set of four matching units together to make the blocks.

5 Repeat steps 1–4 to make a total of 12 blocks.

## Assembling the Quilt

1 Arrange the blocks in four horizontal rows of three blocks each, inserting the light-taupe 1½" x 4" sashing strips between the blocks. Add the taupe sashing squares and sew the block rows and sashing rows as shown. Press. Sew the rows together and press.

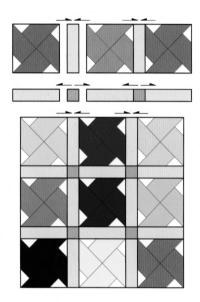

2 Add the light-taupe 1½" x 17½" inner-border strips to the sides of the quilt. Press.

3 Sew a taupe 1½" corner square to each end of the light-taupe 1½" x 13" inner-border strips. Press. Sew the strips to the top and bottom of the quilt.

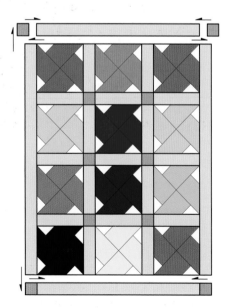

4 Sew the purple-floral 3½" x 19½" outer-border strips to the sides. Press.

5 Sew an assorted 3½" corner square to each end of the purple-floral 3½" x 15" outer-border strips. Press. Sew the strips to the top and bottom of the quilt.

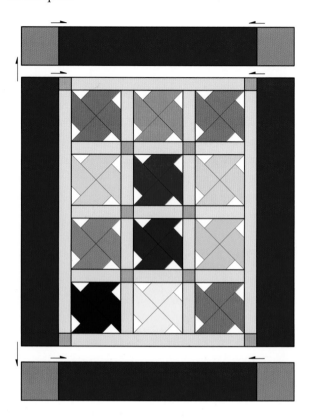

## Finishing the Quilt

Layer, baste, quilt as desired, and add the dark-print binding. This quilt was quilted in the ditch, with parallel lines in the sashing and border, and with crescent shapes inside the Pinwheel blocks.

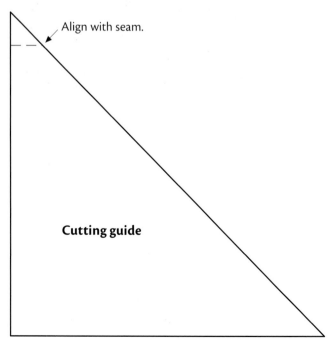

Align with seam.

**Cutting guide**

# One Patch

*This quilt was inspired by an antique doll quilt Kathleen saw. It would be perfect for teaching a beginner or child some simple piecing techniques.*

By Kathleen Tracy

FINISHED QUILT SIZE: 25½" x 25½"    FINISHED BLOCK SIZE: 2" x 2"

## Materials

*Yardage is based on 42"-wide fabric unless otherwise noted.*

⅜ yard of dark Civil War reproduction print for outer border

¼ yard of purple print for middle border

⅛ yard of gold print for inner border

⅛ yard *total* of assorted shirting prints for quilt center

⅛ yard *total* of assorted indigo prints for quilt center

6" x 12" scrap *each* of black print and light-tan print for quilt center

3" x 6" scrap *each* of blue print, blue-striped print, and pink print for quilt center

3" x 3" scrap of gold print for quilt center

¼ yard of black print for binding

⅞ yard of fabric for backing

30" x 30" piece of low-loft cotton batting

# Cutting

*All measurements include ¼"-wide seam allowances.*

**From the black print for quilt center, cut:**
8 squares, 2½" x 2½"

**From the light-tan print, cut:**
8 squares, 2½" x 2½"

**From the blue print, cut:**
4 squares, 2½" x 2½"

**From the blue-striped print, cut:**
4 squares, 2½" x 2½"

**From the pink print, cut:**
4 squares, 2½" x 2½"

**From the gold print for quilt center, cut:**
1 square, 2½" x 2½"

**From the assorted shirting prints, cut:**
10 squares, 2⅞" x 2⅞"

**From the assorted indigo prints, cut:**
10 squares, 2⅞" x 2⅞"

**From the gold print for inner border, cut:**
2 strips, 1½" x 14½"
2 strips, 1½" x 16½"

**From the purple print, cut:**
2 strips, 2" x 16½"
2 strips, 2" x 19½"

**From the dark reproduction print, cut:**
2 strips, 3½" x 19½"
2 strips, 3½" x 25½"

**From the black print for binding, cut:**
3 strips, 2" x 42"

## Making the Quilt Center

1 Using two light-tan 2½" squares, one black 2½" square, and a blue 2½" square, make a four-patch unit as shown. Press the seam allowances toward the darker squares. Make four.

Make 4.

2 Sew a pink 2½" square and a blue-striped 2½" square together and press. Make four.

Make 4.

3 Sew two units from step 2 together with the gold-print 2½" square as shown. Press.

Make 1.

4 Arrange the four-patch units, the units from step 2, and the unit from step 3 as shown. Sew into rows. Press. Join the rows to make the center of the quilt top.

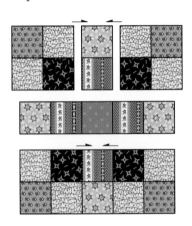

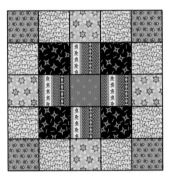

5 Draw a diagonal line from corner to corner on the wrong side of each shirting 2⅞" square. Layer a marked square on top of an indigo 2⅞" square, right sides together. Stitch ¼" from the line on both sides and cut on the drawn line. Press the seam allowances toward the darker fabric. Make 20 half-square-triangle units.

Make 20.

6 Sew five half-square-triangle units together into a strip. Press. Make four strips.

Make 4.

7 Sew two of the strips from step 6 to the sides of the quilt top, arranging them as shown. Press. Sew a black 2½" square to each end of the remaining two half-square-triangle strips and press. Sew these to the top and bottom of the quilt top and press.

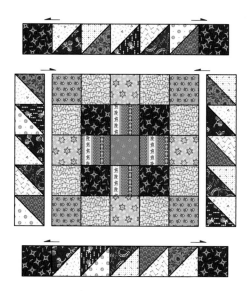

## Assembling the Quilt

1 Sew the gold-print 1½" x 14½" strips to the sides of the quilt top and press the seam allowances toward the border. Add the two gold-print 1½" x 16½" strips to the top and bottom of the quilt top. Press.

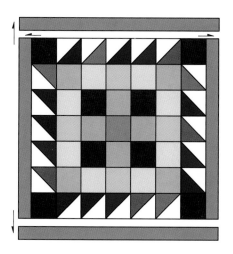

2 Sew the purple-print 2" x 16½" strips to the sides of the quilt top and press the seam allowances toward the border. Add the two purple-print 2" x 19½" strips to the top and bottom of the quilt top. Press.

3 Sew the dark-print 3½" x 19½" strips to the sides of the quilt top and press the seam allowances toward the border. Add the two dark-print 2" x 25½" strips to the top and bottom of the quilt top. Press.

## Finishing the Quilt

1 Layer the quilt top, batting, and backing; pin or baste the layers together.

2 Quilt as desired. This quilt was machine quilted with a simple crosshatching design.

3 Attach the black-print binding to the quilt.

# Lincoln's Platform

*Abraham Lincoln was elected president in November 1860 and inaugurated in March 1861. The name of the Lincoln's Platform quilt block was inspired by his position on slavery.*

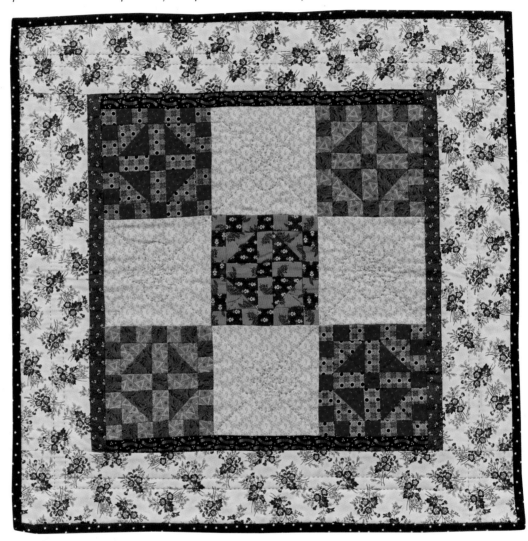

By Kathleen Tracy

FINISHED QUILT SIZE: 24¾" x 24¾"   FINISHED BLOCK SIZE: 5¼" x 5¼"

## Materials

*Yardage is based on 42"-wide fabric unless otherwise noted.*

½ yard of beige-floral print for outer border

¼ yard of light-blue print for setting squares

⅛ yard of black-and-blue print for inner border

⅛ yard of medium-blue print for inner border

Scraps of 3 blue prints (*OR* 3 fat quarters) for blocks

Scraps of 2 red prints (*OR* 2 fat quarters) for blocks

Scrap of butternut-gold print (*OR* 1 fat eighth) for center block

¼ yard of indigo print for binding

1 yard of fabric for backing

28" x 28" piece of cotton batting

# Cutting

*All measurements include ¼"-wide seam allowances.*

**From *each of 2* of the blue-print scraps, cut:**

4 squares, 2⅜" x 2⅜" (8 total)

8 rectangles, 1¼" x 2" (16 total)

24 squares, 1¼" x 1¼" (48 total)

**From the *remaining* blue-print scrap, cut:**

2 squares, 2⅜" x 2⅜"

13 squares, 1¼" x 1¼"

**From *each* of the 2 red-print scraps, cut:**

4 squares, 2⅜" x 2⅜" (8 total)

26 squares, 1¼" x 1¼" (52 total)

**From the butternut-gold print, cut:**

2 squares, 2⅜" x 2⅜"

4 rectangles, 1¼" x 2"

12 squares, 1¼" x 1¼"

**From the light-blue print, cut:**

4 squares, 5¾" x 5¾"

**From the black-and-blue print, cut:**

2 strips, 1¼" x 16¼"

**From the medium-blue print, cut:**

2 strips, 1¼" x 17¾"

**From the beige-floral print, cut:**

2 strips, 4" x 17¾"

2 strips, 4" x 24¾"

**From the indigo print, cut:**

3 strips, 2" x 42"

# Making the Blocks

There are four blue-and-red Lincoln's Platform blocks; two are made from one set of blue and red prints and two are made from a different set of blue and red prints. The block in the center is made from a butternut-gold print and a medium-blue print. Select the fabrics for each block before you begin in order to simplify piecing the blocks.

1 Draw a diagonal line from corner to corner on the wrong side of each blue 2⅜" square. Layer a marked blue square on top of each red 2⅜" square, right sides together. Layer the remaining blue 2⅜" squares with the gold 2⅜" squares. Stitch ¼" from the line on both sides. Cut on the drawn line. Press the seam allowances toward the darker fabric. Make

16 red/blue half-square-triangle units and 4 gold/blue half-square-triangle units.

Make 16.  Make 4.

2 Sew matching red/blue half-square-triangle units together with one matching blue 1¼" x 2" rectangle to make the top and bottom rows of the block. Press the seam allowances toward the rectangle. Sew two matching blue 1¼" x 2" rectangles and a matching red 1¼" square together to make the middle row. Press the seam allowances toward the rectangles. Sew the rows together. Press. Make four red/blue blocks. Repeat with the gold and blue pieces to make one block.

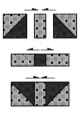  

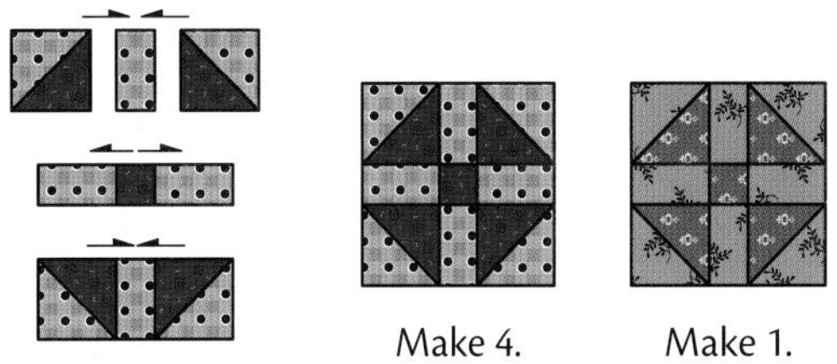

Make 4.  Make 1.

3 Using matching prints for each block, sew two blue 1¼" squares together with three red 1¼" squares to make side units for each block. Press the seam allowances toward the darker fabric. Sew these units to the sides of a block. Sew four blue 1¼" squares together with three red 1¼" squares to make top and bottom units for each block. Press toward the darker fabric. Sew these to the top and bottom. Sew gold and blue 1¼" squares together in the same manner for the gold/blue block.

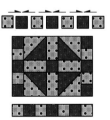

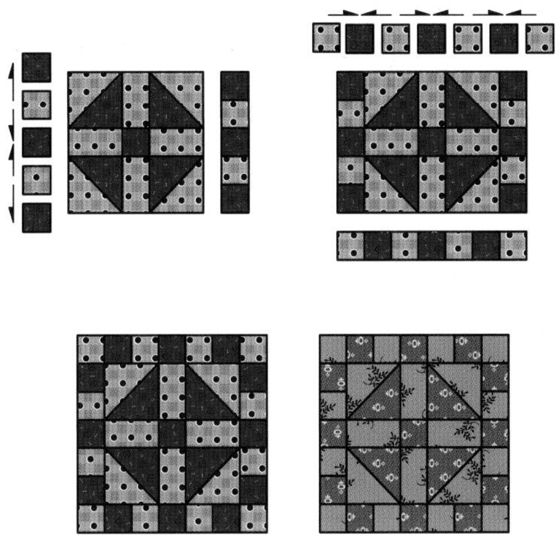

Make 4.  Make 1.

## Assembling the Quilt

1 Lay out the blocks and light-blue squares as shown. Sew the blocks and squares into rows. Press the seam allowances toward the setting squares. Sew the rows together. Press.

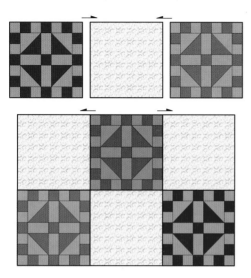

2 Sew the black-and-blue 1¼" x 16¼" strips to the top and bottom of the quilt top. Press the seam allowances toward the border. Sew the medium-blue 1¼" x 17¾" strips to the sides of the quilt top. Press toward the border.

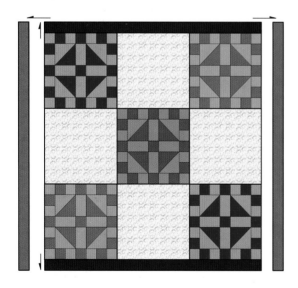

3 Sew the beige-floral 4" x 17¾" strips to the sides of the quilt top, pressing the seam allowances toward the outer border. Sew the two beige-floral 4" x 24¾" strips to the top and bottom of the quilt top. Press toward the outer border.

## Finishing the Quilt

1 Layer the quilt top, batting, and backing; baste the layers together.

2 Quilt a flower design in the plain blue squares and in the ditch along the inner border. Quilt an X in the Lincoln's Platform blocks. Using a bowl, trace a scallop design with a quilt-marking pencil in the outer border; then quilt the scallops.

3 Attach the indigo binding to the quilt.

# Do Not Put Your Elbows on the Table

*Indulge your desire to do something different by making this unusual pattern. If you haven't used templates or tried hand stitching, this is a perfect place to begin.*

By Mary Etherington and Connie Tesene of Country Threads

FINISHED QUILT SIZE: 20" x 28"    FINISHED BLOCK SIZE: 4⅛" x 2"

## Materials

*Yardage is based on 42"-wide fabric unless otherwise noted. Charm squares are 5" x 5".*

31 charm squares in a variety of prints and colors
¼ yard of blue print for border
¼ yard of red-checked fabric for binding
1 yard of fabric for backing
26" x 34" piece of batting
Hand-sewing needle
Template plastic *OR* acrylic template for Church Windows (honeycomb shape; available from your local quilt shop or Country Threads: www.CountryThreads.com)

## Cutting

*All measurements include ¼"-wide seam allowances.*

**From each charm square, cut:**
2 honeycomb shapes using pattern on page 185 (62 total)

**From the blue print, cut:**
3 strips, 2½" x 42"

**From the red-checked fabric, cut:**
3 strips, 2¼" x 42"

## Assembling the Quilt

1 On the wrong side of each honeycomb piece, use a pencil and a small ruler to lightly mark the short seam lines and the dots.

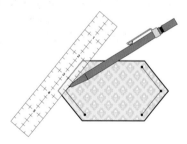

2 Using your sewing machine, sew the long sides of the honeycomb shapes together to make three rows of 12 honeycombs and two rows of 13 honeycombs. Do not stitch into the seam allowances, but backstitch at the beginning and end of each seam.

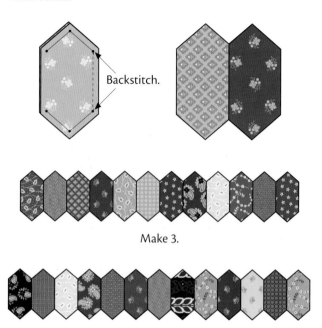

Make 3.

Make 2.

3 Lay a 12-honeycomb row right sides together with a 13-honeycomb row and sew the rows together by hand, working on one small section at a time. Start and stop ¼" from the edge. Do not stitch into the seam allowance. Sew all the rows together in this manner, alternating the longer rows with the shorter rows. Press the seam allowances open.

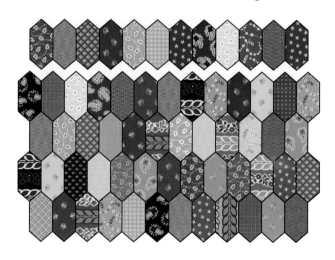

**4** Trim the edges of the quilt to form a rectangle.

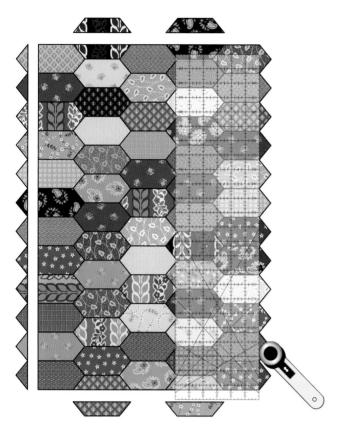

**5** Measure the width of the quilt and cut two pieces from one of the blue 2½"-wide strips to this measurement. Sew them to the top and bottom of the quilt, pressing the seam allowances toward the blue strips.

**6** Measure the length of the quilt and cut two borders from the remaining blue strips to this measurement. Sew them to the sides of the quilt

and press the seam allowances toward the blue borders.

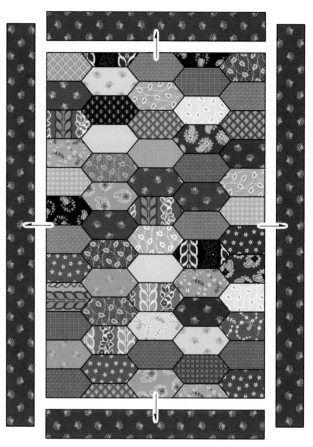

## Finishing the Quilt

Make a quilt back approximately 26" x 34". Layer the quilt top with batting and backing. Baste, and then quilt as desired. Trim the excess batting and backing; then bind with the red 2¼"-wide strips.

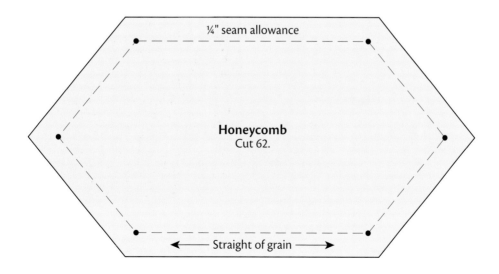

¼" seam allowance

**Honeycomb**
Cut 62.

← Straight of grain →

# Friends Remembered

*Sharing the love of quilting is a time-honored tradition. Swap charm squares with friends or utilize remnants from previous quilts to create your own memorable friendship quilt.*

By Lori Smith of From My Heart to Your Hands

**FINISHED QUILT SIZE: 16" x 20"    FINISHED BLOCK SIZE: 3¾" x 3¾"**

## Materials

*Fat quarters measure approximately 18" x 21"; fat eighths measure 9" x 21".*

1 fat eighth of dark-brown print for border
1 fat eighth of medium-brown print for sashing
3 fat eighths *total* of assorted dark, medium, and light-medium prints for blocks
1 fat quarter *total* of assorted light background prints for blocks
1 fat quarter of rose print for sashing squares and binding
1 fat quarter of fabric for backing
18" x 22" piece of batting

## Cutting

*Each block is made from 3 different print fabrics and a background fabric. Cut the pieces as indicated for each block. Repeat the cutting directions to make 12 blocks, keeping the fabrics for each block separate. All measurements include ¼"-wide seam allowances.*

### For 1 Block (Cut 12 total.)

**From a dark print, cut:**
8 squares, 1⅜" x 1⅜"
**From a medium print, cut:**
4 squares, 1⅜" x 1⅜"
**From a contrasting dark or medium print, cut:**
1 square, 1⅜" x 1⅜"
**From a light background print, cut:**
2 squares, 1½" x 1½"; cut in half diagonally to make 4 triangles
2 squares, 2½" x 2½"; cut into quarters diagonally to make 8 triangles

## For Sashing, Border, and Binding

**From a medium-brown print, cut:**
17 rectangles, 1¼" x 4¼"
**From the rose print, cut:**
6 squares, 1¼" x 1¼"
**From the dark-brown print, cut:**
2 strips, 1⅞" x 16½"
2 strips, 2⅛" x 17¾"
**From the binding fabric, cut:**
4 strips, 1¾" x 20"

## Making the Blocks

1 Arrange the squares and triangles for one block in diagonal rows as shown. Sew the squares and triangles in rows, pressing the seam allowances as indicated.

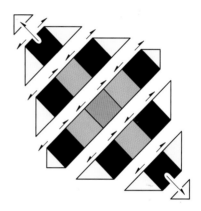

2 Use a shorter-than-normal stitch length to sew the rows together. Press the seam allowances open to reduce bulk. The block should measure 4¼" x 4¼".

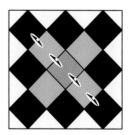

3 Repeat steps 1 and 2 to make a total of 12 blocks.

# Assembling the Quilt

1 Arrange the blocks, medium-brown sashing rectangles, and rose sashing squares on a design wall.

2 Sew the blocks, sashing, and sashing squares into rows as shown. Press the seam allowances toward the sashing.

4 Sew the dark-brown 2⅛" x 17¾" border strips to the sides of the quilt. Press the seam allowances toward the borders. Sew the dark-brown 1⅞" x 16½" border strips to the top and bottom of the quilt top; press.

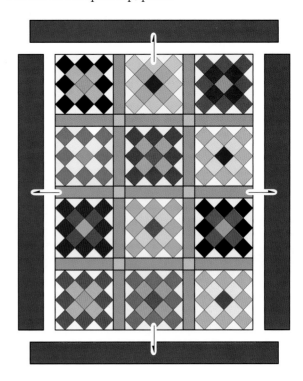

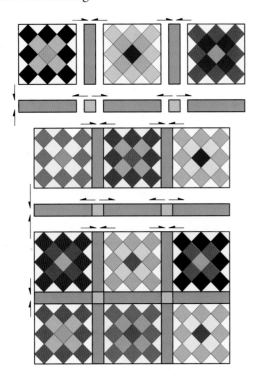

3 Sew the rows together. Press the seam allowances toward the sashing rows.

# Finishing the Quilt

Layer the quilt top, batting, and backing. Baste the layers together and quilt as desired. Add the binding and enjoy.

# Orange Peel

*This Orange Peel quilt contains a perfect blend of scraps and shirting prints. The border for the quilt was inspired by the floral striped fabric seen in day dresses of the nineteenth century.*

By Kathleen Tracy

FINISHED QUILT SIZE: 37" x 37"    FINISHED BLOCK SIZE: 6½" x 6½"

## Materials

*Yardage is based on 42"-wide fabric unless otherwise noted.*

¾ yard *total* of assorted scraps of light prints or shirtings for block backgrounds

⅝ yard of blue-striped print for outer border (for crosswise stripe; ⅞ yard needed for lengthwise stripe)

¼ yard of brown print for inner border

Assorted scraps of medium to dark prints for appliqué

⅜ yard of medium-brown print for binding

1¼ yards of fabric for backing

44" x 44" piece of cotton batting

Template plastic

## Cutting

*All measurements include ¼"-wide seam allowances.*

**From the scraps of light prints or shirtings, cut:**

64 squares, 3¾" x 3¾"

4 squares, 4½" x 4½", from 1 print

**From the brown print, cut:**

2 strips, 1¾" x 26½"

2 strips, 1¾" x 29"

**From the blue-striped print, cut:**

4 strips, 4½" x 29"

**From the medium-brown print, cut:**

4 strips, 2" x 42"

## Making the Blocks

1 Using the pattern on page 191, trace the appliqué shape onto template plastic and cut out on the line. With a water-soluble marking pen, trace the shape onto the right side of the assorted medium to dark scraps. Cut out the shapes, adding a scant ¼" seam allowance all around. Cut 64.

2 Prepare the appliqué shapes using your favorite method. Fold the light-print 3¾" squares in half diagonally and finger-press. Place the appliqué shapes on the folded line right side up and appliqué in place. Make 64 units.

Make 64.

3 Sew four units together to make an Orange Peel block as shown. Press. Make 16 blocks.

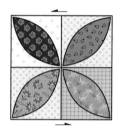

Make 16.

## Assembling the Quilt

1 Lay out the blocks in four rows of four blocks each. Sew the blocks together into rows and press the seam allowances in opposite directions from row to row. Sew the rows together and press.

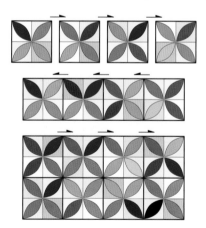

2 Sew the brown-print 1¾" x 26½" strips to the sides of the quilt top and press the seam allowances toward the border. Sew the brown-print 1¾" x 29" strips to the top and bottom of the quilt top. Press toward the border.

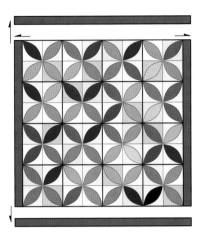

3 Sew two of the blue-striped 4½" x 29" strips to the sides of the quilt top and press the seam allowances toward the outer border. Sew a light-print 4½" square to each end of the remaining blue-striped strips and press toward the borders.

Sew these to the top and bottom of the quilt top and press toward the outer border.

## Finishing the Quilt

1 Layer the quilt top, batting, and backing; baste the layers together.

2 Quilt as desired. This quilt was machine quilted with a stipple design.

3 Attach the medium-brown binding to the quilt.

**Orange peel**
Cut 64.

Pattern does not
include seam allowance.

# Simply Charming

*This medallion-style quilt is simply charming and a joy to make from start to finish! Create it from a variety of colors and prints for maximum appeal.*

By Lori Smith of From My Heart to Your Hands
FINISHED QUILT SIZE: 16" x 20"

## Materials

*Fat quarters measure approximately 18" x 21"; fat eighths measure 9" x 21".*

1 fat quarter of light print for appliqué background

1 fat quarter of brown-striped fabric for middle border

1 fat eighth of gold print for inner border

1 fat quarter *total* of assorted light to medium prints for pieced border

1 fat quarter *total* of assorted medium to dark prints for pieced border and appliqués

Scrap (6" x 6") of red print for border corner squares

Scrap (5" x 5") of rose print for border corner squares and appliqués

Scrap (4" x 4") of dark-brown print for border corner squares

1 fat quarter of fabric for binding

1 fat quarter of fabric for backing

18" x 22" piece of batting

# Cutting

*All measurements include ¼"-wide seam allowances.*

**From the light print, cut:**
1 rectangle, 8½" x 12½"

**From the gold print, cut:**
2 strips, 1¼" x 8"
2 strips, 1¼" x 12"

**From the dark-brown print, cut:**
4 squares, 1¼" x 1¼"

**From the brown-striped fabric, cut:**
2 strips, 2" x 9½"
2 strips, 2" x 13½"

**From the rose print, cut:**
4 squares, 2" x 2"

**From the assorted medium to dark prints, cut:**
14 squares, 2⅞" x 2⅞"; cut in half diagonally to
   make 28 triangles

**From the assorted light to medium prints, cut:**
14 squares, 2⅞" x 2⅞"; cut in half diagonally to
   make 28 triangles

**From the red print, cut:**
4 squares, 2½" x 2½"

**From the binding fabric, cut:**
4 strips, 1¾" x 20"

## Appliquéing the Center

1 Prepare the appliqué pieces using the patterns
on page 194. Cut the stems on the bias.

2 Fold and lightly press the light 8½" x 12½"
background rectangle in fourths. Align the
dashed lines on the appliqué pattern with the
creases in the background fabric. Mark the appliqué
pattern on the background fabric.

3 Arrange the appliqué pieces on the background
and appliqué them in place using your
favorite method.

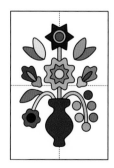

4 Press the appliquéd quilt center from the wrong
side and trim to 8" x 12", centering the design.

## Assembling the Quilt

1 Referring to the assembly diagram, sew the
gold 1¼" x 12" strips to the sides of the appliquéd quilt center. Sew a dark-brown 1¼" square
to each end of the gold 1¼" x 8" strips and sew the
strips to the top and bottom.

2 Sew the brown-striped 2" x 13½" strips to the
sides. Sew a rose 2" square to each end of the
remaining brown-striped strips and sew the strips
to the top and bottom.

3 Sew light or medium triangles to medium or
dark triangles to make 28 half-square-triangle
units. Press seam allowances toward the darker
triangles.

Make 28.

4 Arrange the half-square-triangle units around
the center of the quilt, placing the base of the
darker triangles next to the quilt center. Sew eight
units together for each side border. Sew six half-
square-triangle units together for the top and bottom borders, adding a red 2½" square to each end.

5 Sew the pieced borders from step 4 to the sides
of the quilt; press. Sew the pieced borders from
step 5 to the top and bottom of the quilt; press.

## Finishing the Quilt

Layer the quilt top, batting, and backing. Baste the
layers together and quilt as desired. Add the binding and enjoy.

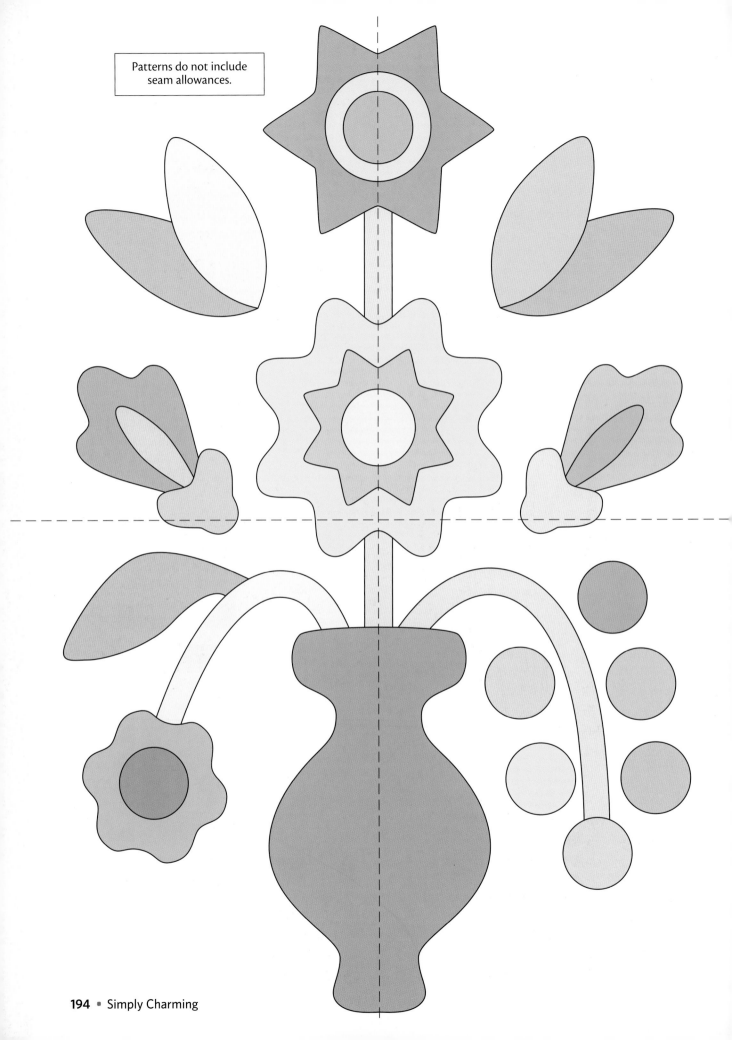

Patterns do not include seam allowances.

# T Is for Temperance

*The official colors of the Women's Christian Temperance Union were blue and white, and there was an abundance of quilts made in these colors toward the end of the nineteenth century.*

By Kathleen Tracy

FINISHED QUILT SIZE: 19½" x 19½"    FINISHED BLOCK SIZE: 6" x 6"

## Materials

*Yardage is based on 42"-wide fabric unless otherwise noted; fat eighths measure 9" x 21".*

¼ yard of medium-blue print for outer border

1 fat eighth *each* of 2 different shirting prints for blocks

1 fat eighth *each* of 2 different blue prints for blocks

⅛ yard of dark-blue print #1 for inner border

¼ yard of dark-blue print #2 for binding

¾ yard of fabric for backing

24" x 24" piece of thin cotton batting

## Cutting

*All measurements include ¼"-wide seam allowances.*

**From *each* of the 2 shirting prints, cut:**

1 square, 4⅞" x 4⅞" (2 total)

5 squares, 2⅞" x 2⅞" (10 total)

**From *each* of the 2 blue prints for blocks, cut:**

1 square, 4⅞" x 4⅞" (2 total)

5 squares, 2⅞" x 2⅞" (10 total)

**From dark-blue print #1, cut:**

2 strips, 1½" x 12½"

2 strips, 1½" x 14½"

**From the medium-blue print for outer border, cut:**
2 strips, 3" x 14½"
2 strips, 3" x 19½"
**From dark-blue print #2, cut:**
3 strips, 2" x 42"

## Making the Blocks

You'll make two pairs of identical blue-and-white T blocks. Pair up your fabrics before you begin, to simplify the piecing.

1 Draw a diagonal line from corner to corner on the wrong side of each light 4⅞" square. Layer a marked square on top of a blue 4⅞" square, right sides together. Stitch ¼" from the line on both sides and cut on the drawn line. Press the seam allowances toward the darker fabric. Make four half-square-triangle units.

Make 4.

2 Draw a diagonal line on the wrong side of each light 2⅞" square. Layer five matching light squares on top of five matching blue 2⅞" squares, right sides together. Stitch ¼" from the line on both sides and cut on the drawn line. Press the seam allowances toward the blue fabric. Make 20 half-square-triangle units in matching sets of 10.

Make 20.

3 Arrange the matching units from steps 1 and 2 as shown; sew the block together in sections. Sew the sections together and press. Make four blocks.

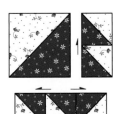 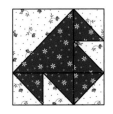

Make 4.

## Assembling the Quilt

1 Sew the blocks together as shown.

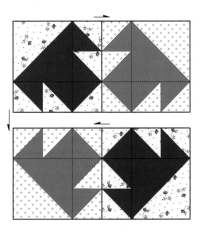

2 Sew the dark-blue 1½" x 12½" strips to the sides of the quilt top, pressing the seam allowances toward the border. Sew the dark-blue 1½" x 14½" strips to the top and bottom of the quilt and press.

3 Sew the medium-blue 3" x 14½" strips to the top and bottom of the quilt top, pressing the seam allowances toward the outer border. Sew the medium-blue 3" x 19½" strips to the sides of the quilt top and press.

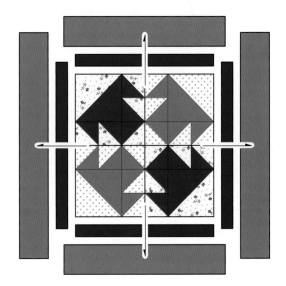

## Finishing the Quilt

1 Layer the quilt top, batting, and backing; baste the layers together.

2 Quilt as desired. The quilt shown was hand quilted in the ditch and with a T motif in the corner triangles.

3 Attach the dark-blue binding to the quilt.

# Break Your Bread, Don't Cut It

*Depending on the number of charm squares you have, you can make this pretty table runner as long or as short as you like. You'll love the look of the half-hexagon shape, and there are no inset seams or difficult bindings in this project.*

By Mary Etherington and Connie Tesene of Country Threads

FINISHED QUILT SIZE: 16" x 8¾"

## Materials

*Yardage is based on 42"-wide fabric unless otherwise noted. Charm squares are 5" x 5".*

15 charm squares in 2 main colors (red and brown)*
⅓ yard of fabric for backing
10" x 17" piece of batting
Template plastic
*You can substitute 6" x 7" scraps of 10 assorted reds and browns. Cut 3 half-hexagons from each scrap.*

## Cutting

*All measurements include ¼"-wide seam allowances.*

**From each charm square, cut:**

2 half-hexagons (30 total) using the pattern on page 198 and template plastic. You can stack up to 6 charm squares and cut all 6 at once.

# Assembling the Quilt

1 Place a red and a brown half-hexagon right sides together and offset so the fabric edges meet at the ¼" seam allowance; stitch. Add a third half-hexagon to the other side of the brown fabric. Alternate the red and the brown fabrics, making about half of the units with two red and one brown fabric and half with two brown and one red fabric.

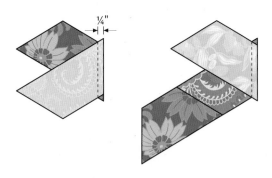

2 Arrange the half-hexagons in 10 columns of three each. Sew the columns together. Press the seam allowances in opposite directions from column to column.

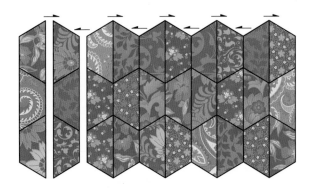

3 Layer the batting, followed by the backing, right side up, and then the quilt, right side down.

4 Stitch along each zigzag edge using a ¼" seam allowance and leaving both ends of the quilt open. With the needle down, pivot at each point and keep stitching. Do not take the quilt out of your machine at each point.

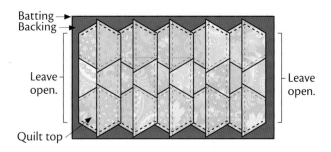

5 Trim the backing and batting around the shape of the runner. Clip up to the seam allowance in the inner points and trim the outer points.

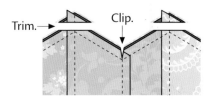

6 Turn the runner right side out. Reach inside with a letter opener or other pointed object to push each of the points out.

7 Close each end by hand, turning in ¼" and slip stitching. Press.

8 Machine quilt ¼" from the edges and as desired.

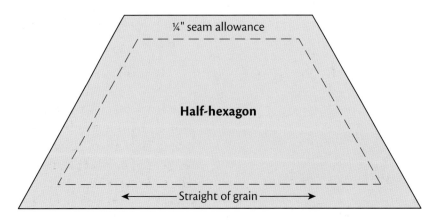

# Evening on the Farm

*The blue and brown combination in the Country Farm blocks gives this quilt a soft, "down home" feel. A nice mix of tan prints—including small-scale florals, plaids, geometrics, and stripes—makes up the background.*

By Shelly Burge

FINISHED QUILT SIZE: 18½" x 22½"    FINISHED BLOCK SIZE: 3" x 3"

## Materials

*Yardage is based on 42"-wide fabric unless otherwise noted.*

6 assorted dark-blue prints, 5" x 5", for blocks

6 assorted dark-brown prints, 5" x 5", for blocks

12 assorted tan prints, 7" x 7", for blocks

½ yard of blue print for borders and binding

¾ yard of tan print for borders*

⅝ yard of fabric for backing

20½" x 24¼" piece of batting

*Select a fabric printed with stripes, scallops, or rows of flowers.*

# Cutting

*All measurements include ¼"-wide seam allowances.*

**From *each* of the assorted blue and brown prints, cut:**

1 square, 2" x 2" (12 total)

2 squares, 2¼" x 2¼"; crosscut into quarters diagonally to make 8 triangles (96 total)

**From *each* of the assorted tan prints, cut:**

1 square, 2¼" x 2¼"; crosscut into quarters diagonally to make 4 triangles (48 total)

4 squares, 1½" x 1½" (48 total)

1 rectangle, 1½" x 3½" (12 total)

1 rectangle, 1½" x 4½" (12 total)

**From the blue print, cut:**

2 strips, 3½" x 25"

2 strips, 3½" x 21"

3 strips, 1¼" x 30"

**Using the print on the tan border fabric as a guide, cut on the *lengthwise* grain:**

2 strips, 2" x 25"

2 strips, 2" x 21"

## Assembling the Quilt

1 Piece 12 Country Farm blocks as shown: six with brown center squares and blue star tips and six with blue center squares and brown star tips. Use tan prints randomly and try not to use a print more than once in each block.

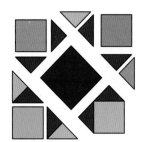
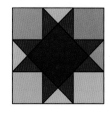

2 Lay out one short tan rectangle, one block, and one long tan rectangle. Arrange as shown above right. When the pieces are arranged correctly, stitch the tan rectangles to the blocks.

3 Arrange the blocks in rows of three, turning the blocks as shown; then join the rows.

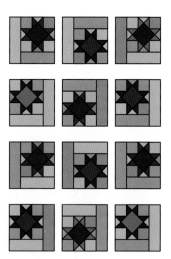

4 Appliqué the tan border strips to the blue border strips. The finished edge of the tan fabric should be ¾" from the inside edge of the blue border strips. Trim the blue fabric under the appliqué to reduce bulk.

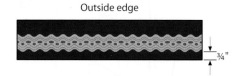

Outside edge

¾"

5 Sew the borders to the quilt top, mitering the corners.

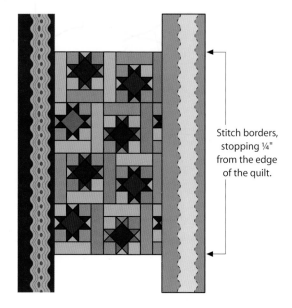

Stitch borders, stopping ¼" from the edge of the quilt.

## Finishing the Quilt

Layer the quilt top with batting and backing; baste. Quilt as desired. Bind the edges with the blue-print strips to finish.

# Reveille

*White nine-patch units and careful color placement combine to create a quilt that looks like it's made from puzzle pieces. A scrappy border adds to the charm.*

By Carrie Nelson; machine quilted by Louise Haley

FINISHED QUILT SIZE: 31½" x 31½"    FINISHED BLOCK SIZE: 6¼" x 6¼"

## Materials

*Yardage is based on 42"-wide fabric unless otherwise noted. Charm squares are 5" x 5".*

⅝ yard of background fabric for nine-patch units and inner border

32 matching *pairs* of assorted charm squares for blocks and outer border (64 total)

⅜ yard of fabric for binding

1⅛ yards of fabric for backing

37" x 37" piece of batting

## Cutting

*All measurements include ¼"-wide seam allowances.*

**From the background fabric, cut:**

5 strips, 2" x 42"; crosscut into 40 strips, 2" x 5"

2 strips, 1½" x 27½"

2 strips, 1½" x 25½"

**From each of the 32 matching pairs of assorted squares, cut:**

1 square, 5" x 5"; crosscut in half diagonally to make 2 triangles (64 total)

1 strip, 2½" x 5" (32 total)

1 strip, 2" x 5" (32 total)

**From the binding fabric, cut:**

140" of 2"-wide bias binding

# Making the Blocks

Use a scant ¼"-wide seam allowance throughout. After sewing each seam, press the seam allowances in the direction indicated.

1 Sort the 2" x 5" assorted strips into two groups of 16 strips each. Using one group of assorted strips and eight background strips, sew assorted strips to both long edges of each background strip as shown to make a strip set. Make a total of eight strip sets. Cut each strip set into two 2"-wide segments. Cut a total of 16 segments

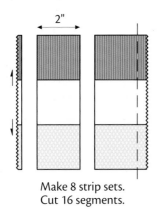

Make 8 strip sets.
Cut 16 segments.

2 Using the remaining assorted strips and 2" x 5" background strips, sew background strips to both long edges of each assorted strip as shown to make a strip set. Make a total of 16 strip sets. Cut each strip set into two 2"-wide segments. Cut a total of 32 segments.

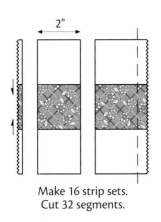

Make 16 strip sets.
Cut 32 segments.

3 Lay out one segment from step 1 and two segments from step 2 as shown. Join the segments to make a nine-patch unit that measures 5" square. Repeat to make a total of 16 nine-patch units.

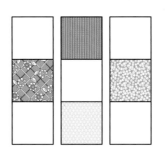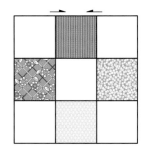

Make 16.

4 Select four triangles; each triangle should match one of the squares in a nine-patch unit. Fold the nine-patch unit in half vertically and horizontally and finger-crease to mark the center of each side. Fold the triangles in half and finger-crease to mark the center on each long side. Sew triangles to opposite sides of the nine-patch unit, matching the center creases. Trim the triangle point that sticks out beyond the seam line.

Sew triangles to the remaining sides of the nine-patch unit to complete the block. The triangles are oversized and will be trimmed in the next step. Make a total of 16 blocks.

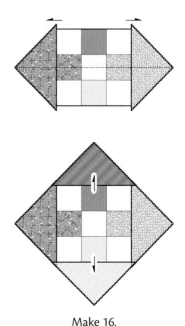

Make 16.

5 Using a square ruler, trim each block to measure 6¾" square. To properly align the ruler, align the 3⅜" lines on the ruler with the corners of the nine-patch unit. The outermost point of the nine-patch unit is just a bit more than ¼" from the outer edge of the block. The most important thing is that the blocks are all trimmed to the same size and that you have at least ¼" seam allowance.

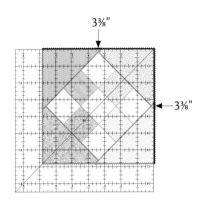

## Assembling the Quilt

1 Lay out the blocks in four rows of four blocks each. Join the blocks into rows and press the seam allowances in opposite directions from row to row. Then sew the rows together and press. The quilt top should measure 25½" square.

2 For the inner border, sew the 25½"-wide background strips to the sides of the quilt top, and then sew the 27½"-long background strips to the top and bottom of the quilt top. Press the seam allowances toward the inner border.

3 For the outer border, sort the 2½" x 5" strips into four groups of seven strips each. You'll have four extra strips, so pick the ones you like best. Join each group of strips end to end to make four long strips. Press the seam allowances in one direction. For the side borders, trim two strips to measure 2½" x 27½". For the top and bottom borders, trim two strips to measure 2½" x 31½".

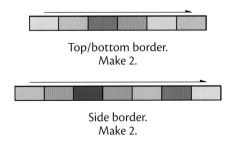

Top/bottom border.
Make 2.

Side border.
Make 2.

4 Sew the border strips to the sides, and then the top and bottom of the quilt top. Press the seam allowances toward the outer borders.

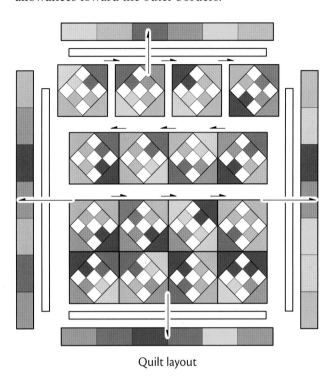

Quilt layout

## Finishing the Quilt

Layer, baste, and quilt as desired. Using the 2"-wide binding strips, make and attach binding.

# Stand Up Straight!

*This quilt is simply bursting with energy! The flash of turquoise really sparkles against the hot orange and yellow, but this block looks terrific in all sorts of colors.*

By Mary Etherington and Connie Tesene of Country Threads

FINISHED QUILT SIZE: 15" x 24"    FINISHED BLOCK SIZE: 3" x 3"

## Materials

*Yardage is based on 42"-wide fabric unless otherwise noted. Charm squares are 5" x 5".*

10 light, 10 dark, and 20 medium charm squares for blocks

⅝ yard of fabric for backing

17" x 26" piece of batting

## Making Do

If you don't have a set of precut charm squares, you'll need 4" x 16" scraps of five different medium-value prints, 4½" x 9" scraps of five different light-value prints, and 4½" x 9" scraps of five different dark-value prints. Cut each medium print into four squares, 3⅞" x 3⅞" (20 squares total); then cut each square in half diagonally to make 40 triangles total. Cut each light print into two squares, 4¼" x 4¼"; then cut each square into quarters diagonally to make four triangles (40 total). Cut each dark print as for the light prints to make 40 dark triangles.

## Cutting

*All measurements include ¼"-wide seam allowances.*

**From *each* of the 10 light charm squares, cut:**

1 square, 4¼" x 4¼"; crosscut into quarters diagonally to make 4 triangles (40 total)

**From *each* of the 10 dark charm squares, cut:**

1 square, 4¼" x 4¼"; crosscut into quarters diagonally to make 4 triangles (40 total)

**From *each* of the 20 medium charm squares, cut:**

1 square, 3⅞" x 3⅞"; crosscut in half diagonally to make 2 triangles (40 total)

**From the fabric for backing, cut:**

1 piece, 17" x 26"

## Assembling the Quilt

1. Sew the dark and light triangles together in pairs, stitching along the short edge with the dark triangle on the left and the light triangle on the right as shown. Mix the fabrics so the combination in each unit is different. Press the seam allowances toward the dark fabric. Make 40 triangle units.

Make 40.

2. Sew a medium triangle to each unit from step 1, stitching along the long edge. Press the seam allowances toward the medium triangles. Blocks should measure 3½" square. Make 40.

Make 40.

3. Lay out the blocks in eight rows of five blocks each, with the medium triangles in the bottom-right corner.

4. Sew the blocks into rows, pressing in opposite directions from row to row. Sew the rows together and press.

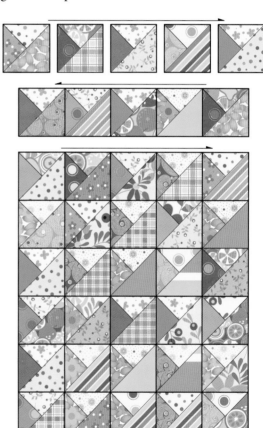

# Finishing the Quilt

This quilt doesn't have binding. Instead, the layers are stitched together, and then turned right side out before quilting.

1 Layer the batting, followed by the backing fabric *right side up,* and then the quilt top *right side down.* The batting and backing are a little larger than the quilt. Pin the layers together around the perimeter of the quilt top.

2 Stitch around the edge of the quilt using a ¼" seam allowance and leaving a 6" opening for turning the quilt right side out.

3 Trim the batting and backing to the size of the quilt top and clip the excess batting out of the corners to reduce bulk.

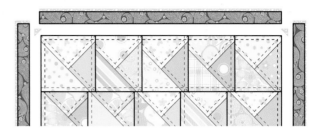

4 Turn the quilt right side out and stitch the opening closed by hand.

5 Press the quilt, and then quilt as desired.

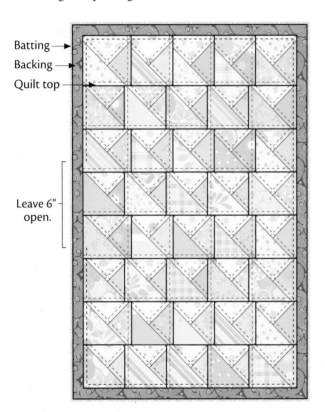

Batting →
Backing →
Quilt top →

Leave 6" open.

# Pinwheel Charm

*The block is a square divided into two equal, odd-shaped, four-sided patches, which creates a tessellated pattern that's lots of fun to piece.*

By Ellen Pahl

FINISHED QUILT SIZE: 26½" x 26½"     FINISHED BLOCK SIZE: 4" x 4"

## Materials

*Yardage is based on 42"-wide fabric unless otherwise noted.*

¾ yard of dark print for blocks and inner and outer borders

⅜ yard *total* of assorted solid fabrics for blocks*

¼ yard of light-solid fabric for middle border

¼ yard of dark print for binding

1 yard of fabric for backing

31" x 31" piece of batting

*Perfect for 5" x 5" charm squares! You'll need 25; 1 charm square is enough for 1 block.*

## Cutting

*All measurements include ¼"-wide seam allowances.*

**From the dark print, cut:**

4 strips, 2½" x 42"

2 strips, 1½" x 20½"

2 strips, 1½" x 22½"

2 strips, 1½" x 24½"

2 strips, 1½" x 25½"

**From the assorted solid fabrics, cut a *total* of:**

25 strips, 2½" x 7"*

**From the light-solid fabric, cut:**

2 strips, 1½" x 22½"

2 strips, 1½" x 25½"

**From the dark print for binding, cut:**

3 strips, 2⅛" x 42"

*If you're using charm squares, cut each charm square in half to make 2 strips, 2½" x 5.*

## Cutting and Making the Blocks

1 Prepare a paper cutting guide using the pattern opposite. Include the stitching lines to help maintain accuracy when cutting.

2 Layer two dark-print 2½" x 42" strips together, right sides up, and press. Trim and square up one end of the layered strips.

3 Place the paper guide on the strips, aligning it with the cut edges of the strips as shown. Place a ruler over the paper, positioning the ¼" line of the ruler on the stitching line, and cut with a rotary cutter. Rotate the cutting guide and make a cut along the straight edge. You should be able to cut about 25 patches from each 42" strip. Prepare the

two remaining dark-print 2½" x 42" strips as in step 2, and continue cutting until you have cut a total of 100 pieces.

Cut 100.

4 Layer the solid strips in pairs and cut four matching pieces for each block to make a total of 100.

5 Place the narrow end of each solid piece right sides together with the wide end of a print piece, offsetting the points by ¼". Sew and press. Make four matching units for each block.

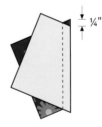

¼"

Make 4 matching units for each block (100 total).

6 Arrange four matching units as shown and sew into rows. Press. Sew the rows together to make the block. Repeat to make a total of 25 blocks.

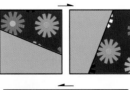

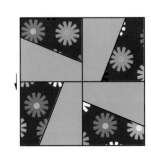

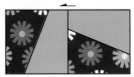

Make 25.

## Assembling the Quilt

1 Arrange the blocks in five rows of five blocks each, rotating the blocks as needed so that the seams will butt together. Sew into rows and press. Sew the rows together; press.

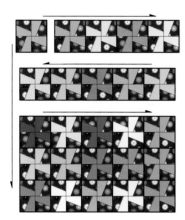

2 Sew the dark-print 1½" x 20½" strips to the sides of the quilt. Press. Sew the dark-print 1½" x 22½" strips to the top and bottom. Press. Add the light-solid 1½" x 22½" strips to the top and bottom.

3 Sew the light-solid 1½" x 25½" strips to the dark-print 1½" x 25½" strips. Press.

4 Add the border units from step 3 and the dark-print 1½" x 24½" strips to the quilt using a partial seam to begin. Start in the center of the top edge of the quilt, sewing the dark-print strip to the quilt as shown. Work counterclockwise around the quilt to add the borders, finishing the top seam last. Press all seam allowances outward.

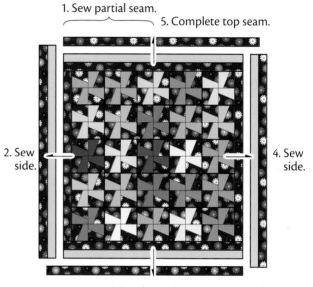

1. Sew partial seam.  5. Complete top seam.

2. Sew side.  4. Sew side.

3. Sew bottom.

## Finishing the Quilt

Layer, baste, and quilt. The quilt shown is quilted in the ditch of the blocks and borders and has two different straight-line designs in the solid patches. Make and attach the dark-print binding.

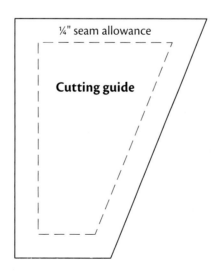

¼" seam allowance

**Cutting guide**

# Use a Napkin Only for Your Mouth

*Of course there are exceptions to this rule. You may also use a napkin to keep something from spilling on your quilt, especially one like this where you can use all of your favorite fabrics.*

By Mary Etherington and Connie Tesene of Country Threads

**FINISHED QUILT SIZE: 30" x 30"    FINISHED BLOCK SIZE: 9" x 9"**

## Materials

*Yardage is based on 42"-wide fabric unless otherwise noted. Charm squares are 5" x 5".*

36 assorted charm squares in your favorite prints\*

⅜ yard of dark fabric for block connector squares and border

⅓ yard of fabric for binding

1⅛ yards of fabric for backing

36" x 36" piece of batting

*\*You can substitute ¼ yard or fat quarters of 6 assorted prints. Cut 5" squares from each.*

## Cutting

*All measurements include ¼"-wide seam allowances.*

**From the dark fabric, cut:**

2 strips, 2½" x 42"; crosscut into 36 squares, 2½" x 2½"

3 strips, 2" x 42"

**From the fabric for binding, cut:**

4 strips, 2¼" x 42"

## Assembling the Quilt

1 Sew a dark 2½" square to one corner of each charm square. Trim the outside corner of the connector square and press the seam allowances toward the triangles.

Make 36.

2 Sew four of the units from step 1 together to make a block, arranging the dark triangles to meet in the center. Press the seam allowances in opposite directions. Repeat to make nine blocks.

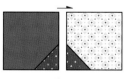
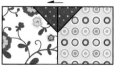

Make 9.

3 Sew the blocks together into three rows of three blocks each. Press in opposite directions from row to row. Sew the rows together and press.

4 Sew the three dark 2"-wide strips together end to end. Measure the length of the quilt and cut two strips to this length. Sew them to the sides of the quilt. Press the seam allowances toward the strips. Measure the width of the quilt. Cut two strips to this length and sew them to the top and bottom of the quilt. Press the seam allowances toward the strips.

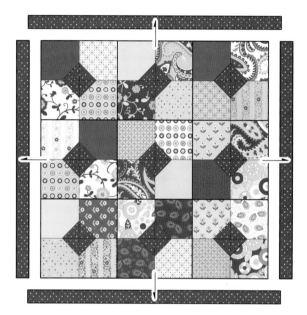

## Finishing the Quilt

Make a quilt back approximately 36" x 36". Layer the quilt top with batting and backing. Baste, and then quilt as desired. Trim the excess batting and backing and bind the quilt with the 2¼" x 42" strips.

# Xs and Os

*Here's your chance to show off some of the batiks in your own collection. The X block is a standard Pinwheel, but with the corners cut off. Here it's paired it with an O block just for fun.*

By Ellen Pahl

FINISHED QUILT SIZE: 20" x 20"    FINISHED BLOCK SIZE: 4" x 4"

## Materials

*Yardage is based on 42"-wide fabric unless otherwise noted.*

⅝ yard of light batik for blocks

13 pieces, 4" x 6", of medium to dark batiks for X blocks

12 pieces, 6" x 6", of medium batiks for O blocks

¼ yard of light plaid for binding*

¾ yard of fabric for backing

25" x 25" piece of batting

*\*If you want to use a plaid cut on the bias, a fat quarter will yield longer bias strips for fewer seams.*

## Cutting

*All measurements include ¼"-wide seam allowances.*

**From the light batik, cut:**

2 strips, 2⅞" x 42"; crosscut into 26 squares, 2⅞" x 2⅞". Cut each square in half diagonally to make 52 triangles.

5 strips, 1⅝" x 42"; crosscut into 100 squares, 1⅝" x 1⅝"

1 strip, 1¾" x 42"; crosscut into 12 squares, 1¾" x 1¾"

**From *each* 4" x 6" batik piece, cut:**

2 squares, 2⅞" x 2⅞"; cut in half diagonally to make 4 triangles (52 total)

**From _each_ 6" x 6" batik piece, cut:**
2 rectangles, 1¾" x 1⅞" (24 total)
2 rectangles, 1⅞" x 4½" (24 total)
**From the light plaid, cut:**
2⅛"-wide bias strips to total 94"

## Making the X Blocks

1 Sew a medium or dark 2⅞" triangle to a light 2⅞" triangle along the long edges to make a half-square-triangle unit. Press. Make four identical units.

Make 4.

2 Sew the four units together as shown to make a Pinwheel block.

3 Draw a line diagonally on the wrong side of each light 1⅝" square. Position a square on each corner of the Pinwheel block as shown and sew on the drawn lines. Trim the extra fabric to leave a ¼" seam allowance and press outward.

4 Repeat steps 1–3 to make a total of 13 X blocks.

## Making the O Blocks

1 Sew matching medium 1¾" x 1⅞" rectangles to opposite sides of a light 1¾" square. Press.

2 Sew matching medium 1⅞" x 4½" rectangles to the top and bottom of the unit from step 1. Press.

3 Position a marked light 1⅝" square on each corner of the block and sew on the drawn line. Trim the extra fabric to leave a ¼" seam allowance and press inward.

4 Repeat steps 1–3 to make a total of 12 O blocks.

## Assembling and Finishing the Quilt

1 Arrange the X and O blocks in five rows of five blocks each, alternating them as shown. Sew the blocks into rows and press. Sew the rows together; press.

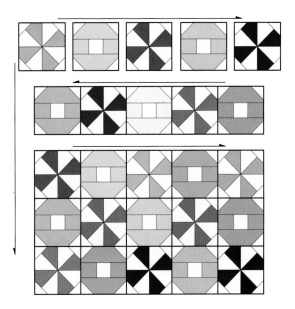

2 Layer, baste, quilt, and add the plaid binding.

# Take Turns

*Pink and brown is a classic color combination, but any charm pack with two dominant colors is all you need.*

By Mary Etherington and Connie Tesene of Country Threads

**FINISHED QUILT SIZE:** 20" x 30"    **FINISHED BLOCK SIZE:** 4" x 4"

## Materials

*Yardage is based on 42"-wide fabric unless otherwise noted. Charm squares are 5" x 5".*

14 assorted pink charm squares for blocks and outer border*

14 assorted brown charm squares for blocks and outer border*

½ yard of tan print for blocks and inner border

½ yard of pink print for Star block, sashing cornerstones, and border corners

¼ yard of brown print for Star block, sashing strips, and outer border

¼ yard of fabric for binding

¾ yard of fabric for backing

24" x 34" piece of batting

*You can substitute 3" x 21" strips of 7 assorted pink and 7 assorted brown prints. Double the number of pieces for each charm square in the cutting instructions.*

## Cutting

*All measurements include ¼"-wide seam allowances. When cutting your charm squares, be very careful not to waste any fabric. Measure to the outside of pinked edges. Do not straighten the edges; you'll need every square inch of fabric.*

**From *each* pink charm square, cut:**

2 squares, 1½" x 1½" (28 total)

1 square, 2⅞" x 2⅞"; cut in half diagonally to make 2 triangles (28 total)

1 rectangle, 1¾" x 2½" (14 total; 2 will be extra)

**From *each* brown charm square, cut:**

2 squares, 2½" x 2½" (28 total)

1 rectangle, 2½" x 5" (14 total)

**From the tan print, cut:**

2 strips 1⅞" x 42"; crosscut into 32 squares, 1⅞" x 1⅞". Cut each square in half diagonally to make 2 triangles (64 total).

4 squares, 1½" x 1½"

3 strips, 1½" x 42"; crosscut 1 of the strips into 2 strips, 1½" x 14½". Trim the other 2 strips to 1½" x 26½".

**From the pink print, cut:**

4 squares, 1⅞" x 1⅞"; cut in half diagonally to make 8 triangles

8 squares, 1½" x 1½"

4 squares, 2½" x 2½"

**From the brown print, cut:**

4 squares, 1⅞" x 1⅞"; cut in half diagonally to make 8 triangles

3 strips, 1½" x 42"; crosscut into 22 strips, 1½" x 4½"

2 rectangles, 2½" x 5"

**From the fabric for binding, cut:**

3 strips, 1½" x 42"

## Assembling the Quilt

Each 4" Charm block is made from one brown charm square, one pink charm square, and the tan print. All four pieces of pink and both pieces of brown print should match within a block. The Star block is not made with charm squares, but with the brown, pink, and tan prints.

1 Place a tan triangle right sides together with a pink charm square, aligning the short edges of the triangle with two sides of the square, and stitch. Press the seam allowances toward the triangle. Sew the short edge of another tan triangle to a side of the pink square as shown. Press toward the triangle. Be careful not to stretch the long side of the tan triangles. Repeat to make two units from each pink charm square (14 matching pairs; 28 total).

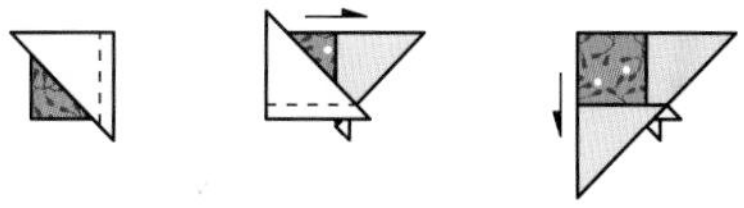

Make 14 pairs.

2 Sew a pink 2⅞" charm triangle to each of the units from step 1, matching fabrics. You will have 14 matching units (28 total).

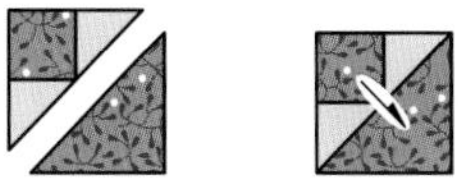

Make 14 matching units.

3 Arrange two matching units from step 2 with two matching brown squares so the pink squares are on the outside of the block. Sew the squares and units together and press. Make 14 Charm blocks.

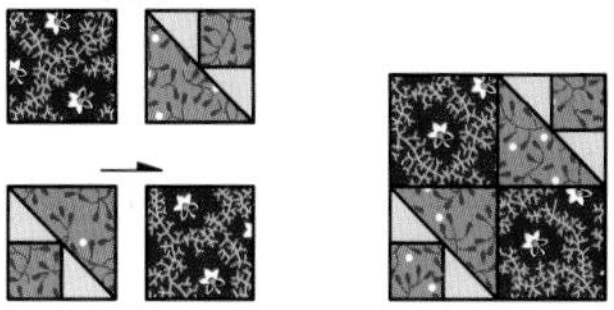

Make 14.

4 For the Star block, sew four pink-print 1⅞" triangles to four tan triangles as shown. Sew four brown-print triangles to four tan triangles. Sew four pink-print triangles to four brown-print triangles. Press the seam allowances as shown.

Make 4 of each.

5 Arrange the triangle units from step 4 with the four tan 1½" squares as shown. Sew into rows and sew the rows together. It can be difficult to press the seam allowances in a direction that makes it easy to match the points. One solution is to press the seam allowances open instead of to one side.

Make 1.

6 Arrange the 14 Charm blocks and the Star block in three columns of five blocks each, with the Star block in the center. In the sample, all of the Charm blocks are oriented in the same direction. Place the brown-print 1½" x 4½" sashing strips between the blocks. Alternating five sashing strips and four pink-print cornerstones as shown, arrange sashing rows between the block rows. Sew into rows and sew the rows together. Press toward the sashing strips.

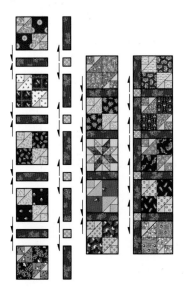

7 For the inner border, sew the tan 1½" x 14½" strips to the top and bottom of the quilt top, easing as needed to fit. Sew the tan 1½" x 26½" strips to the sides of the quilt top. Press toward the borders.

8 The outer border is made from the leftover fabrics. Your brown rectangles should measure about 2½" x 5". The 2½" measurement is the border width. If the scraps are a little narrower, trim them all to the narrowest width (either 2¼", or 2"). Trim the pink 1¾" x 2½" rectangles and the four 2½" squares to this same width. For example, if your border pieces are 2¼", cut the pink rectangles 1¾" x 2¼" and the corner squares 2¼" x 2¼".

9 Sew two pink rectangles between three brown rectangles to make a side border. Make two, and check the fit. Borders are too long? Just trim to fit. Borders are too short? Substitute the brown print for one of the rectangles and cut it longer than the others. Sew the side borders to the quilt top. Press toward the inner border. Sew four pink rectangles between five brown rectangles to make the top border. Check the fit and add or trim as needed. Sew a pink-print corner square to each end. Repeat to make the bottom border. Sew the top and bottom border strips to the quilt top. Press as shown.

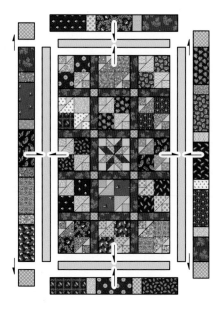

## Finishing the Quilt

Layer the quilt top with batting and backing; baste. Quilt as desired. Sew the 1½"-wide binding strips together end to end to make one long strip. Use this strip to bind your quilt.

# People Will Find You Interesting If You're Interested in Them

*If you're shy talking to people you don't know, ask them questions about themselves. Or show off this quilt—it can spark a conversation. Its small size makes it the perfect project to practice your points.*

By Mary Etherington and Connie Tesene of Country Threads

FINISHED QUILT SIZE: 15" x 19"    FINISHED BLOCK SIZE: 3" x 3"

## Materials

*Yardage is based on 42"-wide fabric unless otherwise noted. Charm squares are 5" x 5".*

30 assorted medium to dark charm squares for blocks and pieced border

18 assorted light to medium charm squares for block backgrounds

¼ yard of pink print for setting triangles

¼ yard of brown print for binding

⅝ yard of fabric for backing

20" x 24" piece of batting

## Making Do

If you don't have a set of precut charm squares, you'll need one fat eighth (9" x 20") *each* of nine assorted medium to dark fabrics. Cut two 2⅞" squares and eleven 1⅞" squares from each fabric; you may need a couple of additional small squares for the border. You'll also need one fat eighth *each* of six assorted light to medium fabrics for the backgrounds. Cut six 1⅞" squares and three 1½" squares from each fabric.

## Cutting

*All measurements include ¼"-wide seam allowances.*

**From *each of 18* medium to dark charm squares, cut:**

1 square, 2⅞" x 2⅞"; cut in half diagonally to make 2 triangles (36 total)

3 squares, 1⅞" x 1⅞"; cut each square in half diagonally to make 2 triangles (108 total)

**From the remaining *12* medium to dark charm squares, cut:**

4 squares, 1⅞" x 1⅞"; cut each square in half diagonally to make 2 triangles (96 total, 4 will be extra)

**From *each* of the light to medium charm squares, cut:**

2 squares, 1⅞" x 1⅞"; cut each square in half diagonally to make 2 triangles (72 total)

1 square, 1½" x 1½" (18 total)

**From the pink print, cut:**

3 squares, 6" x 6"; cut into quarters diagonally to make 12 triangles (2 will be extra)

2 squares, 4½" x 4½"; cut each square in half diagonally to make 2 triangles (4 total)

**From the brown print, cut:**

2 strips, 2¼" x 42"

## Creating the Quilt

Each block is made from two medium/dark 2⅞" triangles, four medium/dark 1⅞" triangles, four light/medium 1⅞" triangles, and one light/medium 1½" square. Many, but not all, of the blocks have matching light/medium pieces.

1 Sew two different 2⅞" triangles together, being careful not to stretch the bias edges. Press the seam allowances in one direction. Repeat with all the 2⅞" triangles to make 18 half-square-triangle units.

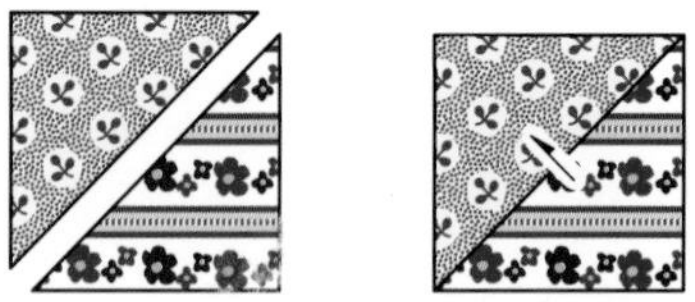

Make 18.

2 Pair four matching light/medium 1⅞" triangles and four assorted medium/dark triangles. Sew the triangle pairs together and press the seam allowances in one direction. Make 72 half-square-triangle units for the blocks. Repeat with the remaining 1⅞" triangles to make approximately 64 additional units for the borders.

Make 72 for blocks.  Make 64 for borders.

3 Sew a unit from step 1, four half-square-triangle units from step 2, and a light/medium 1½" square together to make a block. Press as indicated. Make 18 blocks. Many (but not all) of the blocks in this quilt have the same light/medium background fabric; this helps the individual blocks show more clearly.

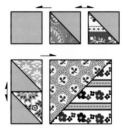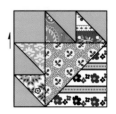

Make 18.

4 Arrange the blocks, pink side triangles, and pink corner triangles as shown. Sew the blocks and side triangles into diagonal rows. The pink triangles are cut oversized and will extend beyond the pieced blocks. Sew the rows together and add the pink 4½" triangles on each corner. Trim the quilt top ¼" outside the block corners.

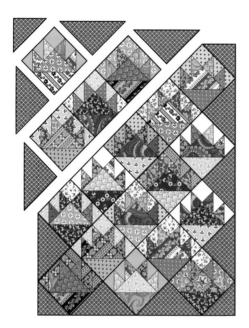

5 Sew 13 half-square-triangle units together, orienting the triangles in the same direction. Make two units and sew one to the top and one to the bottom of the quilt. Sew 19 half-square-triangle units together for each side border. Don't worry about fitting everything together perfectly. With this many seams, it can be difficult to make the borders exactly the same size as the quilt center. If it's too long, cut it off. If it's too short, add more triangle units! You can also adjust the border lengths by taking a little larger or smaller seam allowance between some of the triangle squares.

## Finishing the Quilt

Make a quilt back approximately 20" x 24". Layer the quilt top with batting and backing. Baste, and then quilt as desired. Trim the excess batting and backing and bind the quilt with the brown 2¼"-wide strips.

# Roundabout

*This quilt is made from rectangles stitched around a center square—yet the block looks like a circle or the letter O.*

By Carrie Nelson; machine quilted by Louise Haley

FINISHED QUILT SIZE: 32½" x 32½"    FINISHED BLOCK SIZE: 5¼" x 5¼"

## Materials

*Yardage is based on 42"-wide fabric unless otherwise noted. Charm squares are 5" x 5".*

⅞ yard of background fabric for blocks and inner border

50 assorted charm squares for blocks

17 assorted charm squares for outer border

⅜ yard of fabric for binding

1¼ yards of fabric for backing

38" x 38" piece of batting

## Cutting

*All measurements include ¼"-wide seam allowances.*

**From the background fabric, cut:**

8 strips, 2¼" x 42"; crosscut into 125 squares, 2¼" x 2¼"

2 strips, 1⅜" x 28½"

2 strips, 1⅜" x 26¾"

**From *each* of the 50 assorted squares for blocks, cut:**

2 rectangles, 2¼" x 4" (100 total)

**From *each* of 16 assorted squares for outer border, cut:**

2 rectangles, 2¼" x 5" (32 total)

**From the 1 remaining assorted square, cut:**

4 squares, 2½" x 2½"

**From the binding fabric, cut:**

145" of 2"-wide bias binding

## Making the Blocks

1 Draw a diagonal line from corner to corner on the wrong side of four of the background squares. Place a marked square on one end of an assorted rectangle, making sure the square is position exactly as shown. Sew along the marked line and trim, leaving a ¼" seam allowance. Repeat to make a total of four pieced rectangles.

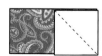
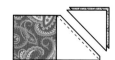

Make 4.

2 Lay out the four pieced rectangles and a background square as shown.

3 Sew a rectangle to the top of the background square, stitching a little more than halfway as shown.

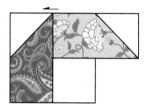

4 Sew the next rectangle to the left edge of the unit from step 3.

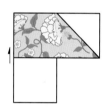

5 Sew a third rectangle to the bottom of the unit, and then sew the last rectangle to the right edge of the unit as shown.

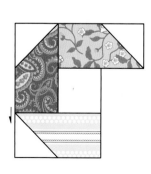
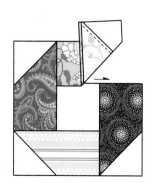

6 Complete the partial seam stitched in step 3. You can start where you stopped stitching and sew toward the outside raw edge, or you can start at the outside edge and sew toward the center square, whichever you prefer. The block should measure 5¾" square. Repeat to make a total of 25 blocks.

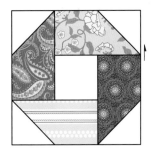

Make 25.

# Assembling and Finishing the Quilt

1 Lay out the blocks in five rows of five blocks each. Sew the blocks together in rows. Press the seam allowances in opposite directions from row to row. Sew the rows together and press. The quilt center should measure 26¾" x 26¾".

2 For the inner border, sew the 26¾"-long background strips to opposite sides of the quilt center, and then sew the 28½"-long background strips to the top and bottom of the quilt top. Press the seam allowances toward the inner border.

3 For the outer border, sort the 2¼" x 5" assorted strips to make two sets of 16 strips each. Select one set of strips and sort it into two groups of eight strips each. Join each group of eight strips side by side. Press the seam allowances in one direction. Make two pieced sections. Each section should measure 10" x 14¼". Repeat to make a second set of two pieced sections.

4 Cut each pieced section in half lengthwise to make eight pieced outer-border strips, and then sort them into two groups of two matching sets.

5 Join one set of strips to make a 2½" x 28½"-long pieced outer-border strip, keeping the pinked edges on the same side. Press the seam allowances in one direction. Repeat to make a total of four pieced outer-border strips.

6 Sew two outer-border strips to the sides of the quilt top, keeping the pinked edges on the outside. Press the seam allowances toward the outer border.

7 Join 2½" squares to the ends of the two remaining outer-border strips. Press the seam allowances toward the border strip. Sew these borders to the top and bottom of the quilt top and press the seam allowances toward the outer border.

8 Layer, baste, and quilt as desired. Using the 2"-wide binding strips, make and attach binding.

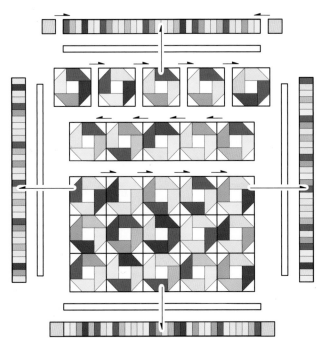

Quilt layout

# Album

Use this friendship quilt to display the names of special people or perhaps favorite quotes or other sentiments. Personalize your album quilt by signing your name (or the names of others) in the light squares.

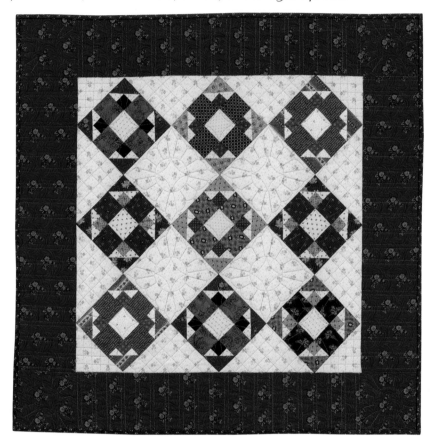

By Kathleen Tracy; machine quilted by Dawn Larsen

FINISHED QUILT SIZE: 36" x 36"     FINISHED BLOCK SIZE: 6" x 6"

## Materials

*Yardage is based on 42"-wide fabric unless otherwise noted.*

¾ yard of red print for border

⅝ yard of light shirting print for setting blocks and triangles

⅝ yard *total* of assorted medium and dark prints for blocks

⅜ yard *total* of assorted light prints for blocks

⅜ yard of dark-blue print for binding

1⅓ yards of fabric for backing

42" x 42" piece of cotton batting

## Cutting

*All measurements include ¼"-wide seam allowances.*

### For 1 Block (Cut 9 total.)

**From one assorted light print, cut:**

1 square, 2½" x 2½"

4 squares, 1⅞" x 1⅞"; cut in half diagonally to make 8 triangles

**From one assorted medium or dark print, cut:**

4 squares, 2½" x 2½"

**From a second medium or dark print, cut:**

2 squares, 2⅞" x 2⅞"; cut in half diagonally to make 4 triangles

**From a third medium or dark print, cut:**

4 squares, 1½" x 1½"

*For the Setting Pieces, Border, and Binding*

**From the light shirting print, cut:**

4 squares, 6½" x 6½"

2 squares, 9¾" x 9¾"; cut into quarters diagonally to make 8 triangles

2 squares, 5⅛" x 5⅛"; cut in half diagonally to make 4 triangles

**From the red print, cut:**

2 strips, 5½" x 26"

2 strips, 5½" x 36"

**From the dark-blue print, cut:**

4 strips, 2" x 42"

## Making the Blocks

1 Sew two matching light-print 1⅞" triangles to adjacent sides of a medium or dark 1½" square. Press the seam allowances toward the triangles. Make four.

Make 4.

2 Sew a medium or dark 2⅞" triangle to the long edge of each unit from step 1. Press the seam allowances toward the larger triangles.

Make 4.

3 Arrange the units from step 2, four medium or dark 2½" squares, and a light-print 2½" square in rows as shown. Sew the rows and press the seam allowances toward the darker squares. Sew the rows together to make the block.

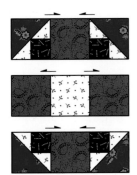

4 Repeat steps 1–3 to make a total of nine blocks.

## Assembling the Quilt

1 Referring to the quilt diagram, lay out the blocks, the light shirting 6½" squares, and the side setting triangles into diagonal rows. Sew the blocks into rows; press the seam allowances toward the setting pieces. Sew the rows together, pressing the seam allowances in opposite directions. Add the corner setting triangles and press toward the triangles.

2 Sew the red-print 5½" x 26" strips to the sides of the quilt top. Press the seam allowances toward the border. Sew the red-print 5½" x 36" strips to the top and bottom of the quilt. Press toward the border.

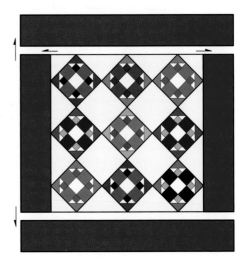

## Finishing the Quilt

1 Layer the quilt top, batting, and backing; baste the layers together.

2 Quilt as desired. This quilt was machine quilted with a medallion design in the center of the blocks and straight lines in the border. Omit the quilting in the center of the blocks if you add signatures.

3 Attach the blue-print binding to the quilt.

# Answer All Invitations That Ask You to RSVP

*It's only polite and proper to respond to invitations in a timely manner. Of course, everyone will want to accept an invitation to see this charming little quilt!*

By Mary Etherington and Connie Tesene of Country Threads

FINISHED QUILT SIZE: 24" x 24"    FINISHED BLOCK SIZE: 8" x 8"

## Materials

*Yardage is based on 42"-wide fabric unless otherwise noted. Charm squares are 5" x 5".*

36 charm squares in an assortment of light, medium, and dark values*

¼ yard of black print for binding

⅞ yard of fabric for backing

30" x 30" piece of batting

*You can substitute fat eighths (9" x 20") of 4 red, 4 light gold, 2 brown, 2 blue, and 2 green fabrics. Cut a total of 36 charm squares, about half lighter in value than the others.*

## Cutting

*All measurements include ¼"-wide seam allowances.*

**From the black print, cut:**

3 strips, 2¼" x 42"

## Assembling the Quilt

Each block is made up of two matching half-square-triangle units and two matching four-patch units.

1 Pair nine light charm squares with nine dark charm squares. Trim each square to 4⅞" x 4⅞" and draw a diagonal line from corner to corner on the wrong side of the light fabrics.

$2$ Place a light square and a dark square from step 1 right sides together and stitch ¼" from the line on each side. Cut in half along the line, creating two matching triangle units. Press the seam allowances toward the darker fabric. Make nine pairs of half-square-triangle units (18 total).

Make 9 matching pairs.

$3$ Layer two charm squares right sides together. Sew ¼" in from each side and cut in half, 2½" from the edge. Press the seam allowances toward the darker fabric.

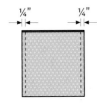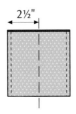

$4$ Layer the two units from step 3 right sides together with the light fabrics opposite the dark fabrics, matching the seams. Sew ¼" in from each side and cut in half, 2½" from the edge. Press the seam allowances open. You'll have two matching four-patch units.

$5$ Repeat steps 3 and 4 to make nine pairs of four-patch units (18 total).

$6$ Pair two matching half-square-triangle units with two matching four-patch units to create one block. Sew the triangle units to the four-patch units as shown and press the seam allowances open. Sew the resulting matching units together and press the seam allowances open. Make nine blocks.

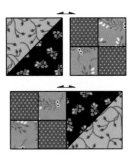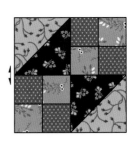

Make 9.

$7$ Arrange the blocks in three rows of three blocks each. Sew the blocks into rows, pressing the seam allowances open. Sew the rows together and press.

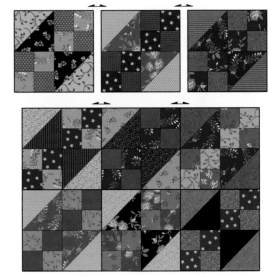

## Finishing the Quilt

Make a quilt back approximately 30" x 30". Layer the quilt top with batting and backing. Baste, and then quilt as desired. Trim the excess batting and backing and bind the quilt with the black-print 2¼"-wide strips.

# Tumbling Blocks

*This quilt was inspired by a photo of a Tumbling Blocks quilt made in 1882 by President Calvin Coolidge when he was a child. If you've never hand pieced before, try it here—you may be surprised to find out how much fun it is.*

By Kathleen Tracy

FINISHED QUILT SIZE: 19½" x 27⅝"    FINISHED BLOCK SIZE: 3" hexagon

## Materials

*Yardage is based on 42"-wide fabric unless otherwise noted.*

⅛ yard of brown reproduction print for border

⅛ yard of tan reproduction print for border

Scraps of assorted prints in light, medium, and dark shades, each at least 2½" x 5", for 168 diamonds

¼ yard of indigo print for binding

⅞ yard of fabric for backing

20" x 30" piece of cotton batting

Template plastic

## Cutting

*All measurements include ¼"-wide seam allowances.*

**From the brown reproduction print, cut:**

2 strips, 1¾" x 24⅛"

**From the tan reproduction print, cut:**

2 strips, 2¼" x 19½"

**From the indigo print, cut:**

2 strips, 2" x 42"

## Making the Blocks

1 Using the pattern on page 229, trace the diamond shape onto template plastic and cut it out on the line. Using a water-soluble marking pen, trace around the template on the right side of the assorted scraps. Cut out each shape, leaving a scant ¼" seam allowance all around. Cut 168.

2 On the wrong side of each diamond, place a small dot where the seams will intersect. Use an accurate ¼" seam allowance.

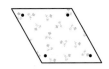

3 For accurate piecing, you'll need to sew a Y seam. With right sides together, sew a light diamond to a medium diamond, sewing from dot to dot and avoiding stitching into the ¼" seam allowances. Sew a dark diamond to one edge of the Y-shaped sewn unit in the same way. Stitch the other edge of the dark diamond to the finished unit. Make 54 blocks. (You will have six diamonds left over; set these aside for later.)

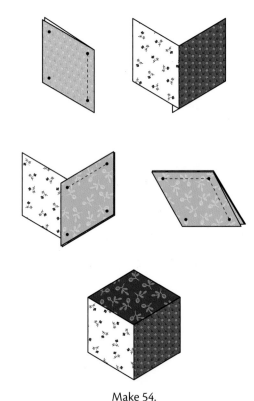

Make 54.

## Assembling the Quilt

1 Lay out the hexagons in nine rows of six blocks each. Sew the hexagons together into rows. Sew six diamond pieces to the bottom edge of the quilt top to fill out the rows. Press.

2 Using a long ruler, trim the top and bottom edges of the quilt, leaving a ¼" seam allowance. Trim the side edges even with the edge of the shorter rows of blocks as shown.

3 Sew the 1¾" x 24⅛" brown strips to the sides of the quilt top. Press the seam allowances toward the border. Sew the 2¼" x 19½" tan strips to the top and bottom of the quilt top. Press toward the border.

## Finishing the Quilt

1 Layer the quilt top, batting, and backing; baste the layers together.

2 Quilt ¼" along the blocks in horizontal rows.

3 Attach the binding to the quilt.

**Diamond**
Cut 168.

Pattern does not
include seam allowance.

# Four-Patch Pinwheels

*This simple Pinwheel block is perfect for using up small odds and ends of fabrics. Choose two background prints that you love—one for the blocks and one for the setting triangles and sashing. The rest can come from your scrap basket.*

By Ellen Pahl

**FINISHED QUILT SIZE: 31½" x 41½"   FINISHED BLOCK SIZE: 6" x 6"**

## Materials

*Yardage is based on 42"-wide fabric unless otherwise noted.*

1 yard of light print #1 for sashing and setting triangles

⅝ yard of light print #2 for block backgrounds

½ yard *total* of scraps of assorted medium to dark fabrics for blocks and sashing squares

⅓ yard of light-dotted print for binding

1½ yards of fabric for backing

36" x 46" piece of batting

# Cutting

*All measurements include ¼"-wide seam allowances.*

**From the assorted medium to dark fabrics, cut a total of:**

89 squares, 1½" x 1½"

72 rectangles, 1½" x 2½"

**From light print #2, cut:**

7 strips, 2½" x 42"; crosscut into 72 rectangles, 2½" x 3½"

**From light print #1, cut:**

9 strips, 1½" x 42"; crosscut into:

    36 rectangles, 1½" x 6½"

    10 rectangles, 1½" x 7½"

    2 rectangles, 1½" x 8½"

3 squares, 11½" x 11½"; cut into quarters diagonally to make 12 side triangles (2 will be extra)

2 squares, 6¾" x 6¾"; cut in half diagonally to make 4 corner triangles

**From the light-dotted print, cut:**

4 strips, 2⅛" x 42"

# Making the Blocks

1 Using the assorted medium or dark pieces, sew a 1½" square to each 1½" x 2½" rectangle. Press. Make 72.

Make 72.

2 Sew each unit from step 1 to a 2½" x 3½" light-print #2 rectangle. Press. Make 72.

Make 72.

3 Sew four units from step 2 together to make a block. Press. Repeat to make a total of 18 blocks.

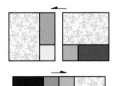
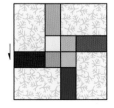

Make 18.

# Assembling the Quilt

1 Arrange the blocks, light-print #1 sashing strips, medium or dark sashing squares, and light-print #1 setting triangles in diagonal rows as shown in the quilt diagram. Sew together into rows and press.

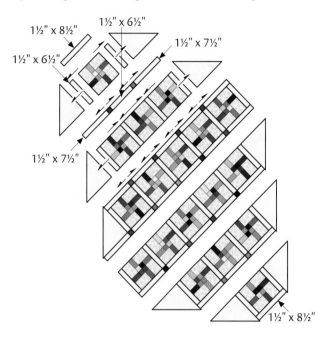

2 Sew the rows together; press. Add the corner triangles last; press.

3 Trim and square up the quilt as needed, making sure to leave ¼" beyond the points of the sashing strips.

# Finishing the Quilt

Layer, baste, quilt as desired, and add the dotted-print binding. The quilt shown features a spiral in each block, partial spirals in the setting triangles, and a random wavy line in the sashing.

# Walk—Don't Run

*"Walk—don't run" is usually good advice, unless of course it's Shop Hop time or your favorite quilt store is having a sale.*

By Mary Etherington and Connie Tesene of Country Threads

FINISHED QUILT SIZE: 23¾" x 38"    FINISHED BLOCK SIZE: 4¾" x 4¾"

## Materials

*Yardage is based on 42"-wide fabric unless otherwise noted. Charm squares are 5" x 5".*

40 assorted charm squares for block backgrounds*
⅛ yard *each* of 4 coordinating fabrics for blocks
¼ yard of red-striped fabric for binding
1⅓ yards of fabric for backing
28" x 42" piece of batting
*You can substitute 5" x 10" scraps of 20 assorted prints. Cut 2 squares, 5" x 5", from each.*

## Cutting

*All measurements include ¼"-wide seam allowances.*

**From the charm squares, cut:**
80 triangles (cut each square in half diagonally)
**From *each* of the 4 coordinating fabrics, cut:**
2 strips, 1½" x 42"; crosscut into 10 rectangles,
    1½" x 8" (40 total)
**From the red-striped fabric, cut:**
4 strips, 1½" x 42"

## Assembling the Quilt

1 Sew a coordinating 1½" x 8" rectangle between two matching triangles as shown. Press the seam allowances toward the triangles. Make 40.

2 Trim the excess from the strip and square up the blocks so they measure 5¼" x 5¼".

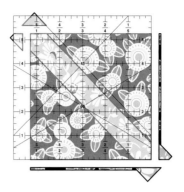

3 Arrange the blocks in eight rows of five blocks each as shown. Sew the blocks into rows and press seam allowances in opposite directions from row to row. Sew the rows together and press.

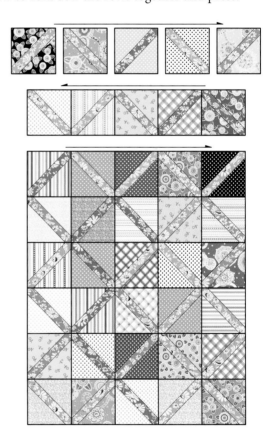

## Finishing the Quilt

Layer the quilt top with batting and backing; baste. Quilt as desired. Sew the 1½"-wide red-striped strips together end to end to make one long strip. Use this strip to bind your quilt.

# Three of Hearts

*The combination of red and white is one of those classic color schemes that never goes out of style. Make this quilt to cheer up a blank wall, use on a table for Valentine's Day, or give as a special treat to brighten someone's day.*

By Ellen Pahl

**FINISHED QUILT SIZE: 26" x 28"**    **FINISHED BLOCK SIZE: 3" x 3"**

## Materials

*Yardage is based on 42"-wide fabric unless otherwise noted. Fat quarters measure approximately 18" x 21".*

1 yard of cream print for background and borders

⅜ yard *total* of assorted red prints for hearts and blocks

⅛ yard *OR* 1 fat quarter *each* of 2 different red prints for sashing

¼ yard of red print for binding*

1 yard of fabric for backing

30" x 32" piece of batting

*\*Or make a scrappy binding with ¼ yard total of assorted red prints.*

## Cutting

*All measurements include ¼"-wide seam allowances.*

**From the cream print, cut:**

1 rectangle, 7½" x 18"

2 strips, 2⅜" x 42"; crosscut into 32 squares, 2⅜" x 2⅜". Cut each square in half diagonally to make 64 triangles.

1 strip, 5½" x 42"; crosscut into 6 squares, 5½" x 5½". Cut each square into quarters diagonally to make 24 side triangles.

1 strip, 3" x 42"; crosscut into 8 squares, 3" x 3". Cut each square in half diagonally to make 16 corner triangles.

1 strip, 4¾" x 42"; crosscut into 2 strips, 4¾" x 17½"

1 strip, 5¾" x 20"; crosscut into 2 rectangles, 5¾" x 9"

**From the assorted red prints, cut a *total* of:**

32 squares, 2⅜" x 2⅜"; cut squares in half diagonally to make 64 triangles

**From *each* of the 2 red prints for sashing, cut:**

2 strips, 1½" x 17½" (4 total)

**From the red print for binding, cut:**

3 strips, 2⅛" x 42" (or strips to total 120")

## Appliquéing the Hearts

1 Prepare the heart appliqués using the template on page 236 and your favorite appliqué method.

2 Fold the cream 7½" x 18" rectangle in half both ways to mark the vertical and horizontal centers. Position and pin the three hearts in place on the rectangle so that they are centered and spaced evenly. The background is cut slightly oversized so that you can trim it to size after stitching the appliqués.

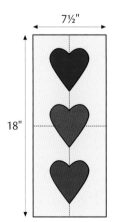

3 Appliqué the hearts in place.

## Making the Pinwheel Blocks

1 Sew each red 2⅜" triangle to a cream 2⅜" triangle along the long edges. Press. Make 64 half-square-triangle units.

Make 64.

2 Sew two different units from step 1 together (you'll need two matching pairs for each block), and then sew matching pairs together to make the Pinwheel block. Arrange the units to make eight blocks with triangles spinning one way and eight blocks spinning the opposite direction.

Make 8 of each.

## Assembling the Quilt

1 Trim the appliquéd center rectangle so that it measures 7" x 17½". Be sure to keep the hearts centered.

2 Sew a red 1½" x 17½" strip to each side of the appliquéd center. Press.

3 Arrange four Pinwheel blocks (spinning in the same direction) with six side triangles and four corner triangles as shown. Sew together into diagonal units, pressing the seam allowances as indicated.

Sew the units together to make a Pinwheel row. Make four Pinwheel rows.

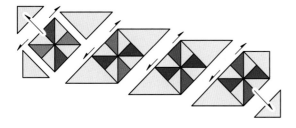

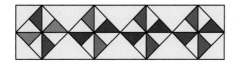

Make 2.

Make 2.

4 Sew matching Pinwheel rows to each side of the quilt center. Press toward the red strips.

5 Sew a cream 4¾" x 17½" strip to each side of the quilt center. Press.

6 Sew a red 1½" x 17½" strip to each of the remaining two Pinwheel rows. Press. Sew a cream 5¾" x 9" rectangle to the right end of each row unit as shown. Press.

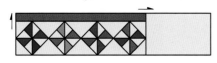

Make 2.

7 Sew the units from step 6 to the top and bottom of the quilt center. Press.

# Finishing the Quilt

Layer, baste, quilt, and add the red-print binding. The quilting shown features a meandering leaf and vine in the background of the hearts and feathers in the outer borders.

Pattern does not include seam allowance.

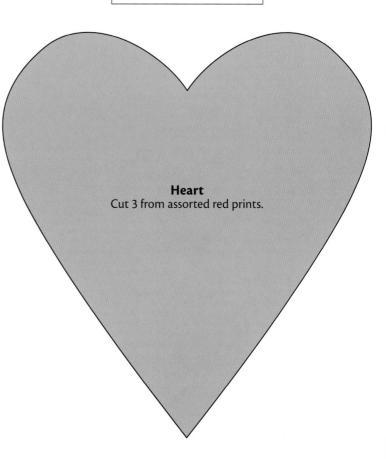

**Heart**
Cut 3 from assorted red prints.

# Vintage Bow Ties

*This quilt was modeled on a darling little antique doll quilt, made with red-and-black polka-dot bow ties and aqua squares. If red's not your thing, you can find dozens of other possibilities!*

By Karen Costello Soltys

FINISHED QUILT SIZE: 15½" x 18½"    FINISHED BLOCK SIZE: 3" x 3"

## Materials

*Fat quarters measure approximately 18" x 21".*

1 fat quarter of red polka-dot fabric for bow ties
1 fat quarter of white-striped shirting fabric for bow
  tie backgrounds

1 fat quarter of turquoise print for alternate blocks
  and binding
1 fat quarter of fabric for backing
18" x 21" piece of batting

# Cutting

*All measurements include ¼"-wide seam allowances.*

**From the red polka-dot fabric, cut:**

4 strips, 2" x 21"; crosscut into 30 squares, 2" x 2"

2 strips, 1¼" x 21"; crosscut into 30 squares, 1¼" x 1¼"

**From the white-striped shirting fabric, cut:**

4 strips, 2" x 21"; crosscut into 30 squares, 2" x 2"

**From the turquoise print, cut:***

3 strips, 3½" x 18"; crosscut into 15 squares, 3½" x 3½"

4 strips, 2" x 18"

*\*To ensure that you'll have enough fabric, cut strips along the 18" width of the fat quarter rather than along the 21" length.*

## Making the Bow Tie Blocks

1 Position a red 1¼" square on the upper-right corner of each white 2" square, right sides together. If you're using a striped fabric, position the stripes vertically for each unit if you want all the stripes to face the same way in the finished blocks. Stitch from corner to corner as shown. Press to set the seam; then flip open the red triangle and press again. Trim away the underneath layers to create a ¼" seam allowance and reduce bulk. Make 30.

Make 30.

2 Sew the units from step 1 to the red 2" squares as shown. Press the seam allowances toward the red squares. Sew the units together to make a Bow Tie block. Make 15.

Make 30.

Bow Tie block.
Make 15.

# Assembling the Quilt

1 Lay out the Bow Tie blocks and the turquoise squares in rows. Notice that the layout isn't exactly symmetrical in the quilt shown. While the blocks and turquoise squares alternate, the top row has bow ties in the corners but the bottom row has turquoise squares in the corners.

Quilt plan

2 Sew the blocks together into rows, pressing the seam allowances toward the turquoise squares. Then sew the rows together. Press all seam allowances in one direction.

# Finishing the Quilt

1 Mark any quilting designs on the quilt top.

2 Place the backing right side down on a table or floor, and lay the batting on top, smoothing out any wrinkles. Then add the pressed quilt top, right side up, on top. Hand or pin baste the layers together.

3 Quilt by hand or machine. The quilt shown was hand quilted. The bow ties and white background pieces feature outline quilting, with stitching ¼" from the seams. Each turquoise square was quilted first with an X from corner to corner, and then an on-point square was added.

4 Using the turquoise 2"-wide strips, make and attach binding.

# Lava Flow

*The strong, hot colors of the pink and orange fabrics might make you think of molten lava flowing from an active volcano, but any group of related colors would be equally effective in this design.*

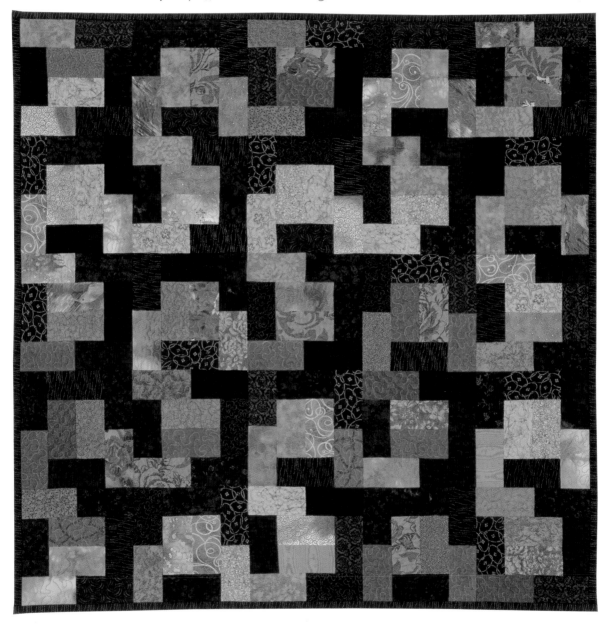

By Margaret Rolfe; quilted by Beth Reid

FINISHED QUILT SIZE: 40" x 40"    FINISHED BLOCK SIZE: 8" x 8"

## Materials

*Yardage is based on 42"-wide fabric unless otherwise noted.*

1 yard *total* of assorted black and navy prints for blocks

1 yard *total* of assorted bright pink, orange, red, and purple prints for blocks

½ yard of navy print for binding

1¼ yards of fabric for backing

44" x 44" piece of batting

## Cutting

*All measurements include ¼"-wide seam allowances.*

**From the assorted black and navy prints, cut a total of:**

100 rectangles, 2½" x 4½"

**From the assorted bright pink, orange, red, and purple prints, cut a total of:**

100 rectangles, 2½" x 4½"

**From the navy print, cut:**

5 strips, 3" x 42"

## Making the Blocks

You'll need a total of 25 pieced blocks for this quilt. Avoid duplicating prints within the blocks.

1 Arrange four black or navy print and four pink, orange, red, or purple print rectangles. Shade the pink, orange, red, and purple prints from light to dark, juxtaposing the pinks with oranges and the reds with purples to increase the vibrancy of the color.

2 Sew the rectangles together as shown; press. Make 25 blocks.

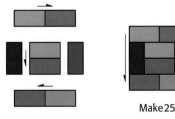

Make 25.

## Assembling the Quilt

1 Arrange the blocks in five horizontal rows of five blocks each. Make sure to rotate the blocks within each row. Place the blocks so that the different values of the red prints flow through the "curves."

2 Sew the blocks together into rows. Press the seam allowances in opposite directions from row to row.

3 Pin and sew the rows together; press.

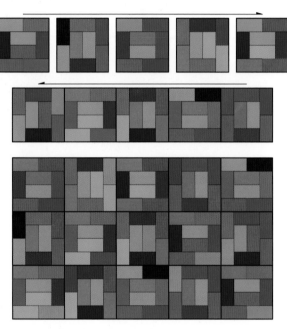

Assembly diagram

## Finishing the Quilt

1 Center and layer the quilt top and batting over the backing; baste.

2 Quilt as desired.

3 Use the navy 3"-wide strips to make the binding. Sew the binding to the quilt.

# Don't Tilt Your Chair at the Table

*If you were a fidgety or restless child, chances are you've heard this rule! On the other hand, tilted blocks are not only attractive in quilts, they're much easier to make than they look.*

By Mary Etherington and Connie Tesene of Country Threads

FINISHED QUILT SIZE: 34" x 40"    FINISHED BLOCK SIZE: 3" x 3"

## Materials

*Yardage is based on 42"-wide fabric unless otherwise noted. Charm squares are 5" x 5".*

80 assorted charm squares for blocks*
½ yard of pink print for inner border
½ yard of turquoise print for outer border
⅓ yard of green fabric for binding

1⅓ yards of fabric for backing
40" x 46" piece of batting
Template plastic *OR* Lil' Twister acrylic template (available from your local quilt shop or Country Threads: www.CountryThreads.com)
*You can substitute 10 assorted strips, 5" x 42"; cut 8 squares, 5" x 5", from each.*

# Cutting

*All measurements include ¼"-wide seam allowances.*

**From the pink print, cut:**
5 strips, 3¼" x 42"

**From the turquoise print, cut:**
4 strips, 4" x 42"

**From the green fabric, cut:**
4 strips, 2¼" x 42"

## Creating the Quilt

1 Sew the charm squares together in 10 rows of eight charm squares each. Press the seam allowances in opposite directions from row to row. Try to place charm squares with good contrast next to each other.

2 Sew the pink 3¼"-wide strips together to make a long strip. Cut two borders the length of the quilt and sew them to the sides of the quilt center. Cut two borders the width of the quilt and sew them to the top and bottom of the center. Press the seam allowances toward the borders.

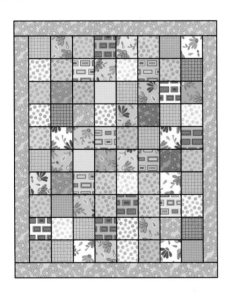

3 If you don't have the purchased acrylic template, cut a square of template plastic, 3½" x 3½". Make a mark on each side of the square 1" from the corner. Connect the marks diagonally to make a tilted X on the template square.

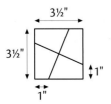

4 Place the template on the quilt top. Align the marks on the template with the seam lines; the template square will be tilted at an angle to the seams. Cut along each side of the template to make a tilted block. Repeat with all the seam intersections, including the pink borders. It's helpful to place the blocks on a work wall as you cut them to keep them in order. You'll have a total of 99 tilted blocks.

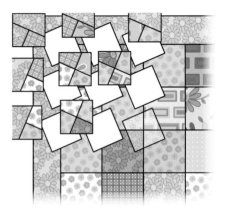

5 Keeping them in order, sew the blocks together in 11 rows of nine blocks each. Press the seam allowances in opposite directions from row to row. Cut two turquoise 4"-wide strips the width of the quilt top and sew them to the top and bottom of the quilt. Cut the remaining turquoise strips the length of the quilt and sew them to the sides. Press toward the borders.

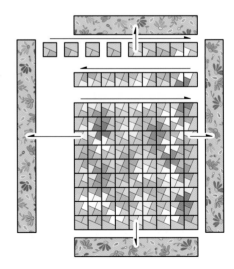

## Finishing the Quilt

Make a quilt back approximately 40" x 46". Layer the quilt top with batting and backing. Baste, and then quilt as desired. Trim the excess batting and backing and bind the quilt with the green 2¼"-wide strips.

# Garden Path

*Pairing appliqué with piecing creates a stunning combination in this traditionally inspired quilt. Framed within a pieced border, the simplified appliqué motifs add to the folk-art charm.*

By Lori Smith of From My Heart to Your Hands

FINISHED QUILT SIZE: 16" x 20"    FINISHED BLOCK SIZE: 2" x 2"

## Materials

*Fat quarters measure approximately 18" x 21".*

1 fat quarter of cheddar fabric for appliqué background and borders

1 fat quarter *total* of assorted light to medium prints for appliqué and blocks

1 fat quarter *total* of assorted medium to dark prints for appliqué and blocks

1 fat quarter of fabric for binding

1 fat quarter of fabric for backing

18" x 22" piece of batting

# Cutting

*All measurements include ¼"-wide seam allowances.*

**From the cheddar fabric, cut:**

1 square, 9" x 9"

2 strips, 2½" x 12½"

2 strips, 2½" x 16½"

**From the assorted light to medium prints, cut:**

18 squares, 3¼" x 3¼"; crosscut in half diagonally to make 72 triangles

**From the assorted medium to dark prints, cut:**

18 squares, 3¼" x 3¼"; crosscut into quarters diagonally to make 72 triangles

**From the binding fabric, cut:**

4 strips, 1¾" x 20"

## Appliquéing the Center

1  Prepare the appliqué pieces using the patterns on page 245. Cut the stems on the bias.

2  Fold and lightly press the cheddar 9" background square in fourths to find the center.

3  Align the dashed lines on the appliqué pattern with the creases in the background fabric. Mark the appliqué pattern on the background fabric.

4  Arrange the appliqué pieces on the background and appliqué them in place using your favorite method.

5  Press the appliquéd quilt center from the wrong side and trim to 8½" x 8½", centering the design.

## Making the Hourglass Blocks and Border

1  Sew together two light and two dark triangles as shown to make an Hourglass block; press. Make 36 Hourglass blocks.

Make 36.

2  Sew four Hourglass blocks together; press. Make two of these strips for the side borders. Sew six Hourglass blocks together for the top and bottom; press. Repeat to make four of these strips.

Make 2.

Make 4.

3  Sew the shorter strips from step 2 to the sides of the appliquéd quilt center; press. Sew the longer strips from step 2 to the top and bottom; press. Sew a second border strip to the top and bottom.

## Assembling and Finishing the Quilt

1  Sew the cheddar 2½" x 16½" strips to the sides of the quilt; press.

2  Sew an Hourglass block to each end of the remaining two cheddar border strips. Sew them to the top and bottom of the quilt.

3  Layer the quilt top, batting, and backing. Baste the layers together and quilt as desired. Add the binding and enjoy.

Patterns do not include seam allowances.

# Wipe Your Feet

*The blocks in this quilt resemble small trees that meet in the center in a miniature forest. And remember, after tromping through the farm or the woods, wipe your feet before entering the house.*

By Mary Etherington and Connie Tesene of Country Threads

FINISHED QUILT SIZE: 26" x 26"    FINISHED BLOCK SIZE: 6" x 6"

## Materials

*Yardage is based on 42"-wide fabric unless otherwise noted. Charm squares are 5" x 5".*

20 charm squares in assorted medium to dark values of brown, red, and green for "trees" and cornerstones

½ yard of brown print for sashing, inner border, and binding

⅜ yard of olive-green plaid for outer border

⅛ yard of tan print #1 for block backgrounds

⅛ yard of tan print #2 for block backgrounds

⅛ yard of dark-brown *OR* black print for tree trunks

1 yard of fabric for backing

30" x 30" piece of batting

## Making Do

If you don't have a set of precut charm squares, you'll need a 4" x 8" strip *each* of nine different prints in medium to dark values of brown, red, and green, and a 4" x 4" scrap of light-brown print. (Using additional fabrics will make your quilt look more like the sample.) Cut the light-brown print into four squares, 1½" x 1½", for cornerstones. Cut each of the nine different prints into two squares, 3⅞" x 3⅞" (18 total). Cut each of these squares in half diagonally to make two triangles (36 total).

## Cutting

*All measurements include ¼"-wide seam allowances.*

**From *each of 2* of the lightest-value charm squares, cut:**

2 squares, 1½" x 1½" (4 total)

**From *each* of the remaining 18 charm squares, cut:**

1 square, 3⅞" x 3⅞"; cut in half diagonally to make 2 triangles (36 total)

**From the dark-brown or black print, cut:**

3 strips, 1¼" x 42"

**From *each* of the tan prints, cut:**

9 squares, 3⅞" x 3⅞" (18 total)

**From the brown print, cut:**

2 strips, 1½" x 42"; crosscut into 12 strips, 1½" x 6½"

2 strips, 1½" x 20½"

2 strips, 1½" x 22½"

3 strips, 1½" x 42"

**From the olive-green plaid, cut:**

2 strips, 2½" x 22½"

2 strips, 2½" x 26½"

## Assembling the Quilt

The blocks in this quilt resemble four small trees that meet in the center. Trees opposite one another are made from matching fabric. The two different background fabrics are used in each block throughout the quilt.

1 Press under ¼" on both long edges of the dark-brown or black print strips. With right sides facing up, lay each strip diagonally on the 3⅞" tan squares to make tree trunks.

2 Topstitch the tree-trunk strips to the tan squares, stitching close to each long edge. Cut the squares apart.

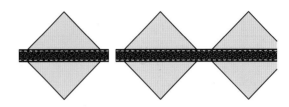

3 Cut each tan square in half diagonally to yield 18 triangles from each of the tan prints (36 total). Trim the tree trunks to the edge of the triangles, keeping triangles of the same fabric together.

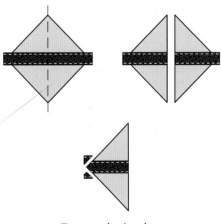

Tree-trunk triangle.
Make 36.

Sew matching tree-trunk triangles to the charm-square triangles along the long edges. Make two matching tree units.

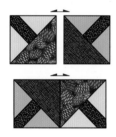

Tree unit.
Make 18 pairs.

 Using two matching tree units with one tan print and two matching tree units with the other tan print, sew the pieced units together. Try to choose two charm-square prints that look different from each other. Press seam allowances open. Make a total of nine blocks.

Tree block.
Make 9.

6 Lay out the blocks and brown 1½" x 6½" sashing strips as shown. Position the four 1½" cornerstones. Sew the blocks, sashing, and cornerstones into rows, and then sew the rows together. Press toward the sashing.

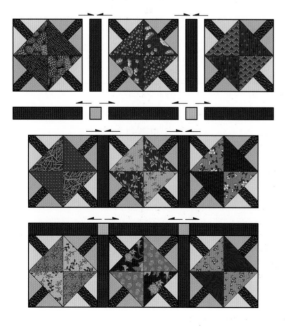

7 For the inner border, sew the brown 1½" x 20½" strips to the sides of the quilt. Press the seam allowances toward the strips. Sew the brown 1½" x 22½" strips to the top and the bottom of the quilt. Press the seam allowances toward the strips. Repeat, using the olive-green plaid strips for the outer border.

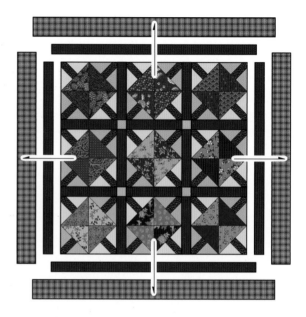

## Finishing the Quilt

Layer the quilt top with batting and backing; baste. Quilt as desired. Sew the brown 1½" x 42" strips together end to end to make one long strip. Use this strip to bind your quilt.

# Never Leave the Table Before the Other Guests

*No one will want to leave a table with this little centerpiece on it. They'll be too busy admiring all the little squares, never guessing that strip-piecing techniques make this a quick and easy project.*

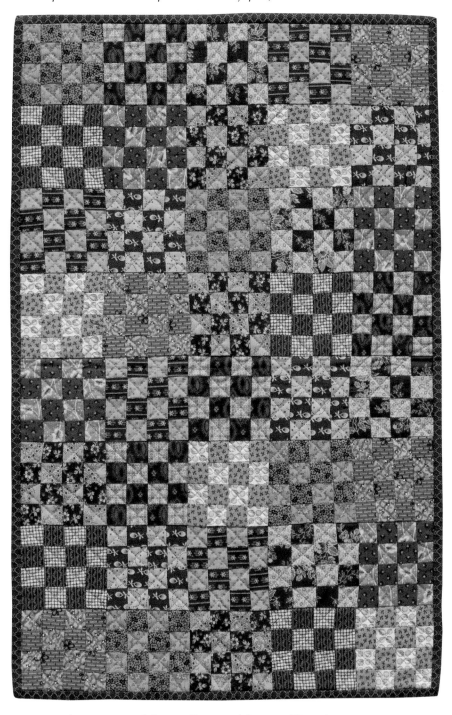

By Mary Etherington and Connie Tesene of Country Threads

FINISHED QUILT SIZE: 15" x 24"    FINISHED BLOCK SIZE: 3" x 3"

## Materials

*Yardage is based on 42"-wide fabric unless otherwise noted. Charm squares are 5" x 5".*

20 assorted medium- to dark-blue charm squares for blocks

20 assorted light-brown and gold charm squares for blocks

⅛ yard of dark-blue print for binding

⅝ yard of fabric for backing

21" x 30" piece of batting

## Making Do

If you don't have a set of precut charm squares, you'll need a minimum of 10 medium- to dark-blue strips, 2½" x 21", and 10 light-brown or gold strips, 2½" x 21". Cut each strip in half lengthwise, and in step 1 below, use the resulting 1¼" x 21" strips to make 10 strip units.

## Cutting

*All measurements include ¼"-wide seam allowances.*

**From each charm square, cut:**

4 rectangles, 1¼" x 5" (80 dark and 80 light total)*

**From the dark-blue print, cut:**

3 strips, 2¼" x 42"

*Keep rectangles of the same fabric together.*

## Creating the Quilt

Each 16 Patch block is made from one dark- or medium-blue fabric and one light-brown or gold fabric.

1 Alternate and sew together two matching blue 1¼" x 5" rectangles and two matching brown or gold 1¼" x 5" rectangles to make a strip unit as shown. Press the seam allowances in one direction. Crosscut the unit into four segments, 1¼" x 5".

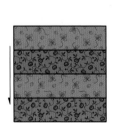

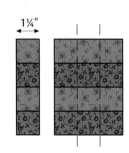

1¼"

2 Rotate every other segment 180° and sew the segments together to make a 16 Patch block. Press the seam allowances in one direction.

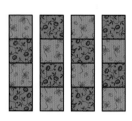

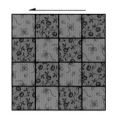

3 Repeat steps 1 and 2 with the remaining charm-square rectangles to make 40 blocks.

4 Arrange the blocks into eight rows of five blocks each, placing the blocks so the checker-board pattern continues throughout the quilt. Sew the blocks into rows and press the seam allowances in opposite directions. Sew the rows together and press.

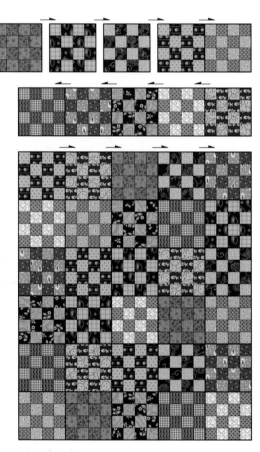

## Finishing the Quilt

Make a quilt back approximately 21" x 30". Layer the quilt top with batting and backing. Baste, and then quilt as desired. Trim the excess batting and backing and bind the quilt with the dark-blue 2¼"-wide strips.

# Log Cabin

*One of the most beloved quilt patterns from the nineteenth century has to be the Log Cabin block. This little quilt, with its light and dark strips resembling the logs in a cabin, is a perfect symbol of rugged pioneer life.*

By Kathleen Tracy

FINISHED QUILT SIZE: 14" x 18½"    FINISHED BLOCK SIZE: 4½" x 4½"

## Materials

*Yardage is based on 42"-wide fabric unless otherwise noted.*

⅛ yard *each OR* scraps of 6 to 12 dark prints for blocks

⅛ yard *each OR* scraps of 6 to 12 light prints for blocks

⅛ yard *total OR* scraps of 4 to 6 pink prints for block centers

¼ yard of medium print for binding

½ yard of fabric for backing

17" x 22" piece of cotton batting

# Cutting

*Cut the pieces in pairs from each fabric. For example, cut a 2"-long and a 2½"-long piece from the same light print and cut a 2½"-long and a 3"-long piece from the same dark print. All measurements include ¼"-wide seam allowances.*

**From the pink prints, cut:**
12 squares, 2" x 2"

**From the light prints, cut:**
12 pieces, 1" x 2"
12 pieces, 1" x 2½"
12 pieces, 1" x 3"
12 pieces, 1" x 3½"
12 pieces, 1" x 4"
12 pieces, 1" x 4½"

**From the dark prints, cut:**
12 pieces, 1" x 2½"
12 pieces, 1" x 3"
12 pieces, 1" x 3½"
12 pieces, 1" x 4"
12 pieces, 1" x 4½"
12 pieces, 1" x 5"

**From the medium print, cut:**
2 strips, 2" x 42"

## Assembling the Quilt

1 Starting with a pink 2" square, sew a light 1" x 2" piece to one side. Press away from the center. Rotate the unit so that the just-added piece is on top. Add a second light piece, 1" x 2½", to the right side of the unit. Press all the newly added pieces away from the center.

2 Rotate the block again and add a dark 1" x 2½" piece to the right side. Press. Turn and add the next dark piece, 1" x 3". Press. Continue adding pieces or "logs" in this way, alternating two light and two dark fabrics until you have three sets of light logs and three sets of dark logs, ending with the dark print.

3 Trim and square up the block, if needed, so that it measures 5" x 5". Make 12 blocks.

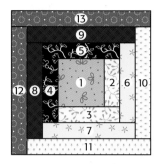

Make 12.

4 Arrange the blocks as shown. Sew together four rows of three blocks each, pressing the seam allowances in opposite directions from row to row. Sew the rows together and press the seam allowances in one direction.

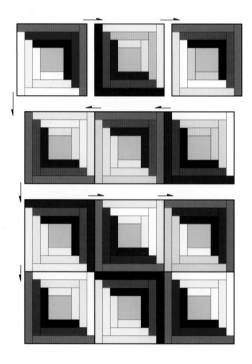

## Finishing the Quilt

1 Layer the quilt top, batting, and backing; baste the layers together.

2 Quilt in the ditch around each strip.

3 Attach the medium-print binding to the quilt.

# Indigo Blue and White

*Quilters in the Gilded Age loved indigo fabric. Just about every quilter had a blue-and-white quilt with fancy quilting she saved for a special occasion or made as an heirloom to celebrate a wedding or birth.*

By Kathleen Tracy

FINISHED QUILT SIZE: 14½" x 18½"    FINISHED BLOCK SIZE: 4" x 4"

## Materials

*Yardage is based on 42"-wide fabric unless otherwise noted.*

¼ yard of dark-indigo print for inner border

¼ yard of white-and-blue print for outer border

¼ yard *total* of assorted indigo prints for blocks

¼ yard *total* of assorted white-and-blue prints or shirtings for blocks

¼ yard of dark-blue fabric for binding

½ yard of fabric for backing

18" x 22" piece of batting

6 buttons, ⅜" in diameter

⅛"-wide dark-blue ribbon (optional)

# Cutting

*All measurements include ¼"-wide seam allowances.*

**From the assorted indigo prints, cut:**

12 squares, 3¼" x 3¼"

**From the assorted white-and-blue prints or shirtings, cut:**

12 squares, 3¼" x 3¼"

**From the dark-indigo print, cut:**

2 strips, 1" x 42"; crosscut into 2 pieces, 1" x 9½", and 2 pieces, 1" x 12½"

**From the white-and-blue print, cut:**

2 strips, 3" x 42"; crosscut into 2 pieces, 3" x 13½", and 2 pieces, 3" x 14½"

**From the dark-blue fabric, cut:**

2 strips, 2" x 42"

## Assembling the Quilt

1 Layer each indigo square with a white-and-blue square, right sides together and with the light square on top. Draw a diagonal line across each light square. Stitch ¼" from the line on both sides and cut on the drawn line. Press the seam allowances toward the darker fabric. Cut these squares on the diagonal as shown to make two triangle units from each square. Sew the triangle units together as shown and press in either direction to make 24 hourglass units.

Make 24.

2 Sew the hourglass units into six blocks as shown, alternating the shades of indigo. Press the seam allowances of each pair in opposite directions and press the joining seam allowances in either direction.

Make 6.

3 Arrange the blocks in three rows of two blocks each. Sew the blocks into rows and press the seam allowances in opposite directions from row to row. Sew the rows together and press the seam allowances in one direction.

4 Sew the two indigo 12½" pieces to the sides of the quilt center, pressing the seam allowances toward the border. Sew the two indigo 9½" pieces to the top and bottom of the quilt center and press again.

5 Sew the two white-and-blue 13½" pieces to the sides of the quilt top, pressing the seam allowances toward the outer border. Sew the two white-and-blue 14½" pieces to the top and bottom of the quilt top and press again.

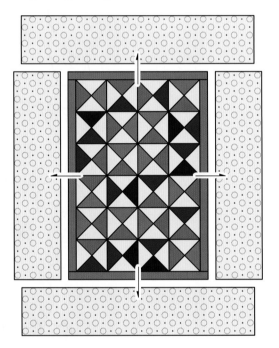

## Finishing the Quilt

1 Layer the quilt top, batting, and backing; baste the layers together.

2 Quilt in the ditch around the six blocks and around the outside edge of the inner border. Quilt the outer border using a decorative stitch on your sewing machine. Sew a button in the center of each block and add a small dark-blue bow to each corner.

3 Attach the binding to the quilt.

# Native American Quilt

*This colorful little quilt was inspired by the many traditional patterns found on Native American baskets, woven blankets, and rugs.*

By Kathleen Tracy
FINISHED QUILT SIZE: 17¼" x 17¼"    FINISHED BLOCK SIZE: 4½" x 4½"

## Materials

*Yardage is based on 42"-wide fabric unless otherwise noted.*

¼ yard of gold print for blocks

¼ yard of medium-blue print for setting square and triangles

⅛ yard of red print for blocks

⅛ yard of indigo print for blocks

⅛ yard of dark-green print for border

⅛ yard of tan print for border

¼ yard of red plaid for binding

⅝ yard of fabric for backing

21" x 21" piece of batting

Red quilting thread

## Cutting

*All measurements include ¼"-wide seam allowances.*

**From the gold print, cut:**

12 squares, 2⅜" x 2⅜"

8 squares, 2" x 2"

**From the red print, cut:**

6 squares, 2⅜" x 2⅜"

2 squares, 2" x 2"

**From the indigo print, cut:**

6 squares, 2⅜" x 2⅜"

2 squares, 2" x 2"

**From the medium-blue print, cut:**

1 square, 5" x 5"

2 squares, 4⅛" x 4⅛"; cut in half diagonally to make 4 corner triangles

1 square, 7⅝" x 7⅝"; cut diagonally into quarters to make 4 side triangles

**From the dark-green print, cut:**

1 strip, 2½" x 42"; crosscut into 2 pieces, 2½" x 13¼"

**From the tan print, cut:**

1 strip, 2½" x 42"; crosscut into 2 pieces, 2½" x 17¼"

**From the red plaid, cut:**

2 strips, 2" x 42"

## Assembling the Quilt

1 Draw a diagonal line from corner to corner on the wrong side of each gold 2⅜" square. Layer a marked gold square on each red 2⅜" square and each indigo 2⅜" square, right sides together. Stitch ¼" from the line on both sides. Cut on the drawn line to make 12 half-square-triangle units of each color combination. Press the seam allowances toward the darker fabric.

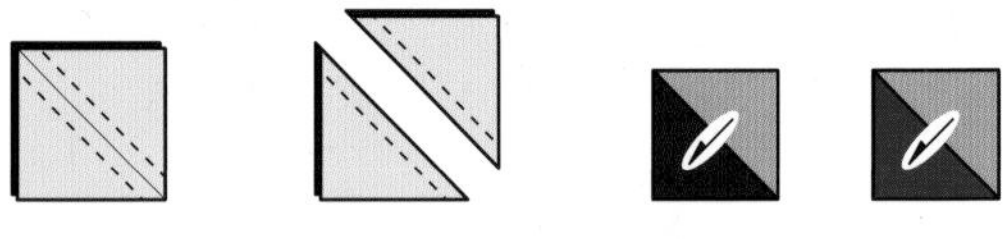

Make 12.    Make 12.

2 Arrange six indigo/gold units from step 1, a red 2" square, and two gold 2" squares in three rows as shown. Sew the units into rows, pressing the seam allowances in opposite directions from row to row. Sew the rows together. Make two blocks.

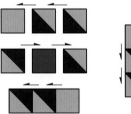 

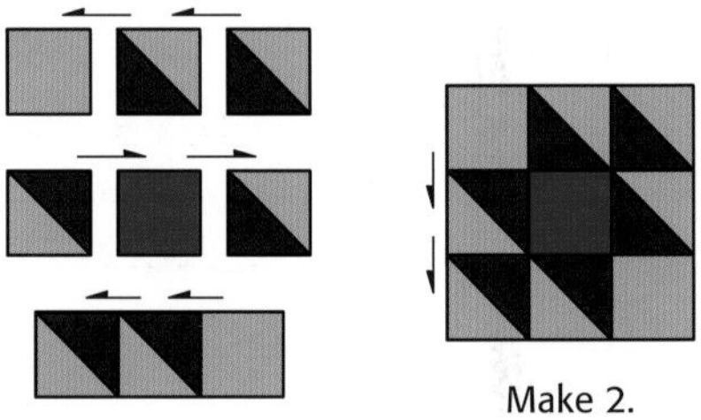

Make 2.

3 Arrange six red/gold units from step 1, an indigo 2" square, and two gold 2" squares in three rows as shown. Sew the units into rows, pressing the seam allowances in opposite directions from row to row. Sew the rows together. Make two blocks.

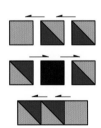 

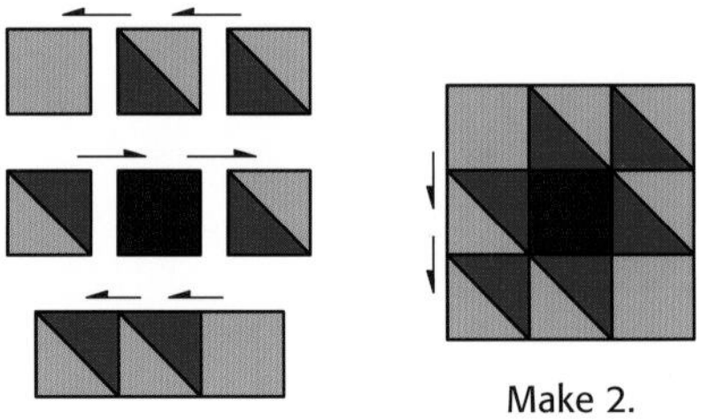

Make 2.

4 Arrange the blocks, the medium-blue 5" square, and the medium-blue setting triangles in diagonal rows as shown. Sew the diagonal rows, pressing away from the pieced blocks. Add the corner triangles and sew the rows together.

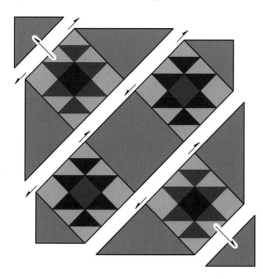

5 Trim and square up the quilt top, leaving ¼" beyond the points of the blocks.

6 Sew the green 2½" x 13¼" strips to the top and bottom of the quilt top. Press the seam allowances toward the border. Add the tan 2½" x 17¼"

strips to the sides of the quilt top, pressing toward the border.

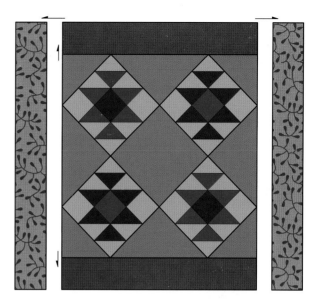

## Finishing the Quilt

1 Layer the quilt top, batting, and backing; baste the layers together.

2 Quilt in the ditch around each block and outline the indigo and red pieces with red quilting thread. Quilt four on-point squares in the central medium-blue square, bisecting the two side squares with vertical lines through the center. Quilt triangles in the medium-blue side setting triangles.

3 Attach the red-plaid binding to the quilt.

# Civil War Baskets

*Women from the Civil War era often used baskets to hold their thread, buttons, scissors, scraps, or a small sewing project. Many of us who like to make scrap quilts today would need more than one basket to hold our scrap collections!*

By Kathleen Tracy

**FINISHED QUILT SIZE:** 22½" x 26¾"  **FINISHED BLOCK SIZE:** 4" x 4"

## Materials

*Yardage is based on 42"-wide fabric unless otherwise noted.*

½ yard *total* of assorted scraps of medium to dark prints for baskets and cornerstones

¼ yard *total* of assorted scraps of light-tan prints for block backgrounds

¼ yard of blue-checked fabric for sashing

¼ yard of brown print for side borders

¼ yard of gold print for top and bottom borders

¼ yard of teal print for binding

⅞ yard of fabric for backing

26" x 31" piece of cotton batting

## Cutting

*All measurements include ¼"-wide seam allowances.*

**From the light-tan prints, cut:**

6 squares, 3¼" x 3¼"; cut into quarters diagonally to make 24 triangles

12 rectangles, 2½" x 4½"

**From the assorted scraps of medium to dark prints, cut:**

6 squares, 3¾" x 3¾"; cut in half diagonally to make 12 triangles (you'll need 1 half-square triangle to match 2 quarter-square triangles cut below)

6 squares, 3¼" x 3¼"; cut into quarters diagonally to make 24 triangles

20 squares, 1¾" x 1¾"

12 bias strips, 1¼" x 6"

**From the blue-checked fabric, cut:**

4 strips, 1¾" x 42"; crosscut into 31 pieces, 1¾" x 4½"

**From the brown print, cut:**

2 strips, 3" x 22¾"

**From the gold print, cut:**

2 strips, 2½" x 22½"

**From the teal print, cut:**

3 strips, 2" x 42"

## Making the Blocks

Each block consists of one light print for the background, one dark or medium print for the basket, and one contrasting bias strip for the handle. Select your fabrics before you piece each block.

1 To make the basket base, sew a medium 3¼" triangle to a light-tan 3¼" triangle. Press. Make 12 pairs.

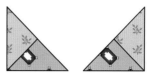

Make 12 pairs.

2 Sew the units from step 1 to the sides of a matching 3¾" triangle. Press.

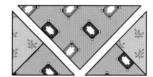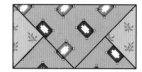

Make 12.

3 Choose a bias-strip handle from a contrasting medium print and position it on a matching light-tan 2½" x 4½" rectangle. Pin in place and stitch the handle to the rectangle. Make 12.

4 Sew each handle unit to a matching unit from step 2. Press. Make 12 blocks.

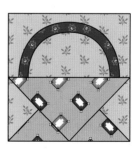

Make 12.

## Assembling the Quilt

1 Sew three blocks together with four blue-checked 1¾" x 4½" sashing pieces to make a row. Press the seam allowances toward the sashing. Make four rows.

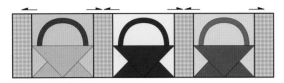

Make 4 rows.

2 Sew three blue-checked 1¾" x 4½" sashing pieces together with four medium 1¾" squares to make a sashing row. Press toward the sashing. Make five sashing rows.

Make 5 rows.

3 Sew the block rows and the sashing rows together, pressing toward the sashing rows.

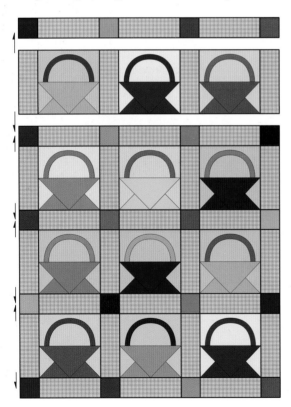

4 Sew the brown 3" x 22¾" strips to the sides of the quilt top and press the seam allowances toward the border. Sew the gold 2½" x 22½" strips to the top and bottom of the quilt top and press toward the border.

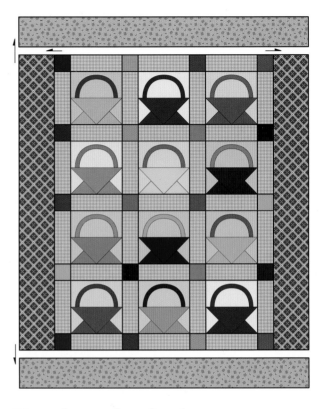

## Finishing the Quilt

1 Layer the quilt top, batting, and backing; baste the layers together.

2 Quilt as desired. The quilt shown was quilted in the ditch along the baskets, with an X in the cornerstone squares, and with a scalloped pattern in the border.

3 Attach the teal-print binding to the quilt.

# Shoofly Potpie

*Filled with unabashed charm and just a hint of spunk, this colorful little quilt embraces the prudent spirit of "making do."*

By Kim Diehl

**FINISHED QUILT SIZE:** 19¼" x 23½"    **FINISHED BLOCK SIZE:** 3" x 3"

## Materials

*Yardage is based on 42"-wide fabric unless otherwise noted. Fat quarters measure approximately 18" x 21"; fat eighths measure 9" x 21".*

1 fat quarter of light print for inner border

1 fat quarter of dark-red homespun for outer border

1 fat eighth OR assorted scraps of dark-blue homespun for border corner squares

6 assorted homespun squares, 3½" x 3½", for setting squares

5 assorted homespun squares, 5½" x 5½", for side setting triangles

2 assorted homespun squares, 3" x 3", for corner setting triangles

Assorted medium and light print scraps for block backgrounds

Assorted medium and dark print scraps for blocks and binding

¾ yard of fabric for backing

25" x 29" piece of batting

## Cutting

*All strips are cut across the width of fabric unless otherwise indicated. One background print and one medium or dark print is used for each block. Please note that in keeping with the spirit of making do, the values for several blocks in this quilt have been reversed. All measurements include ¼"-wide seam allowances.*

**From the assorted medium and light print scraps for block backgrounds, cut:**

24 squares, 1⅞" x 1⅞", in matching sets of 2; cut in half diagonally to make 48 triangles

48 squares, 1½" x 1½", in matching sets of 4

**From the assorted medium and dark print scraps for blocks and binding, cut:**

24 squares, 1⅞" x 1⅞", in matching sets of 2; cut in half diagonally to make 48 triangles

12 squares, 1½" x 1½"

Enough 2½"-wide random lengths to make 95"

**From the assorted homespun squares, cut:**

5 squares, 5½" x 5½"; cut into quarters diagonally to make 20 side setting triangles (use only 2 triangles from each color)

2 squares, 3" x 3"; cut in half diagonally to make 4 corner setting triangles

**From the fat quarter of light print, cut:**

2 strips, 1" x 14¼"

2 strips, 1" x 17½"

**From the fat quarter of dark-red homespun, cut:**

2 strips, 3" x 18½"

2 strips, 3" x 14¼"

**From the fat eighth of dark-blue homespun, cut:**

4 squares, 3" x 3"; or 4 squares cut from assorted blue scraps

## Making the Shoofly Blocks

1 With right sides together, sew an assorted light or medium triangle to a dark triangle along the long side, taking care not to stretch the bias edges. Press the seam allowances toward the dark print. Trim away the dog-ear points. Repeat to make a total of four matching half-square-triangle units.

Make 4.

2 Lay out the four half-square-triangle units from step 1, four light or medium 1½" squares of the same fabric, and one matching dark 1½" square in three rows to form a block. Join the pieces in each row. Press the seam allowances toward the light print. Join the rows. Press the seam allowances toward the center row.

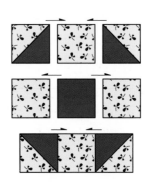

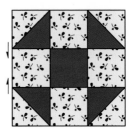

$3$ Repeat steps 1 and 2 to make a total of 12 Shoofly blocks measuring 3½" square.

## Assembling the Quilt Center

$1$ Lay out the 12 blocks on point with the six homespun 3½" squares, 10 side setting triangles, and four corner setting triangles as shown. Join the pieces in each diagonal row. Press the seam allowances toward the setting pieces.

$2$ Sew the pieced rows together and press the seam allowances in one direction. Add the two remaining corner setting triangles to the quilt center. Press the seam allowances toward the corner setting triangles.

## Adding the Borders

$1$ Sew the light 1" x 17½" strips to the right and left sides of the quilt center. Press the seam allowances toward the light print. Sew the light 1" x 14¼" strips to the top and bottom. Press the seam allowances toward the light print.

$2$ Sew the dark-red 3" x 18½" strips to the right and left sides of the quilt top. Press the seam allowances toward the red strips.

$3$ Sew dark-blue 3" squares to both ends of the remaining dark-red strips. Press the seam allowances toward the red strips. Sew these pieced strips to the top and bottom of the quilt center. The finished quilt top should measure 19¼" x 23½".

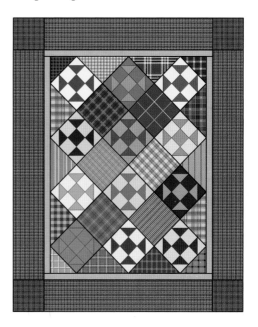

## Finishing the Quilt

Layer the quilt top, batting, and backing. Quilt as desired. The featured quilt was hand quilted ¼" from the seams of the Shoofly blocks and in the ditch around the perimeter of each block. Selected lines of the homespun setting pieces were quilted for texture, and a fan pattern was stitched in the borders. Join the 2½"-wide, random-length strips into one length and use it to bind the quilt.

# Decoy

*Since this quilt uses a block called Duck Tracks, "Decoy" seemed the perfect name. Made in muted blues and reds, this quilt would look great in any color.*

By Carrie Nelson; machine quilted by Louise Haley

FINISHED QUILT SIZE: 30½" x 30½"    FINISHED BLOCK SIZE: 6" x 6"

## Materials

*Yardage is based on 42"-wide fabric unless otherwise noted. Charm squares are 5" x 5".*

⅜ yard of light background fabric for blocks

35 assorted light charm squares for sashing and outer border

26 assorted medium and/or dark charm squares for blocks and inner border

6 assorted accent charm squares for star points and corner squares

⅜ yard of fabric for binding

1⅛ yards of fabric for backing

36" x 36" piece of batting

## Cutting

*All measurements include ¼"-wide seam allowances.*

**From the light background fabric, cut:**

1 strip, 5" x 42"; crosscut into:

    5 squares, 5" x 5"

    2 lengthwise strips, 2" x 15"; crosscut into 12 squares, 2" x 2"

3 strips, 2" x 42"; crosscut into 60 squares, 2" x 2"

**From *each of 22* light squares, cut:**

2 strips, 2" x 5" (44 total)

**From *each of 13* light squares, cut:**

2 strips, 2½" x 5" (26 total)

**From *each of 18* medium and/or dark squares, cut:**

2 strips, 2" x 5"; trim each strip to measure 2" x 3½" (36 total)

**From *each of 8* medium and/or dark squares, cut:**

3 strips, 1½" x 5" (24 total)

**From *1* of the accent squares, cut:**

2 strips, 1½" x 5"; crosscut into 4 squares, 1½" x 1½"

**From the binding fabric, cut:**

140" of 2"-wide bias binding

## Making the Blocks

Use a scant ¼"-wide seam allowance throughout. After sewing each seam, press the seam allowances in the direction indicated by the arrows.

1  Pair an accent 5" square with a background 5" square. Mark diagonal lines from corner to corner. Stitch ¼" on both sides of each line. Cut the squares apart horizontally and vertically, and then cut on the drawn lines. Trim the units to 2" square.

(You'll have four matching units for this block and four units for another block.)

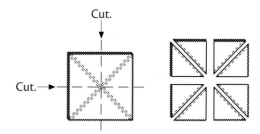

2  Draw a diagonal line from corner to corner on the wrong side of four background 2" squares. Place a marked square on one end of a medium or dark rectangle as shown. Stitch along the marked line and trim, leaving a ¼" seam allowance. Make four star-point units, making sure the direction of the line is the same on all four units and that it matches the diagram.

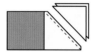

3  Lay out the four star-point units, four half-square-triangle units, and the remaining four background 2" squares as shown. Sew together one background square and one half-square-triangle unit; then add a star-point unit as shown to complete a quadrant. Make four quadrants.

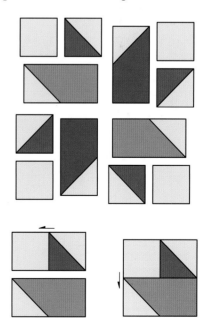

4 Join the quadrants into rows, and then sew the rows together to complete the block. The block should measure 6½" square. Repeat to make a total of nine blocks.

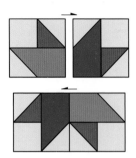

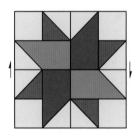

Make 9.

## Assembling the Quilt

1 To piece the sashing strips, divide the light 2" x 5" strips into one set of 20 strips and one set of 24 strips. Sew each set of strips together end to end to make a sashing strip. Press the seam allowances open. Make two strips, one about 90" long and one about 108" long.

2 From the 90"-long strip, cut 12 sashing strips, 2" x 6½".

3 Join three blocks and four sashing strips from step 2 to make a block row as shown in the photo on page 264. Press the seam allowances toward the sashing strips. Make three of these rows.

4 Measure the length of each block row; they should measure 24½". From the 108"-long sashing strip, cut four strips to that length.

5 Join the block rows and sashing strips from step 4. Press the seam allowances toward the sashing strips. The quilt top should measure 24½" x 24½".

6 For the inner border, sort the medium or dark 1½" x 5" strips into four sets of six strips each. Sew the strips together end to end to make four long strips. Press the seam allowances open. The border strips should measure 1½" x 24½".

7 Sew two border strips to the sides of the quilt top. Press the seam allowances toward the inner border. Join 2" accent squares to the ends of the two remaining border strips. Press the seam allowances toward the border strip. Sew these borders to the top and bottom of the quilt top and press the seam allowances toward the inner border.

8 For the outer border, sort the light 2½" x 5" strips into two groups of six strips each for the side borders and two groups of seven strips each for the top and bottom borders. Join each group of strips end to end to make four long strips. Press the seam allowances in one direction. For the side borders, trim the two shorter strips to measure 2½" x 26½". For the top and bottom borders, trim the longer strips to measure 2½" x 30½".

9 Sew the border strips to the sides, and then the top and bottom of the quilt top, keeping the pinked edges on the outside. Press the seam allowances toward the outer border.

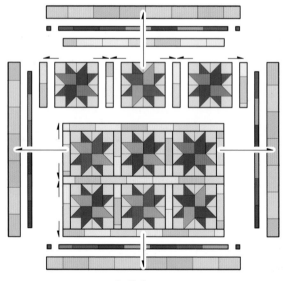

Quilt layout

## Finishing the Quilt

Layer, baste, and quilt as desired. Using the 2"-wide binding strips, make and attach binding.

# Feedsack Flags

*Red reproduction fabrics are quickly sewn into Log Cabin–style flags.*

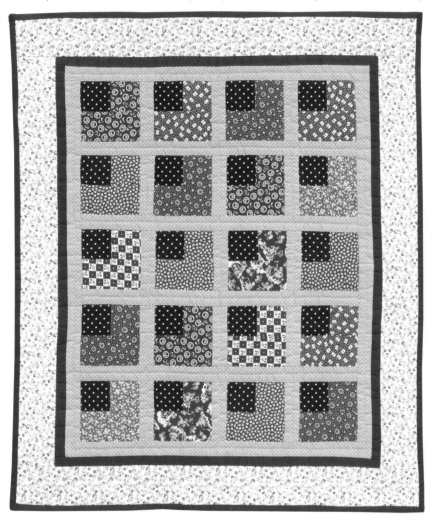

By Alice Berg of Little Quilts

FINISHED QUILT SIZE: 21¼" x 25"    FINISHED BLOCK SIZE: 3" x 3"

## Materials

*Yardage is based on 42"-wide fabric unless otherwise noted.*

⅛ yard of dark-blue pin-dot fabric for flag star fields

¼ yard *total* of assorted red prints for flag bodies

⅜ yard of medium-blue print for sashing and inner border

⅜ yard of red solid for middle border and binding

⅜ yard of light-blue print for outer border

1 yard of fabric for backing

26" x 30" rectangle of thin batting

## Cutting

*All measurements include ¼"-wide seam allowances.*

**From the dark-blue pin-dot fabric, cut:**

20 squares, 2" x 2"

**From the assorted red prints, cut:**

20 *matching sets* of 1 square, 2" x 2", and 1 rectangle, 2" x 3½"

**From the medium-blue print, cut:**

15 strips, 1¼" x 3½"

4 strips, 1¼" x 14¾"

2 strips, 1¼" x 16¼"

2 strips, 1¼" x 18½"

267

**From the red solid, cut:**
2 strips, 1" x 16¾"
2 strips, 1" x 20"
2 strips, 2½" x 42"

**From the light-blue print, cut:**
2 strips, 2¼" x 20½"
2 strips, 2¼" x 20¼"

## Assembling the Quilt

1 Stitch each blue pin-dot 2" square to an assorted red 2" square. Sew a matching red 2" x 3½" rectangle to the bottom of the pieced squares. Press the seam allowances as shown. Make 20 Log Cabin Flag blocks.

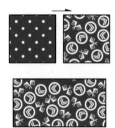 

2 Arrange the blocks and sashing strips as shown. Stitch the blocks and vertical sashing strips together into rows. Press the seam allowances toward the sashing strips. Stitch the block rows and horizontal sashing strips together. Press the seam allowances toward the horizontal sashing strips.

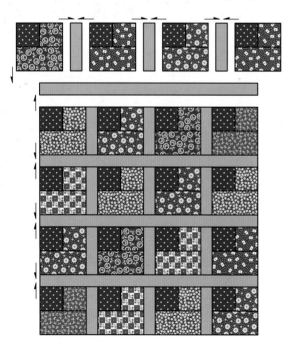

3 For the inner border, sew medium-blue 1¼" x 18½" strips to the sides of the quilt top. Sew the medium-blue 16¼" strips to the top and bottom of the quilt. Press all border seam allowances toward the outer edge of the quilt. Sew the red 1" x 20" strips to the sides of the quilt and the red 1" x 16¾" strips to the top and bottom; press. Sew the light-blue 2¼" x 20½" strips to the sides of the quilt and the light-blue 2¼" x 20¼" strips to the top and bottom. Press.

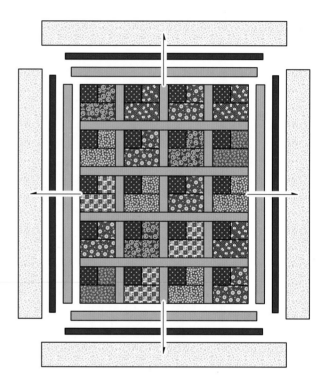

## Finishing the Quilt

1 Layer the quilt top with batting and backing; baste the layers together.

2 Quilt as desired.

3 Bind the edges of the quilt using the red 2½" strips.

# Turkey Tracks

*Turkey red and shades of green were popular colors used in quilts during the nineteenth century. The dotted shirting prints suggest winter snow, providing a nice contrast to the vivid colors of the pattern.*

By Kathleen Tracy

**FINISHED QUILT SIZE: 19½" x 19½"     FINISHED BLOCK SIZE: 6" x 6"**

## Materials

*Yardage is based on 42"-wide fabric unless otherwise noted.*

¼ yard of green print for borders and center square

⅛ yard *each* of 2 red prints for blocks

⅛ yard of white shirting print for blocks

⅛ yard of red-and-white print for sashing

¼ yard of red print for binding

¾ yard of fabric for backing

23" x 23" piece of cotton batting

4 small heart-shaped buttons

## Cutting

*All measurements include ¼"-wide seam allowances.*

**From *each* of the red prints for blocks, cut:**

8 squares, 2½" x 2½" (16 total)

4 squares, 2¼" x 2¼"; crosscut into quarters diagonally to make 16 triangles (32 total)

8 squares, 1½" x 1½" (16 total)

**From the white shirting print, cut:**

8 squares, 2⅞" x 2⅞"; crosscut in half diagonally to make 16 triangles

8 squares, 2¼" x 2¼"; crosscut into quarters diagonally to make 32 triangles

4 squares, 2½" x 2½"

**From the red-and-white print, cut:**

4 rectangles, 2½" x 6½"

**From the green print, cut:**

1 square, 2½" x 2½"

2 strips, 3" x 14½"

2 strips, 3" x 19½"

**From the red print for binding, cut:**

3 strips, 2" x 42"

## Making the Blocks

1 For each block, sew a red 2¼" triangle to a white 2¼" triangle, right sides together. Press the seam allowances toward the red fabric. Make four and four reversed with matching red fabrics.

Make 4 of each.

2 Sew one triangle unit and one reversed triangle unit to adjoining sides of a matching red 1½" square. Make four.

Make 4.

3 Sew a white 2⅞" triangle to the unit from step 2. Make four.

Make 4.

4 Lay out four matching units from step 3, four matching red 2½" squares, and one white 2½" square as shown. Sew the units together in rows. Press the seam allowances toward the red squares. Sew the rows together. Press. Make two blocks from each of the red prints.

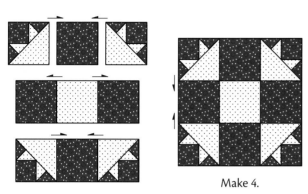

Make 4.

## Assembling the Quilt

1 Lay out the blocks, the four red-and-white 2½" x 6½" rectangles, and the green 2½" square in rows.

2 Sew the blocks, rectangles, and square into rows. Press the seam allowances toward the rectangles. Sew the rows together and press.

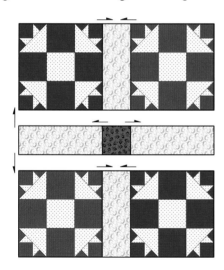

3 Sew the green 3" x 14½" strips to the sides of the quilt top and press the seam allowances toward the borders. Sew the 3" x 19½" strips to the top and bottom of the quilt top and press toward the borders.

## Finishing the Quilt

1 Layer the quilt top, batting, and backing; baste the layers together.

2 Quilt as desired. The quilt shown was quilted in the ditch around each block, with an X in the sashing pieces, a flower in the center square of each Turkey Tracks block, and a diamond shape outlining the center square of each block. The border was quilted with diagonal lines spaced 1½" apart.

3 Attach the binding to the quilt.

4 Add a small button to the center of each Turkey Tracks block.

# Americana Nine Patch

*Snowball and Nine Patch quilts are a familiar sight to most quilters. While the pattern is simple, it's easy to vary the look of the quilt by altering the color placement within the blocks.*

By Karen Costello Soltys

**FINISHED QUILT SIZE: 21½" x 21½"    FINISHED BLOCK SIZE: 3" x 3"**

## Materials

*Yardage is based on 42"-wide fabric unless otherwise noted. Fat quarters measure approximately 18" x 21".*

⅜ yard of light print for blocks

1 fat quarter *each* of medium-blue and dark-blue print for blocks

1 fat quarter of red print for Nine Patch blocks and border

1 fat quarter of blue print for binding

¾ yard of fabric for backing

24" x 24" piece of batting

## Cutting

*All measurements include ¼"-wide seam allowances.*

**From *each* of the medium-blue and dark-blue prints, cut:**

3 strips, 1½" x 21" (6 total)

24 squares, 1½" x 1½" (48 total)

**From the light print, cut:**

2 strips, 3½" x 42"; crosscut into 12 squares, 3½" x 3½"

4 strips, 1½" x 42"; crosscut in half to make 8 strips, 1½" x 21" (1 will be extra)

**From the red print, cut:**

2 strips, 1½" x 21"

4 strips, 3½" x 15½"

**From the blue print for binding, cut:**

5 strips, 2" x 21"

## Making the Nine Patch Blocks

1 Join one dark-blue, one light-print, and one medium-blue strip along their long edges as shown. Press the seam allowances toward the blue strips. Repeat to make three of these strip sets. From the strip sets, cut 34 segments, 1½" wide.

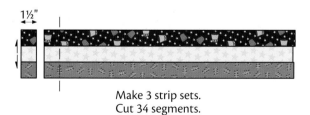

Make 3 strip sets.
Cut 34 segments.

2 In the same manner, make a strip set using two light strips and one red-print 1½" x 21" strip. Press the seam allowances toward the red print. Repeat to make two strip sets. From these strip sets, cut 17 segments, 1½" wide.

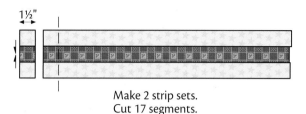

Make 2 strip sets.
Cut 17 segments.

3 Arrange the segments from steps 1 and 2 into Nine Patch blocks. You'll need two segments with blue squares and one with a red square for each block. Be sure to rotate the blue segments as shown so that the medium-blue squares are diagonally opposite one another. Sew the segments together and press the seam allowances toward the blue segments. Make a total of 17 blocks.

Make 17.

## Making the Snowball Blocks

1 Mark a diagonal line from corner to corner on the wrong side of the medium-blue and dark-blue 1½" squares. Then position medium-blue squares on diagonally opposite corners of a light 3½" square, right sides together. Sew along the marked lines and trim away the corner fabric, leaving a ¼" seam allowance. Press the resulting blue triangles open. Make 12 of these units.

Make 12.

2 Repeat step 1, sewing the dark-blue squares to the remaining two corners of each block to complete 12 Snowball blocks.

Make 12.

## Assembling the Quilt

1 Lay out 13 of the Nine Patch blocks and the 12 Snowball blocks in five rows of five blocks each. Start with a Nine Patch block in each of the outer corners and alternate with the Snowball blocks. Position the blocks so that the Nine Patch blocks all have medium-blue squares in the upper-left corner. The Snowball blocks should have dark-blue triangles in the upper-left corner. This way, the medium-blue and dark-blue patches will be adjacent, forming a secondary pattern when the blocks are stitched together.

2 Sew the blocks together into rows, pressing the seam allowances toward the Nine Patch blocks. Then sew the rows together and press the seam allowances all in one direction.

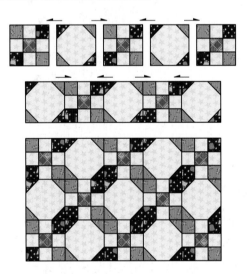

3 Sew red-print strips to the left and right sides of the quilt top. Press the seam allowances toward the borders.

4 Sew the remaining Nine Patch blocks to the two remaining red-print strips. To continue the design, make sure that the medium-blue squares are in the upper-left corners, as shown, for both borders. Press the seam allowances toward the red strips, and then sew the borders to the top and bottom of the quilt top, matching the seam intersections. Press.

## Finishing the Quilt

1 Mark any quilting designs on the quilt top.

2 Place the backing right side down on a table or floor, and lay the batting on top, smoothing out any wrinkles. Then add the pressed quilt top, right side up, on top. Hand or pin baste the layers together.

3 Quilt by hand or machine. The quilt shown was hand quilted, first with straight lines creating an X in each Nine Patch, and then with curved lines in each Snowball block, emphasizing the diagonal movement of the design. The border is quilted in a diagonal crosshatch pattern.

4 Using the blue 2"-wide strips, make and attach binding.

# Little Red Schoolhouse

*The cherished Schoolhouse block has been a favorite of quiltmakers for years.*

By Kathleen Tracy

**FINISHED QUILT SIZE: 16" x 16"     FINISHED BLOCK SIZE: 4" x 4"**

## Materials

*Yardage is based on 42"-wide fabric unless otherwise noted. Fat eighths are approximately 9" x 21".*

⅜ yard of blue-floral print for Hourglass blocks and border

⅛ yard *each OR* scraps of 5 light prints for Schoolhouse blocks

⅛ yard *each OR* scraps of 4 red prints for Schoolhouse blocks

¼ yard or 1 fat eighth of red polka-dot print for Hourglass blocks

¼ yard or 1 fat eighth of light-tan print for Hourglass blocks

⅛ yard *OR* scraps of medium-blue print for Schoolhouse block

Scraps of 4 different blue-checked fabric and prints for roofs

Scrap of red-checked fabric for roof

¼ yard of light print for binding

⅝ yard of fabric for backing

19" x 19" piece of cotton batting

# Cutting

*All measurements include ¼"-wide seam allowances.*
*Make templates using the patterns on page 277.*

**From *each* of the 4 red prints, cut:**

2 squares, 1" x 1" (8 total)

4 pieces, 1" x 2" (16 total)

2 pieces, 1" x 2½" (8 total)

2 pieces, 1" x 3" (8 total)

1 piece using template 2 (4 total)

**From *1* of the red prints, cut:**

2 squares, 1" x 1"

**From *each* of the 5 light prints, cut:**

2 pieces, 1" x 1¼" (10 total)

3 pieces, 1" x 2" (15 total)

1 piece, 1" x 2½" (5 total)

1 piece using template 1 (5 total)

1 piece using template 1 reversed (5 total)

**From the medium-blue print, cut:**

4 pieces, 1" x 2"

2 pieces, 1" x 2½"

2 pieces, 1" x 3"

1 piece using template 2

**From the red-checked fabric, cut:**

1 piece using template 3

**From *each* of the 4 blue scraps, cut:**

1 piece using template 3 (4 total)

**From the red polka-dot print, cut:**

1 square, 5¼" x 5¼"; crosscut into quarters
  diagonally to make 4 triangles

**From the light tan print, cut:**

1 square, 5¼" x 5¼"; crosscut into quarters
  diagonally to make 4 triangles

**From the blue-floral print, cut:**

2 squares, 5¼" x 5¼"; crosscut into quarters
  diagonally to make 8 triangles

2 strips, 2¼" x 42"; crosscut into 2 pieces,
  2¼" x 12½", and 2 pieces, 2¼" x 16"

**From the light print for binding, cut:**

2 strips, 2" x 42"

# Assembling the Quilt

1 To make a red Schoolhouse block, sew two
matching red-print 1" x 2½" pieces to the sides
of a light-print 1" x 2½" piece. Press toward the red
print. Add a red-print 1" x 2" piece to the top of the
unit. Press and set aside.

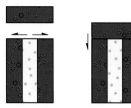

2 Sew three red-print 1" x 2" pieces and two
light-print 1" x 2" pieces together as shown. Sew
red-print 1" x 3" pieces to the top and bottom of the
unit, as shown. Press and set aside.

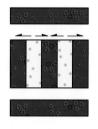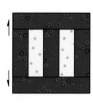

3 Sew two red-print 1" squares, two light-print
1" x 1¼" pieces, and a light-print 1" x 2" piece
together as shown. Press.

4 Using the pieces cut from templates, sew the
roof and background pieces together as shown.
Use a pin to align the dots at the seam intersections
and pin before sewing. Remove the pins as you get
to them. Press.

5 Piece the block units together as shown. Repeat
steps 1 through 5 to make four red school-
houses with blue roofs and one blue schoolhouse
with a red-checked roof.

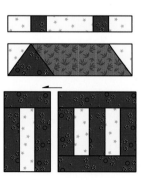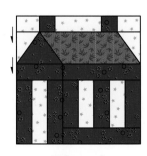

Make 4 red.
Make 1 blue.

6 To make the Hourglass blocks, sew a red polka-dot triangle to a blue-floral triangle; then sew a light-print triangle to a blue-floral triangle. Press. Sew the units together and press. Make four.

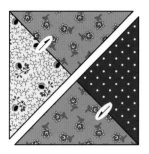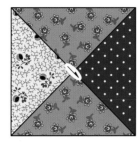

Make 4.

7 Arrange the Schoolhouse blocks with the Hourglass blocks into three rows. Sew the blocks into rows and press. Sew the rows together and press the seam allowances toward the middle row.

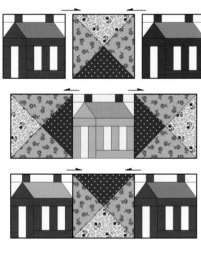

8 Sew the blue-floral 2¼" x 12½" strips to the top and bottom of the quilt top. Press the seam allowances toward the border. Add the blue-floral 2¼" x 16" strips to the sides of the quilt top, pressing the seam allowances toward the border.

## Finishing the Quilt

1 Layer the quilt top, batting, and backing; baste the layers together.

2 Quilt in the ditch around each block and window rectangle.

3 Attach the light-print binding to the quilt.

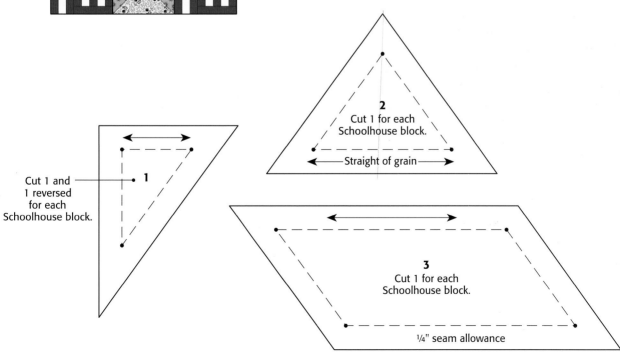

Cut 1 and 1 reversed for each Schoolhouse block.

1

2
Cut 1 for each Schoolhouse block.
←—— Straight of grain ——→

3
Cut 1 for each Schoolhouse block.

¼" seam allowance

# Strippy Triangles

*Piecing triangles together from scraps and assembling them into strips, as in this cute quilt, provided an easy way for little girls to learn sewing skills.*

By Kathleen Tracy

**FINISHED QUILT SIZE: 13½" x 18"     FINISHED BLOCK SIZE: 1¾" x 1¾"**

## Materials

*Yardage is based on 42"-wide fabric unless otherwise noted.*

⅜ yard *total* of assorted shirting fabrics or light-print scraps for blocks

⅛ yard of pink print for blocks

⅛ yard of medium-blue print for blocks

⅛ yard of dark-blue print for blocks

⅛ yard of gold print for blocks

⅛ yard of blue-green print for blocks

⅛ yard of red print for blocks

⅛ yard of tan print for borders

⅛ yard of blue print for binding

½ yard of fabric for backing

17" x 21" piece of batting

## Cutting

*All measurements include ¼"-wide seam allowances.*

**From the assorted shirtings or light prints, cut:**

30 squares, 2¾" x 2¾"

**From the pink print, cut:**

5 squares, 2¾" x 2¾"

**From the medium-blue print, cut:**

5 squares, 2¾" x 2¾"

**From the dark-blue print, cut:**

5 squares, 2¾" x 2¾"

**From the gold print, cut:**

5 squares, 2¾" x 2¾"

**From the blue-green print, cut:**

5 squares, 2¾" x 2¾"

**From the red print, cut:**

5 squares, 2¾" x 2¾"

**From the tan print, cut:**

1 strip, 1¾" x 42"; crosscut into 2 pieces, 1¾" x 18"

**From the blue print for binding, cut:**

2 strips, 2" x 42"

## Assembling the Quilt

1 Layer each of the assorted light 2¾" squares on top of a print 2¾" square, right sides together. Draw a diagonal line across each light square. Stitch ¼" from the line on both sides and cut on the drawn line. Press the seam allowances toward the dark fabric. Trim each block to 2¼" x 2¼".

Make 10 of each color.

2 Sew 10 triangle squares of the same color into a vertical row as shown. Repeat to make six rows, each a different color. Arrange the rows side by side. Press the seam allowances in opposite directions from row to row.

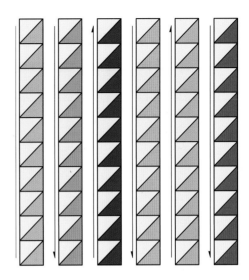

3 Sew the rows together to make the quilt center. Press the seam allowances in one direction.

4 Sew the tan-print 18" strips to the sides of the quilt center and press the seam allowances toward the borders.

## Finishing the Quilt

1 Layer the quilt top, batting, and backing; baste the layers together.

2 Quilt diagonal lines through the center of the blocks. You may also wish to quilt in the ditch along the inside edge of each border.

3 Attach the blue-print binding to the quilt.

# Don't Interrupt!

*A perfect gift for the hectic holidays, this quilt won't take too much time and is simple to make. You might even get it made without being interrupted!*

By Mary Etherington and Connie Tesene of Country Threads

FINISHED QUILT SIZE: 24" x 24"    FINISHED BLOCK SIZE: 4" x 4"

## Materials

*Yardage is based on 42"-wide fabric unless otherwise noted. Charm squares are 5" x 5".*

33 Christmas-print charm squares for blocks*
¼ yard of brown Christmas print for borders
¼ yard of dark-red print for blocks and binding
1 yard of fabric for backing
28" x 28" piece of batting

*You can substitute 1½" x 42" strips of at least 15 different Christmas prints, 4 of them predominantly red. Cut a total of 100 rectangles, 1½" x 4½". You won't have to cut a 1½" x 4½" rectangle from the dark-red binding fabric.*

## Cutting

*All measurements include ¼"-wide seam allowances.*

**From *each* of the charm squares, cut:**
3 rectangles, 1½" x 4½" (99 total; see illustration below)

**From the brown Christmas print, cut:**
2 strips, 2½" x 20½"
2 strips, 2½" x 24½"

**From the dark-red print, cut:**
3 strips, 1½" x 42"; from 1 of these strips, cut 1 rectangle, 1½" x 4½"

## Assembling the Quilt

1  Sew the 1½" x 4½" rectangles together in pairs. (One rectangle comes from the red binding fabric.) Sew two pairs together to make a four-rectangle block. Repeat to make 25 blocks total.

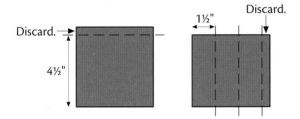

Make 25.

2  Lay out the blocks in five rows of five blocks each, alternating the direction of the rails from horizontal to vertical. Study the diagrams when placing the red strips. If you choose to discard a red strip that isn't as dark as the others, you can use leftover dark-red binding fabric for the red rails.

3  When you're satisfied with the block arrangement, sew the blocks into rows, and then sew the rows together. Press.

4  Sew the brown 20½"-long strips to the top and bottom of the quilt top and press the seam allowances toward the borders. Repeat, using the brown 24½"-long strips for the sides of the quilt.

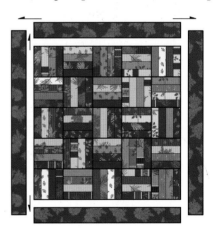

## Finishing the Quilt

Layer the quilt top with batting and backing; baste. Quilt as desired. Sew the dark-red 1½"-wide strips together end to end to make one long strip. Use this strip to bind your quilt.

# Antique Diamonds

*You can make this easy diamond quilt using any color palette—even thoroughly modern bright colors that kids would love. At least 30 fabrics were used for this little gem. The more, the merrier!*

By Karen Costello Soltys

FINISHED QUILT SIZE: 24" x 25"

## Materials

*Yardage is based on 42"-wide fabric unless otherwise noted.*

30 assorted 2"-wide strips, at least 21" long, for diamonds*

⅓ yard of blue print for outer border

2 red- or pink-print strips, 2" x 21", for inner border

1 fat quarter of dark-blue print for binding

⅞ yard of fabric for backing

26" x 27" piece of batting

*Strips can be fat-quarter length (21") or longer.*

## Cutting

*All measurements include ¼"-wide seam allowances.*

**From the assorted fabric strips, trim each strip:**

2" wide x varying lengths (from 21" to 42")

**From the blue print, cut:**

2 strips, 3" x 21"

2 strips, 3¼" x 24"

**From the dark-blue print, cut:**

6 strips, 2" x 21"

## Piecing the Chevron Strips

1 Randomly select three 2" strips. Staggering the ends by 2" each, sew the strips together along their long edges. Press all seam allowances in one direction. Repeat to make five strip sets staggered to the right and five sets staggered to the left.

Make 5 strip sets.

Make 5 strip sets.

2 Using a rotary cutter and a ruler with 45° markings, align the 45° line with the seam line of a strip set as shown. Trim off the irregular end of the strip set.

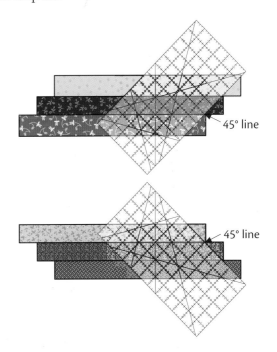

45° line

45° line

3 Rotate the strip set 180°. Measure 2" from the freshly cut end of the strip set and cut a 2"-wide segment. Repeat, cutting 2" segments from all the strip sets for a total of 36 segments.

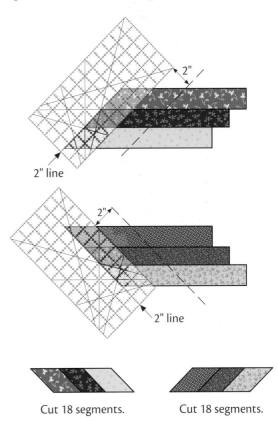

2"

2" line

2"

2" line

Cut 18 segments.          Cut 18 segments.

4 Sew three segments together end to end to make one strip for the chevron. Repeat, making a total of six strip sets slanting in each direction. Press all seam allowances in one direction.

Make 6.

Make 6.

5 Lay out the strips side by side, placing them so that the diamonds slant in opposite directions from one strip to the next and rotating them so the seam allowances will butt together. When you're pleased with the color arrangement, pin to match the seam intersections, and then stitch the strips together.

6 Trim the ends of the quilt center to square it up. Make sure you leave ¼" of fabric past the last seam intersection for the seam allowance.

Trim ends to square up.

7 Measure the width of the quilt top. Trim the two pink or red strips to this length. Sew the strips to the top and bottom of the quilt. Press the seam allowances toward the border strips.

8 Measure the length of the quilt top. Trim the two narrower blue strips to this length. Sew the strips to the sides of the quilt top and press the seam allowances toward the blue borders.

9 In the same manner, measure the width of the quilt top. Trim the remaining blue strips to this length and attach them to the top and bottom of the quilt. Press.

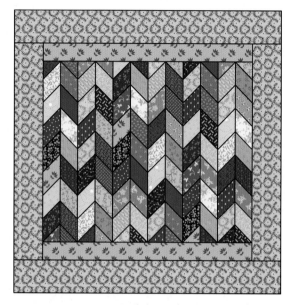

Quilt layout

# Finishing the Quilt

1 Mark any quilting designs on the quilt top.

2 Place the backing right side down on a table or floor and lay the batting on top, smoothing out any wrinkles. Then add the pressed quilt top, right side up, on top. Hand or pin baste the layers together.

3 Quilt by hand or machine. The quilt shown was hand quilted ¼" inside each diamond. The pink borders were quilted in a series of three parallel straight lines at each seam line in the chevron pattern. The outer border was quilted with a large crosshatching pattern.

4 Using the dark-blue 2"-wide strips, make and attach binding.

I f you've enjoyed the projects in this book, look for these other books by the project designers. Ask for them at your local quilt shop, or go to ShopMartingale.com.

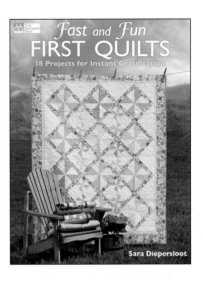

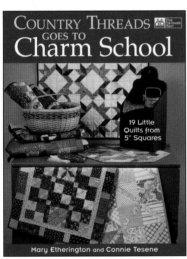

All Buttoned Up
*12 Quilts from the Button Box*
Loraine Manwaring and Susan Nelsen

another BiTE OF SCHNiBBLES
24 quilts from 5" or 10" squares
Carrie Nelson

PINWHEEL *party*
12 FUN AND UNIQUE QUILTS
ELLEN PAHL

TRIANGLE TRICKS
*One Easy Unit, Dozens of Gorgeous Quilts*
Introduction by Sally Schneider

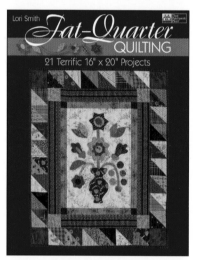

Lori Smith
*Fat-Quarter* QUILTING
21 Terrific 16" x 20" Projects

Bits *and* Pieces
*18 Small Quilts from Fat Quarters and Scraps*
Karen Costello Soltys

DECK THE HALLS
*Quilts to Celebrate Christmas*
CHERYL ALMGREN TAYLOR

*Quilts from* Aunt Amy
COUNTRY THREADS
CONNIE TESENE & MARY TENDALL ETHERINGTON

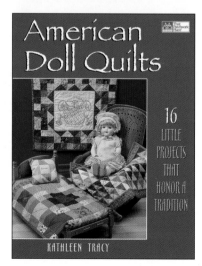

American Doll Quilts
16 LITTLE PROJECTS THAT HONOR A TRADITION
KATHLEEN TRACY

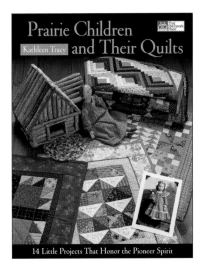